The Writing Process

The Writing Process

PREWRITING, WRITING, REVISING

Robert J. Marzano
University of Colorado
at Denver

Philip DiStefano
University of Colorado
at Boulder

 D. Van Nostrand Company
New York Cincinnati Toronto London Melbourne

To our parents: Lou and Sue, Vic and Rose

D. Van Nostrand Company Regional Offices:
New York   Cincinnati

D. Van Nostrand Company International Offices:
London   Toronto   Melbourne

Library of Congress Catalog Card Number: 80-53126
ISBN: 0-442-26055-5

Published by D. Van Nostrand Company
135 West 50th Street, New York, N.Y. 10020

10 9 8 7 6 5 4 3 2 1

PREFACE

The Writing Process offers a unique approach to composition instruction. Intended for freshmen and sophomore students, the text presents writing as a process that consists of three integrated phases: prewriting, writing, and revising. The prewriting phase includes motivation, topic identification, format identification, consideration of audience, and information gathering. Only after these elements are considered can writing take place smoothly and naturally. Given adequate preparation by means of these prewriting activities, the process of composing becomes a relatively simple task.

The objective in the writing phase of the composing process is to get ideas on paper while allowing the mind to retrieve and organize the information collected during prewriting in as unencumbered a fashion as possible. Revision begins immediately after ideas have been put to paper. Revision is the most involved part of the composing process and the one most heavily emphasized in the text. It includes consideration of the overall logic and organization of a paper, paragraphing, expanding and reducing, vocabulary, and mechanics.

Following this model of the writing process, chapters 2, 3, 4, and 5 are devoted to prewriting and include the topics of motivation, topic identification, audience and format, and collecting information, respectively. Chapters 6, 7, 8, and 9 deal with the writing and revising phases of composing as a set of interconnected actions. Specifically, these chapters cover putting thought to paper and revising for logic (chapter 6), revising to expand and reduce (chapter 7), revising for vocabulary (chapter 8), and revising for mechanics (chapter 9).

The three-part composing process is demonstrated in chapter 10 in the context of a research paper. In that chapter students are guided through the writing of a hypothetical research paper from its assignment by an instructor to the final typing. Chapter 11 discusses a specific type of writing commonly encountered in colleges and universities—essay examinations. This chapter presents techniques for preparing for and efficiently taking essay examinations.

The last section of the text, a Grammar and Usage Handbook, contains information on spelling, capitalization, punctuation, commonly confused terms, and trite expressions, along with sections on parts of speech and parts of a sentence. The Grammar and Usage Handbook is designed as a reference section for problems that students might have with specific grammar and usage rules or with terminology that is used in the text. The inclusion of this handbook makes any supplemental readers or handbooks unnecessary. Consequently the text can serve as the sole source for a composition course.

An instructor's manual, available from the publisher, contains techniques for diagnosing a student's ability in selected phases of the writing and revising process. This diagnostic orientation enables the instructor to set goals for the student and prescribe activities to help meet these goals. The instructor's manual also contains supplementary exercises and suggestions for integrating the text into various types of first-year composition programs.

We would like to express gratitude to Charles B. Dodson, of the University of North Carolina at Wilmington, J. F. Kobler, of North Texas State University, and Elizabeth Cowan, of Texas A & M University, whose critiques of the manuscript in preparation were invaluable. We sincerely hope that readers find The Writing Process interesting and informative and that it provides a framework around which various types of compositions can be structured.

R.J.M.
P.D.

CONTENTS

PART THREE   WRITING AND REVISING

PART FOUR   SPECIAL TOPICS

PART FIVE   A GRAMMAR AND USAGE HANDBOOK

part
1

Introduction

CHAPTER ONE

AN OVERVIEW

TWO WRITING STORIES

What happens when a writer composes something? What process occurs when an individual writes an exemplary paper in a college course? Is it the same process that occurs when someone writes a letter or a poem or a story? To answer these questions, consider these two stories about people writing.

Example 1-1. *Pat*

She awoke, that first summer morning back home, in a good mood. From the moment Pat opened her eyes she was full of energy and enthusiasm and eager to enjoy the exciting things she anticipated the day would bring. It was her first day back home in Michigan after two years of school abroad, and she had a lot of friendships to renew—friendships she hoped had not faded over her two-year absence. She decided to start the day by taking a quick jog along the river, a habit she had acquired in Paris. The first mile was pleasant; she enjoyed the sun and the foliage along the banks of the Grand River, which ran close to her house. As she neared the site of the newly opened bauxite plant, constructed after she had left for Europe, the tone of her morning jog started to change. She began to notice dead fish floating by the bank, and she thought she could detect a thin, slimy film covering the water. The farther she ran, the more dead fish she saw and the thicker the film appeared to be. She finally stopped in amazement when she came upon a large underground pipe, apparently coming from the plant, emptying what seemed to be a raw chemical into the river. In the water around the area where the chemical was being dumped there were dead fish everywhere. Even a few rodent carcasses lined the bank.

Pat aborted her run and headed home. At the house she anxiously quizzed her father, who told her that the plant had been built about a year ago, that it had created 500 jobs for the townspeople, and that the plant owners had assured the townspeople that all necessary precautions were being taken to protect the environment. When Pat told her father about what she had seen, he reacted with mild disbelief. When she brought him to the spot where the pipe was emptying its waste, however, he too was shocked and felt that whatever was going on was a clear violation of the promises the company had made to the townspeople.

By the time they had walked back home, Pat's amazement had turned to outright anger. She would expose this injustice to the public. But how? She first thought of writing a letter to her congressman. She then thought of writing a detailed description of what she had seen and passing it out to the townspeople. She finally decided on a letter to the town newspaper. She went into her father's study and sat down at the typewriter. About four lines into the letter she realized that she hadn't much to say. She wasn't positive the pipe led to the factory; she didn't know what the chemical was; she wasn't positive that it was killing the fish. She needed more information.

The next few days were filled with telephone calls to old friends who might have some answers, to some reading up on the waste products of bauxite production, and to some Sherlock Holmes-type snooping around the plant. Her information gathering indicated that: (1) the chemical was probably sodium triacitate, which was a known cancer causer in rats and in large doses was lethal; (2) the company had promised they would bury the sodium triacitate in canisters at a site some fifty miles away from the town; (3) the chemical did not dilute quickly in water and could possibly stay in its highly concentrated form until it reached the water-processing plant, which produced the town's drinking water, twenty miles down river. Now her letter was quite easy to write. Facts flowed and mixed well with her angry words. When the letter was completed, she spent a few minutes reading it over for errors. She found a few, corrected them, and sent the letter off. It appeared in the Sunday paper along with a full-page editorial apparently inspired by her efforts.

Example 1-2. *Greg*

Greg had been working on the paper for about three hours straight. It was worth one third of his history grade for that semester. As usual he had waited until the day before it was due to start working on it, and now he was paying the price. He would stay up all night if he had to, and the way things were progressing, that seemed more and more probable by the minute. Actually the topic should have been a simple one for him—an essay comparing Hitler's advance into Russia with that of Napoleon. The assignment had been to write a comparative essay on two historic figures covered in class—a minimum of five pages, double spaced. Greg had skimmed through his class notes and immediately singled out Napoleon and Hitler. He had always been a war buff and had read a great deal about the military strategies employed by Napoleon and Hitler even before he took this course. Because both military leaders made the same mistakes in invading Russia, it should have been easy to write a five-page comparative essay on them. Greg knew enough about the topic to sit down and write pages of facts without even consulting a textbook: Within the first half hour he had written over seven pages of information about the two campaigns. But information wasn't going to cut it—at least not with Professor Bradley, who demanded that all papers be well written and logical, a fact he had found out after receiving a C− on the first assignment. No, Bradley wasn't impressed with quantity of facts; it was how you put them together that differentiated the A's from the B's from the C's. And Greg had already put the facts for this paper together in two different ways, and each time he knew it wasn't right. The result? Two different sets of papers were filed in the wastebasket, and time was running out. He had to allow for an hour's worth of typing, and he also had to consider fatigue.

He decided to take a new tack. Instead of trying to get the information down perfectly the first time, he'd concentrate more on revising and reworking what he had written. He retrieved his last attempt at the paper from the wastebasket. He read over what he had written and decided that there was a great deal of extraneous information—facts stated with no apparent purpose. He crossed those out. He also decided that a little rearranging was in order: paragraph four could actually be stated in one sentence and placed at the end of paragraph three; the second sentence of paragraph eight needed more information to back it up, so he added a couple of sentences. This rearranging process went on for another half hour. Sentences were dropped, added, and reshuffled so that the paper, at the end of the process, looked very different from what he had taken out of the wastebasket a little earlier.

He was fairly happy with the arrangement of ideas now, but he noticed that he tended to use the same words over and over to express the same ideas. He went to his thesaurus and quickly solved that problem. He read through the paper again, this time aloud to himself. Doing this made it apparent that he had written a few words and phrases that were acceptable in everyday speech but that didn't sound right in a formal paper. The final reading of the paper was to look for spelling and punctuation errors. He always had a great many of those. He finally leaned back in his chair and smiled. The paper was good—very good, probably the best he had ever written. It was logical, concise, and highly polished. It was just the type of essay Dr. Bradley liked. Greg placed a fresh page in the typewriter, knowing that his work now was mechanical. Typing the final draft would take about an hour. He still might have time for a decent night's sleep before class in the morning.

These two stories were contrived to make the point that there is a great deal of commonality in all instances of writing. In both stories, we can identify seven different steps that should be a part of all writing:

1. *Motivation.* Both Pat and Greg were motivated to write, but in vastly different ways. Pat's motivation was "inner directed." Something in her life spurred her to communicate: She was compelled to write. Greg's motivation was "outer directed." He did not have an intrinsic desire to write about Napoleon and Hitler's campaigns. Instead, he was forced to write because he was assigned an essay to complete for his history grade.

2. *Topic identification.* Both Pat and Greg had to be concerned with topic identification and exactly what was to be said about the topic. For Pat, topic identification and motivation were basically the same process: The topic itself motivated her to write. This is generally the case with inner-directed writing, in which the topic springs from a motivating experience. For Greg, motivation and topic identification were separate events. He was motivated to write by his desire to receive a good grade in history class. But he had to go through a separate process to identify his topic. That process was to skim over his class notes. This scenario is typical of outer-directed writing: A topic is generally not defined for you, and a good part of the writing task becomes the identification of what to write about.

3. *Audience.* The audience of a paper is whom the paper is written for, the person or persons who will read it. For Greg, the audience was defined for him. He knew that only Dr. Bradley was going to read the paper. Even though Greg did not have to worry about audience identification, "audience" was still a

major consideration for him. He had to identify and weigh heavily the expectations of his audience, Dr. Bradley. Pat not only had to consider her audience but also had to identify it. She could have written to a single individual (a member of congress) or to a group of people (the townspeople). The content, style, and format of what she wrote would have been different for the two types of audiences.

4. *Format.* Format can be defined as the form the writing takes (for example, a story, a poem, a letter). Format is influenced by the audience for whom the information is intended. With outer-directed writing, the format is oftentimes defined for the writer. For example, Greg knew he had to write a comparative essay. He even knew its length and typing format. For Pat the format was undefined. She could have written an angry letter, published a pamphlet, or written a story. For inner-directed writing format will always be a major decision for the writer.

5. *Adequacy of information.* Both writers had to decide whether or not they had enough information to complete their respective writing tasks. Pat concluded that more research was necessary before she could begin writing. Greg, however, was familiar enough with the topic to begin writing without further investigation. Generally any attempt to write without adequate information will end in frustration and failure.

6. *Putting thought to paper.* At some point in the writing process, every writer has to sit down and put his or her thoughts on paper. The more information you have about a topic, the easier this phase becomes. For example, Pat's first attempt at writing produced only four lines of a letter. She didn't have enough information about the topic and therefore found it difficult to write. Greg, on the other hand, had information and was therefore able to write seven pages about the topic on the first sitting.

7. *Polishing.* Both writers had to consider possible revisions to be made; we will call this **polishing.** In Pat's case, this meant correcting a few errors. For Greg, however, the polishing of the paper was the most involved part of the writing process. In general, the more formal your composition, the more time you must spend on revision. Pat was writing a letter, and the language in a letter is usually similar to that used in everyday speech. Therefore, little revision was necessary. Greg's writing was far more formal and the type of language to be used was restricted. Hence he had to revise his essay a number of times before it met the formal standards set by Professor Bradley.

In summary, there are at least seven factors common to all writing or seven tasks that all writing must attend to:
1. Motivation
2. Topic identification
3. Audience identification and consideration
4. Identification of format
5. Collection of information
6. Putting thought to paper
7. Polishing

All seven steps are integral parts of writing, although, some tasks are more important than others in different writing situations. For example, in formal writing polishing is probably the most critical of the seven tasks, as is evidenced by Greg's story. And most writing done in connection with college courses is formal. The chapters of this text reflect that varying importance—we have devoted more chapters to polishing than to any other phase of writing.

The rest of the text is divided into four parts. Part 2 is entitled Prewriting and deals with the components of the writing process that occur before you begin to write. The four chapters in Part 2 cover the topics of motivation (Chapter 2), topic identification (Chapter 3), audience and format (Chapter 4), and collecting information (Chapter 5).

Part 3 of the text is entitled Writing and Revising. In Chapter 6 we discuss putting thought to paper and in chapters 7, 8, and 9 we consider polishing. The fourth part of the text is called Special Topics. The chapters in this section deal with such concerns as footnoting, bibliographies, and title pages. There is also a chapter on the research paper as a special form of writing, and a chapter on taking essay exams. Part 5 is entitled A Grammar and Usage Handbook. In it are sections on grammar rules, terminology, parts of speech, spelling, capitalization, punctuation, and common usage errors.

Prewriting

CHAPTER TWO

MOTIVATION

Motivation is a primary factor in all human behavior and a crucial component in the writing process. Because of its importance, we will briefly delve into motivation theory in this chapter to identify some theoretically sound and yet practical techniques to help in writing situations.

As we have seen, motivation for writing can be either inner directed (Pat's story) or outer directed (Greg's story). Motivational problems can occur in both situations; however, they usually stem from somewhat different sources. Because outer-directed writing is the most common type of writing in a college or university setting (for example, an instructor gives you an assignment in class), we will consider motivation as it relates to outer-directed writing first and then discuss motivation as it relates to inner-directed writing. But before discussing techniques for motivation we will first discuss motivation in general terms.

WHAT IS MOTIVATION?

Webster's New Encyclopedic Dictionary defines the verb "to motivate" as "to impel, to induce." Hence we can say that motivation is the amount of impetus or inducement you have to complete a task.

But how do you develop or improve motivation for a task? To begin answering this question we'll consult a rather unusual source—a book about tennis.

In his book *The Inner Game of Tennis*,[1] W. Timothy Gallwey generates some fascinating hypotheses about how our minds function. He believes that all human actions are governed by one of two selves operating in all of us. Gallwey says that he discovered the two selves one day while he was teaching tennis. (He is a tennis pro.) One afternoon when he was in a relaxed mood, he decided to do a little less teaching and more observing of his students. He noticed that they would make mistakes (which he would ordinarily call to their attention) and then gradually correct their own errors without any intervention from an instructor. Later he noticed that when he stepped in to try to correct their errors in his usual fashion ("Keep your eye on the ball." "Bring the racket back in a straight line.") the students would automatically tense up and perform less well. All of this led him to try an experiment. With one of his new students, he decided to skip his usual explanation to beginning players about the proper grip, stroke, and footwork for the basic forehand shot. Instead, he hit ten forehand shots himself and instructed the student to watch him carefully—not to analyze what he was doing but instead to try to obtain a strong visual image of the proper way to hit a forehand shot. To Gallwey's amazement, when he handed the student a racket and told him to hit some forehand shots, the student was able to accomplish the stroke remarkably well—much better than other beginning students do in their first attempts.

From this experience Gallwey reasoned that there are two selves working in all humans, one that is intuitive (self 2—the subconscious) and one that is judgmental and analytical (self 1—the conscious). He reasoned that if self 2 is given appropriate and strong mental images it will automatically make the body function in such a way as to actualize those images, provided that self 1 does not interfere with the process once the goals are given.

The foundation of Gallwey's ideas may be found in a relatively new field of study called cybernetics. Cybernetics is the science of control and communication within living and nonliving things. Cybernetic theories are now being applied to almost all aspects of life and society. Gregory Bateson, a well-known anthropologist, has said, "I think that cybernetics is the biggest bite out of the fruit of the tree of knowledge that mankind has taken in the last 2,000 years."[2]

In general, cybernetics postulates that all systems of control and communication must have a purpose or goal in order to function.

Also, all goal-oriented systems take in information (input), organize that information (processing) and do something as a result of processing that information (output). Recently, such men as Maxwell Maltz and Kenneth Sayre have attempted to apply cybernetic theory to the explanation of motivation in man.[3] Maltz in his book *Psycho-Cybernetics* (the application of cybernetics to psychology) states that what we used to call the subconscious mind (Gallwey's self 2) is not really a mind at all but a cybernetic system—one that, by definition, handles input, processes it, and has some type of output. Because it is a cybernetic system the subconscious mind must have goals in order to function, and these goals are given to the subconscious mind via the conscious mind (Gallwey's self 1).

Maltz goes on to say that our subconscious, cybernetic self 2 is impersonal. It does not make judgments about the goals given it; it simply motivates us to act in such a way as to accomplish those goals. Present it with success goals and the subconscious mind will function as a success mechanism, handling new situations in such a way as to make us successful; present it with failure goals and it will act as a failure mechanism.

Like Gallwey, Maltz believes that goals are given to the subconscious mind primarily in the form of mental images. In other words, when we envision ourselves doing something, we are actually giving our subconscious mind some goals for its cybernetic motivational system. If this is true, it suggests that people have the capability of "programming" or "motivating" themselves for success, so to speak, by consciously concentrating on mental images of themselves performing whatever task they want to accomplish. In his book, *The Conquest of Happiness*, Bertrand Russell, the famous philosopher and mathematician, discusses how he used mental programming in his writing:

> I have found, for example, that if I have to write upon some rather difficult topic, the best plan is to think about it with great intensity—the greatest intensity of which I am capable—for a few hours or days, and at the end of that time give orders, so to speak, that the work is to proceed underground. After some months I return consciously to the topic and find that the work has been done. Before I had discovered this technique I used to spend the intervening months worrying because I was making no progress; I arrived at the solution none the sooner for this worry, and the intervening months were wasted, whereas now I can devote them to other pursuits.[4]

A remarkable claim for the power of changing one's behavior using self-programming can be found in Dr. Elwood Worcester's book, *Body, Mind and Spirit*. Dr. Worcester, a scientist, states that up to his fiftieth year he was an unhappy and ineffective man. He lived with a continual sense of gloom and failure and frequently experienced blinding headaches that he attributed to his general state of depression. He had read some of the works of William James and was particularly impressed by James's contention that our beliefs shape our lives. Worcester put this philosophy to the test:

> I decided to limit the period of conscious effort to one month, as I thought this time long enough to prove its value or worthlessness to me. During this month I resolved to impose certain restrictions on my thoughts. If I thought of the past, I would try to let my mind dwell only on its happy, pleasing incidents . . . . In thinking of the present, I would deliberately turn my attention to the desirable elements . . . . In thinking of the future I determined to regard every worthy and possible ambition as within my grasp. Ridiculous as this seemed at the time, in view of what has come to me since, I see that the only defect of my plan was that it aimed too low and did not include enough.[5]

The effects of Worcester's efforts were remarkable. His attitude improved, his writings were published, and he began to receive the scientific recognition he had craved for so long. In effect, he felt he had changed his life by changing his thinking.

As can be seen from these examples, some people believe that you can drastically change your life via proper control and monitoring of your thoughts. We will apply this cybernetic concept of mental programming to the improvement of motivation in writing. Stated in summary form, we can say that the cybernetic theory of motivation is based on four tenets:

1. All people possess a goal-seeking cybernetic mechanism sometimes referred to as the subconscious mind (or self 2).
2. The subconscious mind will automatically motivate us to accomplish the goals that are given it by the conscious mind (or self 1).
3. One of the major ways that the conscious mind gives goals to the subconscious mind is by the use of mental images.
4. Once goals are given to the subconscious mind by the conscious mind, an attempt should be made to stop conscious mind thoughts that are contradictory to those goals.

This theory as it applies to writing suggests that any student can improve motivation for writing by feeding the subconscious mind images of the goals the student wants to accomplish. We will first apply this technique to improving motivation for outer-directed writing assignments.

IMPROVING MOTIVATION FOR OUTER-DIRECTED WRITING

Let us consider the kind of thinking that a typical student might do when faced with an outer-directed writing assignment. Recall that outer-directed writing occurs when you are forced to write. Someone else has requested that you write something; the impetus has not come from within. Such is the case with most assignments in a college or university setting. For example, let's assume that Christine, a college freshman, has been given the assignment of writing a two-page (typed, double-spaced) paper for her chemistry class explaining what a sodium pump is and how it functions in the communication of one neuron with another. Christine's first reaction might be to picture the inconvenience the assignment will cause her. She might think ahead to the ski trip she had planned for the weekend and conclude that the paper was going to spoil it. This would probably cause her to feel anger. She might also envision herself sitting before a blank piece of paper not being able to think of anything to write (What is a sodium pump, anyway?) This would probably cause her to feel frustration. She might picture herself receiving a low grade on the paper. This would cause fear. She might even imagine failing the course and being kicked out of school, all because a paper was assigned. This type of mental response is a type of thinking that many students (and people in the business world) engage in when they are faced with a discomforting task. According to our cybernetic theory of motivation, this type of thinking is a form of negative programming that can be overcome by consciously replacing negative thoughts with positive ones.

A productive type of thinking for Christine might have been to envision herself completing the paper and still being able to go on the ski trip. She could have pictured herself working productively during the week and getting most of the paper finished before the weekend. She then could have imagined herself coming back from the trip refreshed, renewed, and ready to commence writing. She might also have imagined herself handing the paper in and feeling good about what she had accomplished. To complete the mental scenario, she could have envisioned getting the paper back with a good grade on it and let herself experience the feelings she would have as a result of her success. Such thinking would have given self 2 positive goals to work on, goals that Christine's innate cybernetic system would have helped her accomplish.

As Christine's example illustrates, applying the cybernetic model to motivation for outer-directed writing involves the monitoring and control of how you think about writing assignments. This is not an easy task; it takes discipline and effort to change patterns of thought: The simple act of having a few positive thoughts about an assignment is not going to change well-established thought patterns overnight.

Many of us have established a habit of negative thinking regarding writing assignments. Yet this negative thinking (negative programming) must be replaced by positive thoughts if we are to facilitate the motivation process. A useful scheme for accomplishing this is to spend some time each day (a few minutes) forcing yourself to have positive thoughts about the particular writing assignment for which you are trying to improve motivation. These thoughts, as far as possible, should be expressed as mental images. In other words, you should imagine yourself working on the assignment in a highly positive fashion. Of course, the details of the positive images you create will be specific to your situation and consequently would be different from one individual to another. There are, however, some images that apply to almost all outer-directed writing assignments:

1. *Envision the product.* Mentally picture what your essay, composition, or short story will look like in its final form. Picture the typing, the cover page. Imagine it in your hands; feel how heavy it is—let yourself experience the feelings you will have when the paper is completed.

2. *Establish a time line; anticipate the workload and possible problems.* Determine how much time you have to accomplish the assignment and how much work the assignment will require. Mentally determine a work schedule that will allow you to do the recreational activities you have planned and still complete the assignment. Anticipate any obstacles you might have in completing the assignment (for example, no typewriter at home, need to go to the library before you can begin writing) and picture yourself overcoming those obstacles efficiently.

3. *Picture yourself being productive while you work.* Imagine yourself working on the paper, feeling confident and positive

about the experience. Envision yourself attending to the task with a great deal of enthusiasm, effort, and concentration. Picture yourself not worrying about the paper when you are not working on it. Instead, see yourself able to enjoy other things because you feel good about what you have already accomplished on the paper and confident that you will be able to overcome any obstacles.

4. *Anticipate success.* Imagine yourself experiencing success as a result of your efforts. Picture yourself handing the paper in and feeling good about it. Visualize the instructor returning the paper with a high grade on it and allow yourself to experience the emotions you might feel as a result of that.

In addition to the daily practice of focusing on positive images, you should, as much as possible, try to control negative thoughts regarding the writing assignment. At first this is quite difficult, but with practice it soon becomes easy to recognize when you are indulging in nonproductive thinking about an assignment. At such times you should try to block negative thoughts and replace them with positive images.

These two procedures (positive imaging and control of negative thinking), when applied to outer-directed writing, usually produce remarkable results. Most students find that when they use these techniques, their energy level, productivity, and quality of work increases.

IMPROVING MOTIVATION FOR INNER-DIRECTED WRITING

Negative thoughts can inhibit motivation for inner-directed writing as well. Recall what inner-directed writing is. Inner-directed writing usually stems from an experience you have had and about which you want to communicate. You have been moved by something; you have been internally motivated to write.

Does this happen often in a person's life? The answer is a qualified "yes." It has happened to you at least as many times as you have thought, "Somebody should do something about that" or "I wish I could change that." Most people frequently experience things that trigger such thoughts, but few people ever transform such thoughts into written communication. The reason, once again, is a form of negative self-programming that is so ingrained in us that we do not connect the possibility of writing with the

potential inner-motivated writing situations we encounter. We are
going to call this particular type of negative programming specific
to inner-motivated writing "the publication syndrome."

The publication syndrome is a type of self 2 programming that
can be paraphrased as follows:

> Anything I write must be read by someone other than myself
> or it's not worth my time to write it. Consequently, if I don't
> know who is going to read my short story, poem, or essay
> before I write, I might as well not even start.

Of course, the words are different from person to person, but the
statement above characterizes a type of thinking that all writers
tend to indulge in. Like the negative thinking that inhibits
motivation for outer-directed writing assignments, the publication
syndrome can, if you let it, stop you from all inner-directed writing
efforts. The first step in overcoming the publication syndrome is to
recognize the fallacies in it; the second step is to replace it with
some positive self 2 goals and images.

Fallacies of the Publication Syndrome

There are two fallacies inherent in the publication syndrome:

1. that the main purpose for writing is to have someone else read it
2. that you should have a guarantee of an audience before you
   write

It is a popular conception that the main purpose of writing is to
produce a product that will be read by someone other than the
author. However, if you consider what writing is, it becomes fairly
easy to see other purposes. Writing is nothing more than the
recording of conscious thought on paper. When we rearrange and
polish that thought, writing becomes something we want to show
others. However, simply recording one's thoughts can be of great
personal benefit to the writer. Such writing can be a means for an
author to learn about a topic. That writing generates self-knowl-
edge or self-discovery has been verified by many authors:

> Writers find their writing alive under their pen. What they
> have to say is continually evolving beneath the hand . . . As
> writers, we are drawn forward to see what argument comes
> forth in our essays, to find out if hero becomes victim in our
> novels, to discover the reason for an historic event in our

biographies, to experience the image which makes a blurred snapshot in our memory come clear in our poems. I received a magazine assignment to write a report on the elderly imprisoned in county homes. It was never written, but I have published a novel which has taken me inside the body of a young man who is a quadraplegic, who cannot move his arms or his legs. I set out to write a piece of journalism and found a novel. It could as easily have gone the other way. The writer is continually surprised by where language leads.[6]

Jessamyn West echoes these feelings: "I feel the same excitement a reader feels, because my characters say and do things I don't know they are going to say and do."[7] Larry McMurty adds, "the writing of a book is the process of finding out how it turned out that way."[8]

We can conclude that writing is by its nature a creative act, one that allows us to find out what we know or how we feel about a topic. Writing, then, does not have to be read by someone else to be useful. There are a number of situations in which you might want to write for yourself. Some of these are:

1. **A diary.** Get into the habit of writing down things you have experienced during the day that have affected you. It can be information you've learned or feelings or thoughts you've had.

2. **Note keeping.** Some famous writers and scientists (Leonardo DaVinci for one) developed the habit of keeping a notebook with them in which they would record their thoughts and impressions during the day.

3. **Write to alleviate emotions.** When angered or frustrated about something, try writing down your feelings. Read over what you have written. You might then throw the paper away as a symbolic gesture that your frustrations are over.

4. **Write to solve problems.** Some people use writing as a problem-solving technique. After writing out their thoughts on a problem, they look over what they have written, trying to identify errors in their logic and hidden assumptions that could be causing the problem.

5. **Write to make decisions.** Most people find it difficult to make decisions, especially important ones. Some people write out the possible consequences of their decisions as a way of vicariously experiencing different results. In this way they get a feel for what they might experience if they choose different alternatives and can, consequently, pick the one they will probably feel the best about.

We can see the lack of logic, then, in the first fallacy of the publication syndrome. That fallacy states that the main purpose of writing is to produce a product that someone else will read. But what about inner-directed writing that *is* intended for others to read? This brings us to the second fallacy of the publication syndrome.

The second fallacy inherent in the publication syndrome is that you must be guaranteed an audience before you write anything. Unfortunately, a rather hard fact about literary life is that not everything everyone writes is published. Hence there is an inherent risk in writing anything that is inner directed and intended for publication—the risk that no one will ever read your finished product. In effect, you must be willing to take a chance if you are to produce inner-directed writing intended for others.

Fortunately, the risk that your inner-directed writing will not be read can be lessened. Thousands of outlets exist for inner-directed writing. Most colleges and universities have school newspapers or publications sponsored by English departments or literary societies that publish original poems, essays, or short stories. Probably the writer's best source of information concerning outlets for inner-directed writing is a book entitled *Writer's Market*,[9] which comes out once a year. The book lists over 3,000 magazines, newsletters, and publishing houses where one might send a manuscript. A useful characteristic of the *Writer's Market* is that it breaks outlets down by subject. Thus, if you are interested in women's issues, the *Market* will identify for you magazines that accept articles in that area. It also describes how long or short articles should be for particular magazines, whether to include photos, how long the magazine will probably take to inform you whether your manuscript has been accepted, plus a great deal of other information that will facilitate the publishing process. The *Writer's Market* also lists literary societies and writer's guilds by state and the addresses of the people to contact for membership information.

Although the publication syndrome is fallacious, like all negative thoughts it can inhibit the process of inner-directed writing, because it can function as a failure goal used by our self 2 cybernetic motivation system.

The scheme for reversing this negative motivational process is the same for inner-directed writing as it is for outer-directed writing. It requires the daily, systematic imaging of goals and the control of negative thoughts. However, the goals of inner-directed writing are more general than those of outer-directed writing. For example, the following are areas in which goals for inner-directed writing may be established:

1. Your future as a writer. Do you want to develop your writing ability into a career or do you simply want to use it as an outlet for feelings and a way of releasing your creative energies?
2. The type of inner-directed writing you want to engage in. Is your primary interest in writing fiction, poetry, lyrics to music?
3. The amount of time you want to spend engaging in inner directed writing. Should you set up a writing schedule for yourself and begin practicing this art you want to master?

Images related to such goals will be more nebulous than those directed at a particular writing assignment. They will also probably change over time as you begin to clarify what you want to accomplish with your inner-directed writing. Thus, the mental programming used with inner-directed writing is a more long-term and flexible process than that used to improve motivation for a specific assignment. Improving motivation for inner-directed writing must become habitual and allow for the inevitable changes in your writing interests as time passes.

Characteristically, people who do a great deal of inner-directed writing can maintain a positive attitude toward their writing even during the dry times when they receive little or no positive feedback. The use of systematic daily programming should aid the maintenance of such an attitude.

SUMMARY

In this chapter we have identified a cybernetic approach to motivation that postulates that the subconscious mind functions as a goal-seeking mechanism motivating us to accomplish the goals given it by our conscious mind. If the subconscious mind is given negative goals it will work as a failure mechanism; if it is given positive goals it will work as a success mechanism. One way of consciously supplying the subconscious with new, positive success goals is to visualize yourself acting in positive ways or possessing desirable traits. These visualizing exercises should be done systematically for an extended period of time in order to fix the new goals in the subconscious. This technique can be applied to outer-directed writing (school-related writing) by imagining yourself having success and completing the assignment in an efficient and positive fashion. The technique can be applied to inner-directed writing by visualizing the type and amount of inner-directed writing you want to engage in and imagining the behaviors that will aid you in the production of that writing.

Exercises

1. The next time you are given a fairly lengthy assignment in class, monitor your thoughts and record them as soon as possible. Then analyze them for content. Are they primarily thoughts that would tend to make your motivational system work toward success on that assignment or are they thoughts that would program your motivational system to work as a failure mechanism?

2. On a trial basis, spend a few minutes each day positively programming your subconscious (self 2) for success the next time you are given an assignment of any kind. While doing this, keep a journal in which you record your behavior regarding that assignment. At the end of the trial period, evaluate the experience. Did the positive programming work? What actual changes in behavior did you see in yourself? Were there any changes in your attitudes about that particular course? That instructor? Yourself?

3. Identify the ways you would like to act as a student and then contrast your real behavior with your ideal behavior. Again, on a trial basis, spend some time each day for one week visualizing yourself acting in that ideal fashion. Keep a journal during that time in which you record and analyze your behavior. Have there been any real changes?

4. Identify in your life something you do or fail to do that you consider a negative trait. It might be something like not being punctual at meetings with friends, acting aggressively toward your spouse, friends, siblings, or parents, or being afraid to try new things. Once the negative trait has been identified, try to discover the type of thinking that motivates you to act in this negative fashion. In cybernetic terms, try to identify the failure goals you have given your subconscious mind. Where does this type of thinking come from? Where did it originate? Is it something you want to change?

5. Try writing to alleviate emotions. The next time you become frustrated, record your feelings as soon as possible. What is the emotional effect of doing this? Does a release result from expressing your feelings?

6. Use writing to help make your next important decision. Write out the possible outcomes of the various decisions you might reach.

7. Identify the outlets for inner-directed writing that exist in your college or university.

References

1. W. T. Gallwey, the *Inner Game of Tennis* (New York: Random House, 1974).

2. S. Brand, II *Cybernetic Frontiers* (New York: Random House, 1974), p. 28.

3. M. Maltz, *Psycho-Cybernetics* (New York: Pocket Books, 1977); K. M. Sayre, *Cybernetics and the Philosophy of Mind* (Atlantic Highlands, N. J.: Humanities Press, 1976).

4. B. Russell, *The Conquest of Happiness* (New York: Liveright, 1971), p. 154.

5. E. Worcester and S. McComb, *Body, Mind and Spirit* (Boston: Marshall Jones Co., 1931), p. 202.

6. D. M. Murray, "Teach the Motivating Force of Revision," paper presented at Rutgers Invitational Seminar on the Teaching of Composition (New Brunswick, N. J., 1976), p. 2.

7. Murray, p. 1.

8. Murray, p. 1.

9. W. Brohaugh and J. A. Beraha, eds., *Writer's Market* (Cincinnati, Ohio: Writer's Digest, 1979).

CHAPTER THREE

THE TOPIC

Topic considerations are usually very different in inner- and outer-directed writing situations. When writing is inner directed, the topic is closely related to the source of motivation. Something has stirred your emotions or imagination; you know what you want to write about. However, in such situations you might have the problem of narrowing the topic. For example, you might be very angered to find a pile of beer cans ten miles into a backpacking trail in Yosemite National Park, angered enough to want to write about it to effect some change. But specifically, what should you write about—the pile of rubbish you found during your trip, the problem of litter in general, the problem of litter in state parks, the problem of litter in Yosemite National Park? The issue here is not to identify a topic but to narrow a topic.

Topic narrowing can be an issue with outer-directed writing as well. For example, you are given the assignment in a political science class to write a report on suburban crime. Should it be suburban crime related to teenagers, suburban crimes against the elderly, suburban crime increase over the last ten years, five years, or two years? Besides topic narrowing, outer-directed writing can offer another, more basic problem concerning the topic—the problem of topic identification. Often college and university writing assignments are of the form:

Write a five-page descriptive essay on a topic of your choice.
Compare two historical figures of your choice.
Identify and describe an event in the 1960s that had a direct
  impact on the 1970s.

With such writing assignments the topic is not given to you; hence
the problem becomes one of topic identification, and then
narrowing the topic once you've identified it. Thus, there are two
problem areas concerning topics in writing: (1) topic identification,
and (2) narrowing the topic. We will consider each separately.

TOPIC IDENTIFICATION

Before writing this chapter, we asked twenty people (ten were
university students and ten were professional people in the
work force) if they thought they could write a five-hundred-
word essay on nuclear power (certainly a topic that everyone has
heard something about recently). The response of 85 percent of the
people was that they felt they didn't have enough knowledge about
the topic to write five hundred words. Yet when we continued to
talk to those people about nuclear power they were all able to
converse intelligently about the subject for over ten minutes,
during the course of which time they must have spoken five
hundred to one thousand words on the topic of nuclear power.
  This survey demonstrates that any individual has a fair amount
of knowledge about quite a few topics. The problem is really one of
identifying the topics you know the most about. There are two ways
of identifying topics for a writing assignment, or, stated another
way, there are two sources from which one can draw to identify
topics: (1) your own experience, and (2) the experiences of others.

Identifying Topics from Personal Experience

It is a well-known fact that man has an incredible ability to store
information in his brain. Wayne Dyer states that

> the brain, which is composed of ten billion, billion working
> parts has enough storage capacity to accept ten new facts
> every second. It has been conservatively estimated that the
> human brain can store an amount of information equivalent to
> one hundred trillion words, and that all of us use but a tiny
> fraction of this storage space.[1]

We can say, then, that housed in your mind is a wealth of information. This suggests that there are literally thousands of topics you could write about with some ease. The problem is really one of getting the information out. One way of doing this is through the use of "free writing."

In free writing you record (write) all the thoughts that come to mind within a certain period of time (for example, ten to fifteen minutes). The basic idea behind free writing is to allow your pen, pencil, or typewriter to record your thoughts as quickly as possible without attending to grammar, spelling, or punctuation. You shouldn't even try to write in complete sentences. What you put down on paper should be a representation of the random thoughts running through your mind.

Free writing can be either structured or unstructured. In unsructured free writing you put absolutely no constraints on what you write. You simply record anything that comes to mind. Example 3-1 shows unstructured free writing produced by a college student named Amy.

Example 3-1

First year of college. Dormitory life isn't so bad. I remember mom telling me about her first experiences in college—lived in the dorm for a year before pledging tri delta. She wanted me to join but I really don't know about the Greek system. My sister went to college during the 60's when no one was joining sororities. Now, it's the in thing to do—an individual needs to make up her own mind about the decisions in college, such as major, where to live, who to date and so on. One thing I do know—the food in the dorm is as bad as everyone says—the aroma in the cafeteria is almost unbearable. The smell of the food alone will cause me to lose twenty pounds.

Notice the lack of regard for punctuation and grammar in this example. Also notice the many different writing topics that could emerge from this brief exerpt. Amy begins by thinking about past memories: "I remember mom telling me about her first experiences in college." From this statement, Amy could probably produce a narrative composition focusing on the college experiences of her mother. Similarly, based on the statement "I feel that an individual needs to make up her own mind about decisions in college," she might decide to write a composition to persuade the reader that individuals need to make their own decisions. Finally, the statements about the aroma of the dormitory cafeteria ("The smell of the food alone will cause me to lose twenty pounds") could motivate Amy to write a descriptive essay in which she vividly portrays one day's breakfast, lunch, and dinner in the dormitory. The principle, then, underlying unstructured free writing is to record ideas (as many as possible) that can be translated into writing topics.

Structured free writing is the same as unstructured free writing except that your thoughts are restricted in some way. Generally there are considered to be three types of structured free writing: (1) memory; (2) sensory; and (3) reflexive.

The term "memory free writing" describes free writing in which thoughts are focused on events from your past life. The process is one of finding some time (as was mentioned before, about ten or fifteen minutes) and a quiet place, ignoring unrelated ideas, and forcing yourself to think about the past. Clear your mind of all other thoughts and search your memory for some event in your past that has stirred you. It usually doesn't take too long before some memorable event is recalled. It's at that time that you should start recording your thoughts. While writing you should try not to make any judgments about where your mind is taking you. Simply allow your mind to run over, through, and around the topic and let your hand record your experiences as words. Example 3-2 illustrates the results of some memory free writing done by a college freshman:

Example 3-2

It was quiet—I was in bed—my brother wasn't there—about 9 or 10 years old I think—shared a room with Louie—must have been about 2 or 3 in the morning—all the lights were out—I used to be scared as hell of the dark in those days—still am a little—I was probably dreaming but I'm not really sure—I remember sitting up—looking down at the foot of my bed and seeing a boy about my age—just stood there looking at me—even looked like me—didn't move—I think he was smiling or at least had the hint of a smile on his face—I remember he was dressed in a red and black checkered coat—the type you go hunting with—furry and really warm—had a hat on too but I can't remember what it looked like—had blue jeans and boots too—it's amazing how well I remember all this after so many years—strange thing was I wasn't frightened at first—I was sitting up—I'm sure of that—looking—not scared—just interested—then the boy faded away—like they do on Star Trek when they beam down to another planet—he just kind of vanished in front of me—and I still wasn't really that frightened—I did call my mother though—no—I yelled to be exact—guess I was scared after all—when she asked me what had happened I told her I had seen Joey—I never knew Joey though—he died a few days

after he was born—my mom's first baby—then came Louie, then me—I
remember after I said that to her, I didn't know why I said it—I didn't
remember thinking that it was Joey while I was seeing it—but when she
asked what had happened I just automatically said, "I saw Joey"—she
started crying right away and I just sat there amazed at what I had
said—it's been so long that I'm not sure anymore which facts were
accurate and which ones I've filled in—guess I really don't know what
happened back then.

As is true of all free writing, memory free writing is done without
paying any attention to spelling, punctuation, or sentence
structure. As Example 3-2 illustrates, memory free writing is an
attempt to dip into the mind and record the many varied thoughts
you have about a particular event from your past. If you truly
involve yourself in the experience, you will generally find that you
can resurrect some of the emotions associated with the event you
are recalling, as did the student who produced the memory free
writing found in Example 3-2.

Usually memory free writing produces information that can
easily be turned into a story (a narrative). It would be fairly simple,
for example, to transform the account in Example 3-2 into a story
about a boy who receives nocturnal visits from a being only he can
see. A plot could be identified, characters developed, rising and
falling action planned. Of course, narratives are not the only type of
writing that can spring from memory free writing. Example 3-2 also
suggests a scholarly paper on the possibilities of life after death.
Certainly this issue must have been in the mind of the author of the
free writing in this example. Hence that writer might be interested
in such a topic as: "Life After Death: Is There Any Evidence for or
Against?"

A second type of structured free writing is called sensory free
writing. Sensory free writing is accomplished by recording
everything you see, hear, taste, smell, feel during a given period of
time (ten to fifteen minutes). In sensory free writing, attention is
focused on the sensory information (sensations) you are receiving
at the present moment. Any time a sensory-stimulated thought
registers in your mind, record it.

In both sensory free writing and memory free writing, some
selection of thoughts occurs. Example 3-3 contains an example of
sensory free writing.

Sensory free writing usually produces a wider variety of
information from which to select topics than does memory free
writing, because in sensory free writing you focus on information

---

Example 3-3

cars are going by—they're really moving—I never noticed the sound that much before—really close to the freeway—very noisy—some other buzzing out there too—crickets—crazy ecologists—why is it they think that insect and animal noises are any more melodious than automated noises—they should hear those damn frogs about 3 a.m. some morning—nothing pretty about that at all—it's hot—about 95 I would guess—humidity must be about the same—my skin feels really clammy—the south can be unbelievable in August—I remember my visit to Eugene—God I really love the northwest—summers are cool and clear—well, sometimes clear—one of those big caterpillars in a tree outside my window—I wonder how many legs one of those things has—what does a caterpillar do on his day off anyway?—a green MGB just drove by—with a stripe—those things look fantastic on the highway—maneuverable—you can really dart in and out of traffic in them—certainly much better than a Triumph.

---

from different sources of input (your five senses), whereas with memory free writing you limit yourself to a single past event. In Example 3-3, the student focused his attention on the sound of traffic and the sound of insects when he concentrated on his sense of hearing. This in itself suggests a possible writing topic: "Natural vs. Mechanical Noises: Which Are More Melodious?" When the student concentrated on his sense of touch, he noticed the heat and humidity during the summer and then was immediately reminded of his trip to the northwest. This suggests a paper comparing the summer climates of the south and the northwest or one discussing the effects of weather on one's emotions. When the student shifted his attention to what he could see, he noticed an MGB driving by. This too suggests a topic, possibly a comparison of the benefits of an MGB and a TR7.

Sensory free writing also has the characteristic of generating many descriptive words related to sight, touch, taste, sound and smell. Consider Example 3-4.

Example 3-4

I'm on the beach—I don't see why we have to do this—I hate taking classes during the summer—anyway, there's a middle aged lady on the blanket next to me—really tan—with a green bathing suit—looks like a brown mountain with vegetation on it from this perspective—green, brown against a blue sky—kind of interesting—now a thin auburn haired girl has come into view—young—maybe a junior or senior in high school—covered with greasy sun lotion—boy she is with is black—muscular, curly hair—probably an athlete—I'm aware of the sun on my shoulders now—not painful but pleasant—gives the air a thick quality—makes me want to go to sleep or do anything but this—the wind is warm too and kind of sensuous. I can feel it on the bottoms of my feet like a massage, soft, tingly, warmth—the ocean smell is a contrast—not subtle at all—more pungent than anything else—it almost doesn't fit with the rest of the day—it mixes with the odor of mustard (lady on blanket next to me eating a hot dog) to create a strange combination.

A review of the writing in Example 3-4 reveals a number of descriptive sensory words:

Sight   tan
brown mountain
green bathing suit
blue sky
thin
black
auburn hair
muscular
curly hair

Touch   greasy
not painful
thick
sensuous
warm
massage
tingly

Smell   pungent
sharp

Sensory free writing not only helps identify a topic but also provides some vocabulary items that might be used within a particular essay. The words listed above might be used effectively in a descriptive essay about the beach.

The final type of structured free writing is reflexive free writing. Reflexive free writing is begun by focusing on memories or sensations but then gradually moving to opinions. From reflexive writing you can usually generate topics for expository writing that is persuasive in nature. To illustrate, consider the reflexive free writing in Example 3-5. It is an extension of the unstructured free writing by Amy in Example 3-1.

Example 3-5

The smell of the food alone will cause me to lose twenty pounds. Mom said that college food was great when she was in school. Also, it didn't cost her an arm and leg that it is costing me. Inflation has to be the biggest problem today. With gasoline and oil prices so high it is no wonder. I think the oil companies are ripping off the public making sure prices rise very fast so they can make a lot of money. Oil companies are also holding down on alternate sources of energy such as the sun. I know that dad makes more money than five years ago but inflation takes it away. Another cause of inflation is house prices. Since lumber and cement and brick cost more, house prices are going up and up. I think the only solution is mandatory wage and price controls.

As we saw in Example 3-1, Amy began her free writing by focusing on sensations (the smell of food) and memories ("I remember my mother"). But as we see in Example 3-5, Amy's thoughts gradually shifted to an emphasis on opinions as she began to concentrate on inflation. In a sense, the free writing in Example 3-5 reflects back to Amy her beliefs—beliefs she might not be conscious of. The free writing in Example 3-5 might motivate Amy to begin a paper on inflation and its effects on the middle-class American.

Reflexive free writing and the other types of free writing exercises are all effective ways of generating writing topics. Another useful topic-generating technique, similar to free writing, is "brainstorming." Brainstorming is similar to free writing in that thoughts are recorded as quickly as possible without paying attention to spelling, grammar, or punctuation. It is different from free writing in that it emphasizes words rather than sentences or phrases. Another difference is that brainstorming can be done by a small group of people (it is perhaps best done with more than one person) rather than by an individual.

When brainstorming you don't need any particular stimulus to get you started. You begin by recording any words that come to mind. It's usually best if a blackboard is available, but a piece of paper functions just as well. Once the first word is recorded, any other word that the recorded one reminds you of is written. The second word will probably remind you of another word, and so on. The underlying mental process is free association. Example 3-6 contains the product of some brainstorming done by a few university students.

Example 3-6

Football, violence, brutality, super bowl, New Orleans, Pittsburg, Steelers, party, fun, players, cheerleaders, national pastime, Sunday afternoons, fire, drinks, Lynn Swan, ballerina, touchdowns, excitement, halftime shows, boring, Roman Coliseum, lions and Christians, Detroit Lions, New Orleans Saints, players, stars, superstars, O.J., professional, collegians, football, Saturday afternoons, the powerhouses, Notre Dame, Alabama, Ohio State, Michigan, USC, collegians, professionals, future, fame, money, education

---

Once you stop brainstorming, you can look for patterns of thought that suggest possible writing topics. For example, in the brainstorming ideas above, the students begin their free association with *football*, then shift to *violence* and *brutality* and then shift to the *Super Bowl*. The theme of *violence* and *brutality* appears again, this time associated with the Roman *Colisem, lions* and *Christians*, with a swing in thinking back to the *Detroit Lions* and *New Orleans Saints*. This suggests a possible paper focusing on the brutality in football as the major source of interest for the spectators, comparing our modern day extravaganzas with those of the Romans 1,000 years ago. Another pattern of thought can be seen in the words *stars, superstars, professionals, collegians, future, fame,* and *money*. This suggests a paper emphasizing the fact that football is a very lucrative sport and can be the open door to future fame and fortune for many collegians.

Patterns of thought can sometimes be difficult to identify in brainstorming. The technique called "group and label" can facilitate the process of identifying patterns of thought. To illustrate, consider the brainstorming ideas in Example 3-7.

Example 3-7

man—woman—child—toys—baby—home—divorce—stability—happiness—security—food—shelter—emotions—child development—separation—lack of commitment—lure of world—sex—myth—false promises—television—pornography—advertisements—brainwashing—religion—standards—practical—unpopular—"me" generation—missing good things in life—weakening of society

---

The first step in the group and label technique is to group ideas that seem related. Looking over the brainstorming in Example 3-7, we might decide that the following concepts seem to go together:

man
woman
child
baby
toys
child development
home

Another group of related ideas seems to be:

divorce
stability
happiness
security
emotions
separation
weakening of society

A third grouping of ideas might include:

lure of the world
missing good things in life
myth
false promises
lack of commitment
me generation
television
pornography
advertisement
brainwashing

And a final group is:

religion
standards
practical
unpopular

Of course, different people will surely group ideas in different ways. The next step in the process is to label the groups or to try to state the general idea the concepts in a particular group seem to be about.

We might label the general theme of the first group "The Family Unit." The concepts in the second group might be entitled "Elements of Family Dissolution." The third and fourth groups might be labeled "Sources Acting Toward Dissolution" and "Sources Working Toward Unification of Family," respectively. With the groups labeled we now have a clear idea of the patterns of thought produced by our brainstorming. Apparently four basic concepts are illustrated in Example 3-7. Each of these might be pursued as an individual topic or two or more of them combined in some fashion to create a topic for writing.

Free writing and brainstorming, then, are techniques that can be used to generate possible writing topics and even help establish the skeleton of a structure for a paper. Both techniques draw from a person's experiences and identify for the writer ideas and information stored in memory. Many times, though, we might want to identify a topic from someone else's experience.

Identifying a Topic from Someone Else's Experience

Experiencing something as a result of someone else's account of an event is called vicarious experience. For example, if you saw the movie *Jaws*, you probably experienced much of the terror any individual would while being pursued by a three-ton, angry fish with over seventy six-inch teeth. Probably every time you read a book, see a movie, listen to a poem, or hear music you are experiencing and learning something vicariously. Therefore, we can identify many writing topics from our vicarious experiences. Two techniques are useful in identifying topics from vicarious experience: (1) question asking, and (2) use of reference sources.

Question asking is a powerful method of topic identification. When you use the question-asking technique you are role playing, having a discussion with yourself by asking yourself questions that will help identify the vicarious experiences that have interested you the most. A few questions you might ask are:

1. What TV programs, movies, books, have I seen, read, heard that have intrigued me?
2. What was the program (book, etc.) about?
3. Can I identify a general theme or topic that was the cause of my interest?
4. Have I ever had similar experiences to those related in the book, movie, etc.?

5. What else do I know about the topic other than what was presented in the book (movie, etc.)? Where can I go to get more information?
6. Is the topic interesting enough to me that I would be willing to get more information about it?
7. Is the topic one that could be expanded into a paper?
8. What type of paper could be written about the topic?
9. Is the topic one that lends itself to the requirements of the paper (assuming that the writing is outer directed or assigned to you)?

To illustrate how a student could use question asking, let's consider an example. We asked Jeff, a 19-year-old college freshman, to use the question-asking technique to identify a possible writing topic. Below are his answers to the questions:

Question 1: What TV program, movie, or book have I seen (read, heard) that has intrigued me?

Answer: The movie *The Deerhunter* was one I really enjoyed.

Question 2: What was the movie about?

Answer: It was about three friends who grew up and lived in a steel mill town in Pennsylvania. They grew up and worked in the mills together and became very close. The movie took place during the early part of the Viet Nam war in which they all enlisted. They were captured by the Viet Cong and forced to play Russian roulette as a form of entertainment for the guards, who would bet to see which contestant would blow his brains out first. The three escape but are separated during their attempt. All of them make their way to Saigon, though, but none are aware that the others have survived. One, I believe his name was Danny, stumbles upon a game of Russian roulette being played in Saigon. This time, of course, the contestants are volunteers, who apparently receive a large share of the profits from the betting if they win. It seemed as though this was a fairly common form of gambling since there was a large crowd in the gallery watching and betting on the outcome of the various contests. Danny becomes intrigued with the whole thing and eventually stays in Saigon becoming a player in the contests. The other two friends in the set (one's name was Mike, but I can't remember the name of the third person) go back home. Mike returns back to their hometown, but the other one goes to a military hospital because he has lost the use of his legs and one arm. He is ashamed of his condition and doesn't want his wife or parents to ever see him again. Mike learns that his friend is in the hospital and goes to see him. Mike's reaction is pretty profound when he sees his invalid friend. He doesn't react with shock or pity; he simply says: "You look great." They talk and Mike asks if there has been any news from or about Danny. His friend says that he keeps getting money in the mail from Saigon. Fairly large amounts of money. Mike pieces things together and figures that it must be from Danny. He goes back to Saigon, which is about to fall, and tracks Danny down, of course, learning that he has become a regular and highly successful player in the roulette contests. When Mike finds Danny, he does not recognize Mike. Apparently to endure the pressure of being a roulette contestant Danny keeps himself constantly high on drugs. Mike tries to shake Danny back to reality and begs him to come back home. Danny still doesn't respond. Finally Mike has to challenge Danny to a roulette contest so that he can keep talking to him. Throughout the contest, Mike keeps trying to remind Danny of the past and tells him to come back home. Danny loses the contest and blows his brains out, but a moment before he pulled the trigger for the last time, you get the impression that he briefly recognized Mike and realized just how deep Mike's love and friendship ran for him.

Question 3: Can I identify a general theme or topic that was the cause of my interest?

Answer: I'm not sure what there was about the movie that affected me, but something did. I couldn't move for a few minutes when the movie was over. I just had to sit there and compose myself. I think it had something to do with the love and loyalty Mike had for his friends and the power of that. He risked his life for them more than once. But the movie didn't portray that love in an idealistic way. Their friendship was very real and they were very real characters. Many times they were extremely crude and insensitive to one another but it seemed like when things got down to the basics, when they were all facing death, that the power of that love came out and made them, especially Mike, tremendously courageous men. I guess I was moved because I want to believe that we all have that capability, or I'd like to believe that I do but, of course, I'm not sure. I don't know. There's a part of me that thinks I'd turn tail and run if my life were on the line rather than risk it for some friends. But then I've heard stories about very ordinary people doing very courageous things for people they loved.

Question 4: Have I ever had a similar experience to those related in the movie?

Answer: No. Of course not. I mean I've never been to Viet Nam or done anything courageous for a friend. But I have had strong feelings of love for a person before. Oddly enough it was another man—my cousin Paul. He's dead now. Died in Viet Nam, as a matter of fact. We went to different high schools but stayed pretty close. Our senior year he was third in the state in the discus. I usually get jealous at someone else's accomplishment but I didn't with Paul. I was really proud of him and our senior year I did a lot to support him because he was training very hard for the state meet. I even went to a lot of his meets just to kind of cheer him on. And that's really not like me. Maybe the way we felt about each other approached an unselfish love.

Question 5: What else do I know about the topic other than what was presented in the movie? Where can I go to get more information?

Answer: I guess the topic I've identified has something to do with unselfish love but I've never really thought much about it before. I don't know where you go to find out more about that sort of thing. I know of a text used in one of the philosophy courses called *The Art of Loving.* Maybe that talks about different types of love.

Question 6: Is the topic interesting enough to me that I would be willing to get more information on it?

Answer: Yes, definitely.

Question 7: Is the topic one that could be expanded into a paper?

Answer: I don't know yet.

Question 8: What type of paper could be written about the topic?

Answer: I imagine one that discussed different types of love. A comparison.

Question 9: Is the topic one that lends itself to the requirements of the paper?

Answer: This question doesn't apply to me.

As the answers above illustrate, not all questions are relevant to every writing situation. However, many of them open up possible writing topics because they force you to understand your gut reaction and determine what there was about an experience that triggered emotions in you. In Jeff's case, the reason he was affected by *The Deerhunter* was that he had experienced something similar: a genuine, unselfish caring for another person. Even though the context of the movie and Jeff's experience were quite different, the experiences had a strong common thread. The questions were a way of bringing this out—a way of identifying a theme that was important to Jeff.

Identifying topics from vicarious experience via question asking is one way to use the experience of others to generate topics. A second way is through the use of reference sources, which contain information that you may not know from your own personal experiences.

A good place to begin a search for a possible topic is the library card catalogue. Depending on the library that you use, the card catalogue will list books by author, subject, title, or all three. For topic identification purposes, it is perhaps best to use the subject cards. To illustrate, we'll consider how subject matter cards are organized and how they might be used to identify a topic.

Let's say that you are interested in nuclear power and want to find some possible writing topics in that general area. The first thing you would do is to look in the card catalogue under the subject Nuclear. Under this broad heading you would find other headings listed in alphabetical order such as:

Nuclear
Nuclear Age
Nuclear Analysis
Nuclear Astrophysics
Nuclear Chemical Engineering
Nuclear Chemistry
Nuclear Collective Molecules
Nuclear Data
Nuclear Dilemma
Nuclear Diplomacy
Nuclear Electronics
Nuclear Energy
Nuclear Radiochemistry
Nuclear Reactors

These headings would help narrow your topic and identify a more specific topic within the general category Nuclear. For example, suppose you identified nuclear energy and nuclear reactors as something you might want to explore further. You could go to the card file and identify titles of books under those more specific topics. Some of the titles you would find might be:

Nuclear Energy and National Security
Nuclear Energy and U.S. Fuel Economy 1955–80
Nuclear Energy Conversion
Nuclear Energy in Britain During the Last War
Nuclear Energy in Industry
Nuclear Energy in Space
Nuclear Energy in the West
Nuclear Energy: Its Physics and Its Social Challenge
Nuclear Energy Techniques
Nuclear Energy Terms

Nuclear Reactor Analysis
Nuclear Reactor Control Engineering
Nuclear Reactor Engineering
Nuclear Reactor Experiments
Nuclear Reactor Instrumentation
Nuclear Reactor Materials
Nuclear Reactor Metallurgy
Nuclear Reactor Neutrons Energy Spectra
Nuclear Reactor Physics
Nuclear Reactor Plant Data

The next step would be to obtain the books, page through the table of contents of some of them to get an idea about their contents, and single out those you might want to read. You could then begin reading parts of a few selected books to help gather background information. At this stage your reading should be very superficial. Your purpose is not to gather information (we will discuss that in Chapter 5) but simply to get a feel for a topic.

Besides the card catalogue, bibliographies are a good source for identifying topics. Bibliographies list books and magazine articles on selected topics. The following are nine bibliographies commonly found in college and university libraries:

Bibliographic Index
Book Review Digest
Cumulative Book Index
Essay and General Literature Index
International Index

The New York Times Index
Nineteenth-Century Reader's Guide
Reader's Guide to Periodical Literature
Union List of Serials

The most commonly used of the above-mentioned bibliographies is the *Reader's Guide to Periodical Literature*. This bibliography identifies current magazine articles about selected topics. The list of magazines indexed in the *Reader's Guide* is given at the beginning of each volume. The entries are arranged in alphabetical order by subject matter; in addition, there are "See also" entries that refer you to other topics—topics related to the one you have selected. The *Reader's Guide* is published monthly in paperback form and once a year in hard cover. To illustrate how you might use the *Reader's Guide*, assume you have narrowed your topic down to the general area of nuclear reactors. You have browsed through some books on that subject and feel that they are too technical: you still need more information that is at your level. You look up nuclear reactors in the *Reader's Guide* and find a number of articles (see Example 3–8). There you find articles about a specific type of reactor—the breeder reactor. The entries about breeder reactors identify for you the magazine, the title of the article, the volume number of the magazine, the date (issue) of the magazine, and the specific pages on which the article appears. With this information you can then go to those magazines and skim the articles.

One final reference source that can help you identify a topic is the encyclopedia. Students often use the encyclopedia to obtain a general overview of their topic and then use the *Reader's Guide* or books found in the card catalogue to collect more in-depth information.

NARROWING YOUR TOPIC

Identification is not the only issue you must deal with when considering a topic: Often you must also be concerned with narrowing your topic. For example, it is unrealistic to attempt to write a five-page essay on a topic such as "nuclear energy." The books written on that general topic would fill an entire wing of a large library. Something as broad as "nuclear energy" is a general theme or general topic rather than a writing topic. A general topic must be narrowed down to a workable writing topic. For example, the following are all topics that have been derived from the general topic "nuclear energy":

Nuclear Energy Used in the Home
Possible Uses of Nuclear Energy in the Future
Use of Nuclear Energy for Medical Reasons

These topics are easier to write about than "nuclear energy" because they are more specific and hence conducive to discussion within the confines of a short paper. Yet all of these topics were derived from the same general topic by means of limiting. For example, the first topic, "Nuclear Energy in the Home," limits the theme by specifying a place. The second topic, "Possible Uses of Nuclear Energy in the Future," limits the general topic by identifying a specific time frame. The third topic, "Use of Nuclear Energy for Medical Reasons," limits by specifying a reason.

Example 3-8
Reader's Guide to Periodical Literature
March 1977—February 1978*

NUCLEAR powered submarines.
  See Submarine boats, Atomic powered
NUCLEAR-powered warships.
  See Warships, Atomic powered
NUCLEAR reactions
  Analyzing hydrogen with nuclear reactions, S.T. Picraux, bibl il Phys
  Today 30:42-3 + 0 '77
    See also
  Nuclear fission
  Nuclear fusion

NUCLEAR reactors
  Breeder: First prototype shut down for repairs, W. D. Met. il Science 195:972 Mr 11 '77
  Breeder's progress: when a veto is not a veto. W. D. Met. Science 198:710-11 N 18 '77.
  Breeding in light water: the test begins; Shippingport, Pa. il Sci N 112:164 S 10 '77.
  Breeding in the U.S. Sci Am 236:58 Mr '77
  Carter's new plutonium policy: maybe less than meets the eye; effect on Clinch River

reactor. W. D. Metz. Science 196:405-7 Ap 22 '77
Comparative breeding characteristics of fusion and fast reactors. P. Fortescue. il Science 196:1326-9 Je 17 '77
Engineer's memo stirs doubts on Clinch River breeder. D. Shaple. Science 197:350-2 Jl 22 '77.
How states can nuclearize. F.C. Barnabe. il Ann Am Acad 430:29-43 Mr '77
Japan's complete breeder reactor. Sci N 111:22 Ja 8 '77
Landscape of nuclear tombs: decommissioning. A. Park. Progressive 41:30-1 D '77
Nuclear laser power up 100-fold. Sci N 112:69 Jl 30 '77
Possible reprieve for the fast breeder; Clinch River Project. Bus W p31-2 Je 20 '77

Cost
Economic issues of the breeder reactor program. B. G. Chon, bibl il Science 195:551-6 F 11 '77

Fuel
See Nuclear fuels
History
Birth of the atomic reactor. il Sci
  Digest 81:55-8 F '77
  Laws and Regulations
  See Atomic power—Laws and
  regulations
  Maintenance and Repair
Nuclear denting plagues the utili-
ties. Bus W p20-1 Jl 4 '77
Manufacture
See Atomic power industry
Safety devices and measures
Is nuclear energy acceptable? A.
M. Weinberg. bibl Bull Atom
Sci 33:54-60 Ap '77:
Looking back on the Rasmussen
report. F. V. Hippel. bibl il Bull
Atom Sci 33:42-7 F '77.
Reactor safety: Congress hears
critics of Rasmussen report.

P.M. Boff; discussion. Science
194:476-80; 195: 344+;
196:1387-9 0 29 '76, Ja 28, Je 24
'77
Reactor safety: independence of
Rasmussen study doubted. D.
Shap. Science 197:29-30 Jl 1 '77
This month's feature: controversy
over nuclear reactor safety.
Cong Digest 56:34-64 F '77
NUCLEAR security measures. See
Atomic power—Security mea-
sures
NUCLEAR spin
Proton spin surprise. il Sci N
112:196 S 24 '77
Second back bend helps ex-
plain nuclear band crossing.
H. R. Leuchtag. il Phys Today
30:17-19 S '77
NUCLEAR test ban. See Atomic
weapons—Testing.

Narrowing a topic is a process of limiting a general topic, usually in one or more of the following ways:
1. by specifying where the main theme takes place (**location**)
2. by specifying when the main theme takes place (**time**)
3. by specifying the manner of the main theme or conditions surrounding it (**manner**)
4. by specifying the reason for the main theme (**reason**)
5. by specifying the person or thing that is the originator of the action in the main theme (**agent**)
6. by specifying the person or thing that receives the action in the main theme (**receiver**)

Not all general topics can be limited in all ways. The ways in which a theme can be limited depend on the words you select to express the general topic. Topics expressed using action words (verbs) can usually be constrained by most, if not all, of the limitations. General topics expressed using nouns (names of people, places, things) are usually less capable of being specified by all six limitations. We will briefly consider each of the six limitations and then discuss a general technique for limiting or narrowing general themes.

1. **Location.** Most general topics can be limited by location. For example, consider the following:

Nuclear Energy
Jogging
Sports

Each of these can be narrowed by location in the following ways:

Nuclear Energy in the Home
Jogging around Your Own Backyard
Sports under the Large Domes

Usually prepositions are used whenever you limit a topic by location. Some of the more commonly used location-limiting prepositions are: to, toward, at, through, into, up, down, from, across, along, around, near, about, by, beyond, within, upon, on, off, in, inside, above, below, beneath, behind, between, under, among. Thus one way of limiting a general topic is to try out some of these prepositions (along with some other words, of course). Usually if the topic can be limited by location, that limitation will come to mind as you go through the list of prepositions.

Another way of imposing a location limitation on a topic is by attaching a possessive noun to the main theme. For example, we could have written:

Florida's Use of Nuclear Energy
California's Approach to Jogging
Montana Sports

2. **Time.** Most general topics can be limited by time. For example, we could limit our general topics by time in the following ways:

Nuclear Energy Today
Jogging During the Early Morning Hours
Sports of Ancient Greece

Again, certain words are generally used to limit a theme by time. Occasionally prepositions are used, but adverbs can also be used. The following are some commonly used adverbs that limit a theme by time: today, tomorrow, yesterday, tonight, someday, seldom, sometimes, often, never, daily, always, forever, again, yearly, annually, semiannually. Some prepositions that are used as time limiters are: within, on, in between, about, toward, to, at, from, across, around, since.

3. **Manner.** Manner means the specific circumstances or conditions under which the action or events of your general topic

occur. For example, our sample themes can be limited by manner in the following way:

Uncontrolled Use of Nuclear Energy
Violent Sports
Excessive Jogging

Manner limitations on a topic are usually accomplished by using adjectives. In the topics above, "nuclear energy" is limited by the adjective "uncontrolled," "sports" is limited by the adjective "violent," and "jogging" by the adjective "excessive." Unlike prepositions, the number of which is fairly limited in our language, the number of adjectives is very large. The following list gives you ideas for words that can be used as manner-limiting adjectives.

Adjectives describing worth or value: precious, major, main, important, necessary, spare, valuable, special, ordinary, essential, scarce, common, invaluable, worthless

Adjectives describing complexity: plain, simple, bare, uniform, adorned, unadorned, steady, fancy, elaborate, complicated.

Adjectives describing the extent to which something is known: known, unknown, familiar, secret, common, private, public, personal, famous, popular, universal, prominent.

Adjectives describing speed or quickness: slow, sudden, swift, fast, fleet, rapid, sluggish, express, instant, immediate, constant.

Adjectives describing mobility: mobile, moveable, motionless, stationary, static.

Adjectives specifying the time of an event: colonial, medieval, prehistoric, ancient, antique, temporary, permanent, momentary, continual, contemporary.

Adjectives implying a negative judgment: terrible, awful, dreadful, horrible, ghastly, pitiful, useless, ridiculous.

Adjectives implying a positive judgment: exceptional, fabulous, fantastic, marvelous, memorable, outstanding, tremendous, supurb, spectacular, remarkable, extraordinary.

Adjectives describing uniqueness: strange, queer, special, peculiar, irregular, distinctive, uncommon, random, rare, odd, severe, weird.

Adjectives describing ease or difficulty: dangerous, difficult, impossible, easy, grave, harmful, harmless, hazardous, unsafe, tiresome, treacherous, perilous, troublesome.

4. **Reason.** Another way of limiting a general topic is by identifying the reason for the action involved in the theme.

Nuclear Energy Used for Medical Purposes
Jogging to Quit Smoking
Sports as an Outlet for Aggression and Hostility

Commonly the prepositions *for*, *to*, and *as* are used to limit a topic by reason. However, there are a variety of other ways that the same limitation can be accomplished:

Nuclear Energy for the Purpose of . . .
Jogging in Order to . . .
Sports with the Intent of . . .

5. and 6. **Agent** and **Receiver.** We consider agent and receiver together because they are closely related. The agent identifies the initiator or cause of the action in the general topic and the receiver identifies the recipient of the action. Only some general themes can be limited by agent or receiver. For example, out of our three sample themes, only "jogging" can take an agent ("Women Jogging") and none can readily take a receiver. An example of a general topic that can take an agent and receiver is "Aggression." Limiting this theme by specifying an agent and a receiver might yield us:

Women's Aggression toward Men

As can be inferred from this example, certain prepositions mark the receiver of an action. Most commonly those prepositions are: to, toward, for, at. The prepositions *by* and *from* are sometimes used to mark the agent, but more commonly the agent is stated as a noun preceding the main theme. Sometimes those nouns are stated in possessive form:

Men's Aggression
Women's Aggression

As was mentioned previously, most general topics cannot be limited in all six ways, and doing so would yield a topic that would be too specific. For example, limiting the theme of "aggression" in all six ways might give us something like: "Controlled Female Aggression toward Men to Lessen Anxiety during Periods of High Stress in the Home and at Work." Breaking this topic down, we have:

Controlled: Manner Limitation
Female: Agent Limitation

Aggression: Main Theme
toward Men: Receiver Limitation
to Lessen Anxiety: Reason Limitation
during Periods of High Stress: Time Limitation
in the Home and at Work: Place Limitations

This topic might be too specific for a student paper. The reason for limiting a theme or narrowing a topic should be to shrink a topic down to a size that fits well with the length and nature of the paper intended by the author.

To narrow a topic, then one can simply run through the various prepositions, adverbs, and adjectives that commonly mark the different types of limiters, attaching each to the general topic and seeing which stimulus brings to mind usable topics.

A more general way of accomplishing the same task is to ask specific questions about the general topic—questions whose answers limit the topic in the six above-mentioned ways. To accomplish this the following questions can be used:

1. Ask *where* to limit the *location*
2. Ask *when* to limit the *time*
3. Ask *how* to limit the *manner*
4. Ask *why* to limit the *reason*
5. Ask *who* or *what* or *by whom* or *what* to limit the *agent*
6. Ask *to whom or what* or *for whom or what* to limit the *receiver*

To illustrate this technique, let's consider a situation in which you have identified the general topic "sexuality." By asking *where*, you might decide that you want to write about "Sexuality in the United States." By asking *when*, you could further limit your topic by choosing to write about "Sexuality in the United States Since 1970." You could decide to stop limiting the topic here, but for illustrative purposes let's assume that you want to narrow the topic further. Asking *how* or *why* about the topic doesn't seem to fit, indicating that this topic is not easily limited by manner or reason. But asking *who* about the topic might compel you to narrow it still further to "Male Sexuality in the United States Since 1970." Finally, asking *to whom* or *for whom* could lead you to: "Male Sexuality Toward Other Males in the United States Since 1970." Shortening the wording of this would produce "Male Homosexuality in the United States Since 1970." As can be seen, the final wording of the topic can (and probably should) differ from the wording you use when answering the questions. If we wanted, we could take this new topic, "Male Homosexuality in the United

States Since 1970" and ask questions about it until we identify a subtopic. Again, the questions would be used simply as a device to help narrow and limit a topic.

The Thesis Statement

Some authors find it useful to write a thesis statement. The thesis of an essay is its main point, its central idea; it is the reason you are writing the paper. Identifying and narrowing a topic is a major part of formulating a thesis, but the topic is not the thesis itself. For example, suppose we have narrowed the general topic "Sexuality" to "Male Homosexuality in the United States Since 1970." What precisely do we want to say about male homosexuality in the United States since 1970? A thesis statement will help us define this. Of course, about this particular topic there are many possible thesis statements:

> The increase in male homosexuality in the United States since 1970 has added to the general decay of our society and the breakdown of the family unit.

> The increase in male homosexuality in the United States since 1970 has helped liberate mankind both sexually and intellectually.

> The increase in male homosexuality in the United States since 1970 is not really an increase in sexual activity but an increase in honesty about sexual activity.

As can be inferred from the statements above, your thesis represents your preconceived beliefs or hypotheses about the topic. When you begin to collect information and start writing, your beliefs about the topic might change, but this does not negate the importance and usefulness of having a belief or hypothesis from which to start.

A common flaw in thesis-statement writing is to make the statement overly general or self-evident. For example, consider the following thesis statement:

> Teaching hearing-impaired elementary school children is a noble profession.

This thesis statement is far too general to give much direction to the writer. An improved version might be:

The teacher of hearing-impaired elementary school children is responsible for training such students in our most valuable skill—communication.

Here we have specified exactly what it is that makes teaching a noble profession. A specific thesis statement is much easier to research and write about than a general one. The more precise you can be in your thesis statement, the more facile will be the writing process.

SUMMARY

When dealing with topics, two things must be considered: (1) topic identification, and (2) topic narrowing. Topic identification can be accomplished by drawing from your own experiences or drawing from vicarious experiences. Some techniques useful for drawing topics from your own experience are (1) free writing and (2) brainstorming. Identifying topics through vicarious experiences can be accomplished by (1) question asking and (2) use of reference sources. Many times your efforts to identify a topic yield a general rather than a specific topic to write about within the context of a given writing assignment. General topics can be turned into viable topics by limiting them in various ways, such as by (1) location, (2) time, (3) manner, (4) reason, (5) agent, and (6) receiver. One way of determining whether your general topic can be limited in one or more of the six ways is by asking *where, when, how, why, by whom,* and *for whom* about the theme. After a topic has been identified it is also useful to write a thesis statement that summarizes the main point or central idea of the essay.

Exercises

1. Do the sensory free writing and memory free writing exercises described in the chapter, then compare the two products. What differences do you notice in the type of language each elicits? What differences are there in the content of the thoughts produced?

2. With a small group of people, try the brainstorming activity described in the chapter. When you are finished, group the ideas generated into categories. When you have finished grouping ideas, try to label groups. What writing topics do the labels suggest?

3. Below is an example of unstructured free writing. From it identify as many writing topics as possible.

When I began college last fall the first prof I had was a Mr. Zimmer—it was a lecture class which means there were 200 of us stuffed into a hall that held about 150—first impression of Zimmer favorable. Youngish (about 30)—slim—hair on the long side. But when he sat down he made all the noises that an old man would make while sitting—as though he was trying to give the impression of being mature and tired and unimpressed and bored with all of us—he had the mike turned up too high so when he spoke we heard every "p" with a pop and every "s" with a hiss. It also became very apparent very soon (to me at least) that he was flirting with all the women. Every chance he got he would say something like "Doesn't that turn you on." Basically he reinforced my belief that some teachers are up there because they are ego maniacs and use the classroom as a platform to show how incredible intelligent, witty, sexy, compassionate, all of the above, they are.

4. Perform the question-asking exercises described in the chapter using a book or story that you've read and any movie or play that you have seen. Compare your answers for the two mediums of expression (print and visual). Do you see any differences in the answers that are products of the two different modes of expression?

5. For each of the following general topics, identify three books and three articles that would be useful in collecting information about them:

Venereal Disease
Professional Soccer
Teenage Marriages
Life After Death
Corporal Punishment in Public Schools

6. Take the general topics identified in Exercise 4 above and limit them in as many of the six ways listed in the chapter as possible.

7. Write a thesis statement for each of the topics generated from Exercise 6 above.

References

1. W. W. Dyer, *Your Erroneous Zones* (New York: Funk & Wagnalls, 1976), p. 42.

CHAPTER FOUR

AUDIENCE AND FORMAT

The **audience** of your paper is the person or people for whom you are writing; the **format** of your paper is its form or overall organizational pattern. We discuss audience and format in the same chapter because of the close interrelationship between them. That relationship is one of causation: The audience you write for greatly determines the format you use. For example, if you wanted to explain to a group of kindergarteners how important brushing one's teeth is, you might make up a story about a family of teeth that lived on a pink hill in a little girl's mouth. You would go on to state how the teeth were happy when the little girl brushed but became sick and sad when she didn't. Conversely, if you wanted to convey this same information to a group of dental students you would write a scholarly, analytic paper in which you used highly technical terms. With different audiences you would use different formats.

The audience you write for affects far more than the format; it also determines the language you use, the conventions you use, and your choice of words. James Moffett, a well-known writer about writing, speaks of audience in the following way:

The designs a speaker has on his audience and the operation he performs on his subject govern jointly features of discourse from word choice, punctuation and sentence structure, to paragraph development and overall organization.

Whether I call the green film on the surface of a pond "spring algae" or "scum" is of great rhetorical significance because of the difference in effect on my audience.[1]

Some of the effects of audience on writing will be considered in the following section.

AUDIENCE

Considerations of audience include three related areas: (1) your purpose in writing as it relates to your audience, (2) your familiarity with the audience, and (3) your stance in relationship to your audience.

Purpose as It Relates to Audience

Purpose and audience are closely interconnected, yet many writers never consciously consider their overall purpose, probably because they don't realize how drastic an effect it can have on a paper. For example, imagine how differently you might use the same information if your purpose was to persuade rather than inform. If you wanted to inform your audience about how aluminum is made, you might list the processes or steps involved in its production. However, if your purpose was to persuade your audience that producing aluminum is a highly efficient and nonpolluting process, you might interject many subjective comments or words aimed at giving a favorable impression about aluminum production.

The effect of different purposes on writing is most readily seen in advertisements, all of which are meant to persuade an audience that a particular product is useful and highly desirable. For example, one Mexican restaurant chain in the Southwest makes tacos by slicing their meat rather than grinding it. They regularly run an ad in regional magazines in which they state: "They grind it out; we slice it up." The wording of the advertisement illustrates an important point about purpose in writing. Instead of saying "They grind it up; we slice it up," they say, "They grind it out." "Grind it out" implies that something has been taken out of the quality or taste of the meat, but "slice it up" does not. Since the purpose of the authors of this ad is to persuade you that their tacos are better than their competitors', they do so by introducing words, and phrases that carry a value judgment.

It is important to clarify and keep in mind your purpose for writing as well as your audience, because both have profound effects on your product. One artificial yet effective technique for clarifying this is to state your purpose, audience, and topic in one sentence by using the frame: My purpose is to (purpose) (to) (audience) about/that (topic) . For example, using the topic "Jogging for Women to Improve Health in Later Years," we might write:

> My purpose is to persuade a college P.E. instructor that jogging can improve health for women in later years.

The test frame helps clarify for the writer exactly why and to whom he or she is writing.

Familiarity with Audience

Audience in writing is similar to audience in speaking. The way you talk to your friends is different from the way you speak to an English professor: You change your language depending upon your audience, and the same thing happens when you write.

There are many different types of audiences. Usually your paper will be more or less restricted depending on your audience. Generally, the more you know about your audience the less restricted you are in your writing, or the freer you are to use structures, words, and phrases that are not conventional. However, if you don't know much about your audience, you must follow the common conventions of writing. To illustrate this, we'll consider four categories of audiences.

The first category of audience you could write for, and the one that would require the least restriction, is yourself. We saw in Chapter 2 that there are a number of situations in which you might want to write for yourself, including journals and diaries, writing to express strong emotions, writing to solve problems, writing to make decisions, and note keeping. Because you are writing for yourself in these situations, and because you know the audience so well, you can be very informal. You do not have to follow rules or conventions of writing, such as spelling words correctly, or writing in complete sentences. You can make up your own type of code if you want.

Use of a personal code can be found in most diaries. Below is a typical diary entry:

—bad day—no time for #1—tried to talk to J.D. but she was playing Farrah again—can't stand it when she does that—blew that damn history xam—the steelers got in the way—

Note that in this entry the student has taken liberties with standard writing conventions: He has used no particular organizational scheme; sentence structure is nonexistent; there is no formal attention paid to punctuation, capitalization, or spelling. The student has used abbreviations and symbols that probably only he can interpret. In a sense he has developed his own language. An interpretation of this diary entry might be:

> #1 means myself. Thus the student had no time for himself that day, which seemed to be a bad one all around. He tried to talk to J.D., which are probably the initials of a woman, but she was acting snobbish, as a movie star might act (Farrah). The student also did poorly in a history exam (xam), because he spent time watching the Pittsburg Steelers game instead of studying (the steelers got in the way).

When writing to yourself as audience, you can take many shortcuts. As long as you know what the symbols on the page mean, you can write whatever you like. When writing to an audience you know everything about, you are unrestricted in the conventions you can and cannot use.

The next category of audience is that of friends; people you know well. These are people to whom you might send letters, postcards, or notes. Once again, because you know your audience well you can be informal, but not as informal as you are when writing to yourself. For example, you could not write a note to a friend that would look like the journal entry above. But you might write something like the following:

Dear Bill,

Just a brief note to let you know what's happening. Started school a few weeks ago. Taking some pretty tough courses—bio, chem, History (American), English lit and econ. Screwed up my first history exam.

Should of studied the Sunday before but Bradshaw and the boys got in the way. God they look great this year. What do you think? I'm still going (or trying to) go out with Jane but she's been an incredible snob this year. You know, like the way she used to act sometimes back at Jefferson—real beauty queen syndrome. I just can't get close to her when she's like that. Not much else to say. *Write would you, pleeeeeeeeease.* Did you break your arm or just forget how to spell. Put an X on a page and send it—anything—I'll know who its from.

> Take it easy,
> Me

In this letter the author's writing is still fairly unrestricted. He has used words and phrases that convey precise meanings to the person for whom the letter is intended but would not be meaningful to anyone else. For example, "Bradshaw and the boys" conveys the idea of the Pittsburg Steelers football team to Bill, but it would not necessarily do so to the general public. Also, "like she used to act back at Jefferson" probably conveys a whole set of behaviors to Bill that would have to be explained to someone else.

When writing to someone you know very well, then, it is common to use language and symbols that only you and that person understand. You don't have to explain many things. A single word can convey an entire message.

The third category of audience includes teachers, instructors, and professors. Generally, these are the people for whom you write in school. This type of writing is far more formal and restricted than that done for yourself or a friend, because the information you have about the instructor or professor for whom you are writing is usually less than you have about a friend or about yourself. You cannot assume that the instructor will "know what you mean." Things must be explained clearly and stated precisely. When writing for instructors, you almost always have to follow formal writing conventions and watch your spelling, paragraph structure, and word choice.

This does not mean that you can't take some shortcuts. Because you know the instructor's level of knowledge about the topic, it allows you to use language and technical terms you could no use for a more general audience. For example, a dental student writing for a dental school professor would be free to use terminology that couldn't be used if the audience were unknown. Example 4-1 presents a paper that a dental or medical student might write for a professor:

Example 4-1

Periodontal diseases affect the supporting tissues of the teeth. The periodontium consists of the gingiva, which is normally firm, relatively pale in color, and in close apposition to the crowns of the teeth, and the periodontal membrane, containing numerous bundles of collagen fiber which on the tooth side are embedded in the bonelike cementum covering the roots of the teeth and which extends into the adjacent alveolar bone that lines the tooth socket.

One type of periodontal disease is gingivitis, which takes the form of minor inflammatory changes in the gingival margin. Gingivitis may be prevented by such simple measures as regular dental prophylaxis, scaling of calculus, and ordinary toothbrushing. Where the elimination of local irritations fails to remedy the inflammatory process, certain metabolic or nutritional deficiencies may be involved.

Note the terms such as *gingiva, periodontal,* and *collagen,* which convey meaning only to one who is knowledgeable in this field. When you write for an instructor as audience you are more restricted than you would be if you wrote for yourself or a friend, but you are still less restricted than you would be if you knew nothing about your audience. The knowledge that your instructor has a high level of understanding about your topic allows you to convey large chunks of information by using a few highly technical terms.

The fourth and final category of audience is the general public. This is the audience professional writers are usually composing for, and it is the category of audience that a writer knows the least about. When you are writing for many people, there is bound to be a great difference in knowledge, beliefs, and interests among them. In a sense, then, you can't assume anything about this audience. You must spell everything out in detail and write as though they know little or nothing about the topic. This results in a paper that is far less technical than one you might write for a professor. If the essay in Example 4-1 were written for the general public, it might look something like the essay in Example 4-2.

Example 4-2

Gum disease (generally called periodontal disease) affects the supporting tissue of the teeth. The area of the gums called the periodontium is composed of two basic parts: (1) the gingiva, and (2) a protein fiber membrane. The gingiva is the normally firm, pale-colored tissue next to the crowns of the teeth. The protein fibers (sometimes called collagen fibers) are attached to the bonelike part of the teeth found in the gums (called the cementum) and to the part of the jaw bone (called the alveolar bone) that lines the tooth socket.

One type of gum disease is called gingivitis. It takes the form of minor inflammation in the margin between the teeth and the gums. This disease may be prevented by such simple measures as regular dental checkups, removing of an irritation-producing substance called calculus from the teeth, and ordinary tooth brushing. Where the elimination of the irritation fails to stop the disease, certain biological or nutritional deficiencies may be involved.

This essay is much longer than Example 4-1: 175 words instead of 130, because we have had to explain things in more detail than before. Because the level of our audience's knowledge about gum disease is unknown, we must explain technical terms and thus make the essay longer.

We can say, then, that the more you know about your audience, the more you are free to use different types of language, and different formats and to take shortcuts. Most writers agree that they are most successful when they take their audience into consideration as much as possible. We will discuss some techniques for finding out more about your audience if it is the general public, first, and then discuss ways of finding out more about your instructor as audience. The basic technique to use with both types of audiences is to ask a series of questions.

The first question that you might ask yourself about your audience, if it is the general public, is: "What is the age of the people to whom I am writing?" This question is particularly important if your audience is very young. Researchers in reading have found that children are able to comprehend more of what they read when the words and concepts used are at their level. Hence, if you are writing for a young audience, a group of fifth-graders, for example, you must continually ask yourself: "Does a fifth-grader have the background and life experiences to understand this concept or this word?"

A second question one can ask about the general public as audience is: "Where does my audience live?" Growing up or living in a certain part of the country usually affects what you know about. For example, many people who live in Seattle, Washington, are familiar with hydroplanes. Therefore, you could easily write to that audience about speed-boat racing and use such words as *roostertail, gearbox, flying start, five-minute gun,* and *one-minute gun.* However, people from other parts of the country would be baffled by such words.

A third question you should ask about your audience is: "What are their religious, political, or philosophical beliefs?" This is especially important if your basic purpose in writing is to persuade your audience about something. If their beliefs are contradictory to yours, you should word your argument in such a way as to keep their minds open to your point of view. This usually results in a softsell approach. However, if you know that their beliefs are similar to your own, you can be dogmatic in your presentation.

A fourth (and perhaps the most important) question is: "What does my audience already know about the topic?" If your audience has considerable knowledge about what you are writing, it allows you to take liberties and shortcuts. For example, a nuclear physicist addressing a group of laymen about relativity theory would have to spend a great deal of time and use many words explaining the relationship between energy and mass. However, if the physicist were writing or talking to a group of physicists familiar with relativity theory, he or she could simply write $E = mc^2$ and the information would be conveyed.

Thus there are four general areas you should know about your audience. Those are: (1) their age, (2) where they live, (3) their beliefs, and (4) their knowledge about the topic.

Of course these are not the only areas about which you might want to obtain information. Some writers like to identify the general educational level or socioeconomic status of their audience or the extent to which their audience reads. You can identify other things that you feel are important and gather information about them. The basic rule is that the more you know about your audience, the better you will be able to write in a way that is meaningful and understandable to them.

The audience you will spend the most time writing for during your college and university days will be instructors, professors, and teaching assistants. Because they will have the role of "teacher," you will automatically know something about them. For example, you will know their educational level, their level of knowledge about the topic, their age, and, perhaps, some of their beliefs. However, there are some things that aren't obvious about instructors—the knowledge of which can help you greatly in your writing. Instructors have their own biases and quirks and special things to look for in an essay.

Sometimes, if you don't identify what an instructor is looking for, you can receive a low grade on a paper that actually might be well written. This was dramatically illustrated by Paul Diederich,[2] who had professors and professional people from six different academic areas read and grade a set of essays. He found that the raters disagreed widely about the quality of the essays: Some thought particular essays were good, whereas others thought they were poor. The Diederich study illustrates that different instructors look for different things in papers. The better able you are to identify what a particular instructor is looking for, the higher your chances of success in that course.

Some of the more common areas that instructors usually have feelings about are:

1. **Length of paper.** Some instructors prefer lengthy essays, but some have just the opposite bias: long papers tend to "put them off."

2. **Typed papers vs. hand-written papers.** There is almost a unanimous bias among instructors in favor of typewritten papers. Many instructors feel that their students either own or have access to a typewriter and therefore expect that all papers will be typed.

3. **Level of knowledge to be assumed about the reader.** When your audience is the instructor, you know that he or she probably has a greal deal of knowledge about the topic on which you are writing. This fact leads some students to take shortcuts and use words or terms without explaining them. However, sometimes instructors want their students to explain as much as possible in the paper. If you don't know, it's usually best to assume that most instructors consider a paper to be like a test; it is a chance for you to "show off" what you know about a particular topic. Hence, it works to the student's advantage to explain and clarify as much as possible. At times, the student must forget that the instructor is knowledgeable about the topic and write as though the instructor were a layman.

4. **Conventions.** By conventions are meant such things as footnoting, spacing, and topics vs. subtopics. These are areas we will discuss in detail in Chapter 10. With some instructors these conventions are very important. That is, they assume that you will be using a certain type of footnoting procedure, a certain way of signifying headings and subtopics, etc.

This is just a partial list of things that might be important to an instructor and about which you should have some knowledge before you turn in a paper. The best way of obtaining information about these areas is to ask your instructor. Asking questions about such issues is a perfectly legitimate practice in a college or university classroom. Most instructors are more than willing to give you all the specifics about what they expect. Some instructors, when asked, will even provide students with a style sheet listing all conventions to be used in the paper, or they will give students a copy of a past paper that they consider to be a perfect model of what they would like.

The Writer's Stance

How well you know your audience is not your only audience-related consideration. You must also decide the "stance" you, the writer, will take in relationship to your audience. When you consider your stance in writing, you are making decisions about the writer-audience relationship. How writers view their own material is directly related to their perception of their audience. William Irmscher, when discussing the writer-audience relationship, states that "a writer first has to decide whether his audience is on a par with him, whether he must in some way defer to his audience or whether they must defer to him."[3] Irmscher feels that as a writer you can take one of two stances: generalist or specialist. The writer can also consider the audience in one of two ways: as generalists or specialists. This creates the possibility of four types of relationship writers can have with their audiences: (1) specialist to specialist, (2) specialist to generalist, (3) generalist to generalist, (4) generalist to specialist.

If you take the stance of specialist and consider your audience to be specialists, you are assuming that both parties to the writer–audience relationship are knowledgeable about the topic. About the specialist writing to the specialist, Irmscher says:

> There may be differences in interpretation among them, but not great differences in their commitment to the subject. They speak the same language; they have mastered their own jargon. Their common interest bridges their differences and provides them shortcuts in communication.[4]

The specialist-to-generalist writer–audience relationship is the most difficult one for the writer. In this situation, the writer's task becomes that of instructing an audience that is supposedly interested in learning more about the topic but not yet experienced enough to be considered a specialist. The situation is difficult because the author must guess about what his or her audience knows. If the writer explains too much he or she might appear to be condescending; if the writer explains too little he or she might lose the audience. The key to success in such writing is to introduce concepts gradually and to illustrate and exemplify concepts as much as possible.

When the relationship between writer and audience is that of generalist to generalist, the writer is again obliged to explain all concepts. Many free-lance writers necessarily take the generalist-to-generalist stance, because free-lance writing characteristically requires that writers write on topics that are new to them. Free-lance writers contract for a project and then collect background information on that topic. When the writer feels comfortable with the topic, he or she will begin to compose, with the intent of conveying some of the new knowledge acquired. The free-lance writer tries to convey to the audience the fruits of his or her studies and considers the audience just slightly behind in knowledge about the topic.

The final type of writer–audience relationship is that of generalist to specialist. This is the situation most students find themselves in when writing to an instructor or professor as audience. It might appear that a generalist would never have anything of value to say to a specialist. But this is ignoring an important tool generalists have at their disposal—a fresh perspective on the topic:

> What every generalist needs to realize . . . is that his lack of knowledge about a subject can be offset by fresh perception. If it were possible, many specialists would undoubtedly trade some of their knowledge for the completely unencumbered perspective of the newcomer.[5]

The student (generalist) writing for the instructor (specialist) can capitalize on the fresh perspective that a lack of knowledge can bring. For example, a beginning student in literature can bring interpretations to a poem based on his or her past experience that no one else is capable of. Most instructors appreciate these insights, provided that they are expressed clearly and their logic is made evident to the reader.

The consideration of audience is a very important aspect of writing. You must keep in mind your basic purpose for writing and above all, the general characteristics of your audience. Audience controls the style and format we choose to use in our compositions.

FORMAT

Format is the overall organizational pattern of your paper. In this section we will discuss four different overall patterns. Within each major type there are subtypes. The four general patterns are:

1. Time patterns
2. Spatial patterns
3. General-to-specific patterns
4. Comparative patterns

Time Patterns

Three types of papers take an overall time organization: narrative papers, process papers, and cause-and-effect papers. But what is meant by a time organization or time pattern? Let us first consider a narrative paper (see Example 4-3) to determine some of the overall characteristics of time patterns:

Example 4-3

Rainsford sprang up and moved quickly to the rail, mystified. He strained his eyes in the direction from which the reports had come, but it was like trying to see through a blanket. He leaped upon the rail and balanced himself there, to get greater elevation; his pipe, striking a rope, was knocked from his mouth. He lunged for it; a short, hoarse cry came from his lips as he realized he had reached too far and lost his balance. The cry was pinched off short as the blood-warm waters of the Caribbean Sea closed over his head.[6]

A narrative is another name for a story, and a story is a recounting of events. All time-oriented papers share this characteristic: They all state events. In Example 4-3, each sentence relates a different event. In a narrative paper organized around time, you retell events in the sequence they happened.

The second type of time-oriented paper is a process paper. Like the narrative, it too relates events as they happen. However, the events in a process paper lead to a specific outcome. They are the steps one should take to produce the outcome. For example, if you wanted to explain the events leading up to nuclear fission, you would write a process paper. Likewise, if you wanted to describe the steps necessary to make a pie crust, you would select a process format. A process paper generally reads like this:

It's not very easy to catch a snipe.
You must first . . . .
Then you . . . .
After that you . . . .
Finally you must . . . .

The final type of time-patterned paper is the cause-and-effect paper. This is similar to the process paper in that all the events mentioned lead to a particular outcome. However, in the cause-and-effect paper the events that bring about the effect are not steps in a process. That is, they do not have to be done sequentially to bring about the stated outcome. Example 4-4 is an example of a cause-and-effect paper.

Example 4-4

On June 12, 1979, Bryan Allen flew a plane called the Gossamer Albatross across the English Channel using no propulsive power other than that generated by Allen pedalling furiously inside the cockpit. His was the longest human-powered flight in history. When asked why he had succeeded where so many others had failed, Allen listed several reasons.

Probably the most important factor was the brilliant design of the craft, which was engineered solely to win the $210,000 prize money offered by the Winston Foundation for the first human-powered, heavier-than-air crossing of the English Channel. The design of the Albatross was perfect for such an attempt. It weighed only seventy-five pounds, which would have made it highly unstable even in mild winds, had it not been for the oversized stabilizer located on the front of the plane. Its wings were constructed of a material only .0005 inches thick, yet they were longer than those on a DC-9. The retractable landing gear was made of a light alluminum alloy and the steering controls of Kelvar, a space-age material used in the construction of videotape; both materials are highly flexible yet very strong.

The second major reason for the success of the flight was Allen himself. An ex–bike racer, skier, and hang glider, he drew on his diverse background to prepare for the journey. He trained as though for a marathon, sometimes bicycling or running up to 100 miles per week. On the day of the flight he wore running shoes and shorts, a life jacket, a bicycling helmet, and a canteen of water strapped to his waist. Immediately before takeoff he ate a number of hard rolls, bananas, apples, and oranges. Yet with all his preparation it was his will power that allowed him to overcome severe leg cramps and poor wind conditions and keep the Albatross airborne until it reached France. Allen and the Albatross, the man and the machine, had accomplished a task previously thought impossible.

In this essay two causes are given for the success of the Gossamer Albatross: the design of the plane and the actions of Allen. The order of these two causal events is not important. In a process paper, the causes mentioned for a particular outcome generally have to occur in a set sequence. In a cause-and-effect paper, the order is not crucial: In the essay about the Albatross, the author could have discussed Allen first and the design second; the essay would have been basically the same. You can also see that in Example 4-4 quite a few sentences are used to describe only two causes. Some sentences serve functions other than explicating the two causes. We will come back to this essay at the end of this chapter and identify the purposes of some of those other statements.

Narratives, process papers, and cause-and-effect papers all follow a general time pattern. Narratives list events; process papers list steps that culminate in some outcome; cause-and-effect papers list events that are causes of a particular effect but do not necessarily have a sequential relationship to one another. Each of these three types of time patterns can be diagrammed or outlined in such a way as to show the basic, underlying structure. The outline of a narrative is:

Introduction
Event 1
Event 2
Event 3
Conclusion

The outline for a process paper:

Introduction
Step 1
Step 2
Step 3
Conclusion

And the outline for a cause-and-effect paper:

Introduction
Cause 1
Cause 2
Cause 3
Conclusion

A variation on the cause-and-effect theme might be:

Introduction
Cause
Effect 1
Effect 2
Conclusion

The outlines of all three types of time-organized papers can be varied in different ways, but the underlying similarity among these three types of paper is that all use time as the basic organization theme.

A second type of organization pattern is spatial.

Spatial Patterns

Virtually all papers that are organized on a spatial pattern are descriptive in nature. Example 4-5 is a typical descriptive essay.

Example 4-5

Goldmund's eyes traveled from corpse to corpse. The girl's face was already terribly disfigured, but he could see something of her helpless horror of death. In the neck and hair of the mother, who had dug herself so deeply into the bed, one could read rage, fear, and a passionate desire to flee, especially in the wild hair, which could not resign itself to dying. The farmer's face showed stubbornness and held-in pain. He had died a hard death, but his bearded chin rose steeply, rigidly into the air like that of a warrior lying on the battlefield. His quiet, taut, stubbornly controlled posture was beautiful; it had probably not been a petty, cowardly man who had received death in this manner. Most touching was the little corpse of the boy lying on its belly across the threshold. The face told nothing, but the posture across the threshold and the clenched child fists told a great deal: incomprehensible suffering, unavailing struggle against unheard-of pain.[7]

Note the difference between the sentences in this essay and those in Example 4-3. The sentences in the narrative passage are all statements of events; here the sentences are statements of characteristics:

The girl's face was . . .
In the neck and hair of the mother . . . one could read . . .
The farmer's face showed . . . .
His quiet . . . posture was . . .

Hence, a difference between time-organized papers and space-organized papers is that the former mainly state events and the latter describe characteristics. The general outline for descriptive essays is:

Introduction
Descriptive Statement 1
Descriptive Statement 2
Descriptive Statement 3
Conclusion

Usually the descriptive statements have spatial relationship to one another. For example, in Example 4-5 one feels that the bodies were lined up (Goldmund's eyes traveled from corpse to corpse . . .") and that the author describes the first corpse in line, then the next, and so on. Usually a writer follows a pattern organized by depth, horizontal, vertical, or circular orientation. If an author were to describe a scene using depth as the organizing spatial factor, he or she would first mention those things closest to the viewer and then move on to those furthest away (or vice versa):

In the foreground one could see . . .
Behind that was . . .
In the back were . . .

Describing something using a horizontal spatial organization would be accomplished by portraying things as they appear from left to right or right to left. A vertical organization would proceed from top to bottom or bottom to top, and a circular organization would proceed in a clockwise or counterclockwise fashion.

Papers organized around a time or spatial pattern are common in popular literature (novels or short stories), but most papers written in a college or university are analytic in nature. These papers usually fall into one of the last two organizational categories: general-to-specific or comparison–contrast.

General-to-Specific Patterns

Probably the most common way to organize a paper is to state a generalization and then give specifics about it. One type of general-to-specific pattern is called *exemplification*. Example 4-6 is such a paper.

Example 4-6

The size of one's brain has little to do with one's intelligence. Among the most massive brains on record are those of Oliver Cromwell, Ivan Turgenev, and Lord Byron, all of whom were smart but no Albert Einsteins. Einstein's brain, on the other hand, was not remarkably large. Anatole France, who was brighter than many, had a brain half the size of Byron's. Also, during infancy the size of the brain relative to the size of the body is gargantuan, yet infants are certainly not brighter than adults.

Exemplification is the process of explaining or defining a generalization by using examples. In the essay above, the generalization is that the size of one's brain has little to do with intelligence. This generalization is supported by the facts that:

Turgenev, Cromwell, and Byron had very large brains but were not geniuses;
Einstein's brain was not unusually large;
Anatole France had a very small brain;
infants have very large brains relative to their body size.

We can diagram an exemplification pattern in the following way.

Introduction
Example 1
Example 2
Example 3
Conclusion

Enumeration is an overall organizational pattern very similar to exemplification. An enumeration pattern lists and numbers the examples used to support the generalization. For example, if the essay in Example 4-6 had used an enumeration pattern rather than an examplification pattern, it might read as follows:

The size of one's brain has little to do with one's intelligence.
First, among the most massive brains . . . .
Second, Einstein's brain . . . .
Third, Anatole France . . . .
And finally, during infancy . . . .

Another variation on the general-to-specific organizational pattern is that of specific to general. As the name indicates, in such a pattern the writer identifies a series of specifics that together support a generalization. Example 4-7 uses a general-to-specific pattern.

Example 4-7

In my home we now have a microcomputer. A microcomputer is a small computer—a very, very small computer. Ours is about a foot-and-one-half square. Its size, however, is no indication of its capabilities.

Our computer has 48k memory space. The *k* in this parameter means thousands, which indicates that our micro can store forty-eight thousand bits of information (in computer terms, "bytes" rather than "bits"). There is also a disc drive that allows you to store another 116k bits of information. Together this makes one hundred sixty-four thousand bits of information you can manipulate with the micro. My uncle says that our micro has a larger storage capacity than the computer the entire university used when he was getting his degree. What's even more amazing is that the computer he used weighed over two tons and cost $1.5 million; ours weighs fifteen pounds and costs three thousand dollars.

Our computer is being used to keep track of home spending, balance checkbooks, and compute income tax information. My father is also using it for business. He keeps his mailing list of over three thousand customers stored in the computer (on disc, actually). When he wants a set of mailing labels, he presses a button and they are immediately printed for him. Before, this task took an entire week of typing.

Micros are also finding their way into education. The high school I used to go to now has one similar to ours. They use it to keep track of absenteeism, tardiness, library books, and discipline problems.

It seems as though the computer age is here whether we like it or not. Micro computers are inexpensive: almost any family can own one. The computers themselves are capable of performing tasks that formerly required a great deal of time and effort. Their potential usefulness is unimaginable today.

In this essay the student has led the reader up to the generalization stated in the last paragraph by first citing the reasons for it. The specific-to-general pattern accomplishes the same thing as the general-to-specific pattern but in the reverse order. Some people prefer the specific-to-general pattern because they feel it creates an atmosphere of anticipation. Some topics lend themselves better to one pattern than another. Which pattern you should use for a given assignment depends on your topic, purpose, audience, and personal taste.

Comparison and Contrast Patterns

An organizational pattern based on comparison and contrast explains or defines something by telling what it is similar to and what it is different from. Comparison and contrast is the process of describing two or more things by identifying their similarities and differences. Example 4-8 contains a sample of a comparison-contrast paper.

Example 4-8

They were as different as two fighters could be. They were even different in the way they entered the canopied ring. Tate stepped onto the canvas grinning and showing all the confidence expected of the third-ranked world heavyweight contender. He waived repeatedly to the crowd, joking and talking with the spectators in the front rows. One might have thought he was running for public office rather than perparing for a key fight in his quest for the title. Knoetze, on the other hand, came into the ring without any ceremony. At first you could not see his face because it was buried deep in the hood of his navy blue warm-up robe, making him look like a medieval monk. When he finally did appear from its folds, he was wearing a scowl that made him look even more threatening.

The contrast in their entrances was highlighted by the differences in their physical appearance. Knoetze, a 226-pound, 6'1½" white South African, looks the role of a street brawler. His face is hard and lined and seems painted with a permanent look of aggression, one befitting a fighter known for his tendency to pound mercilessly on opponents. Tate, although much larger, has a softer appearance. In spite of his 6'4", 233-pound frame, he looks less conditioned than you would expect of a world contending heavyweight—a fact that led Knoetze to make repeated allusions to Tate's "blubbery body."

They were as different in the way they fought as they were in appearance. From the first round Tate began peppering Knoetze's face with jabs that made Knoetze's lunging right hand leads look ridiculous. Tate kept up the cat-and-mouse game for seven rounds, quickly moving in to score and then retreating while Knoetze threw ferocious, unscoring punches and did little more than create a breeze. In the eighth round Tate landed a right that almost took Knoetze off his feet. He followed up with a series of uppercuts, each of which snapped Knoetze's head back. In a burst of humanity referee Rodriguez rushed in and pulled Tate off the

---

totally helpless Knoetze.

When Knoetze had regained his senses he left the ring. He did so without looking at or speaking to Tate, who again was smiling and chatting with the crowd.

In this essay two boxers are being compared on three different characteristics: how they came into the ring, their physical appearance, and their fighting style. The three characteristics are stated in order and each boxer is described in terms of the particular characteristic being discussed. For example, we are first told what Tate did when he entered the ring, and then Knoetze's antics are described. We are then told of some of Knoetze's physical characteristics, after which Tate's physical appearance is described. Finally, the paper discusses Tate and Knoetze's respective fighting styles, establishing the third comparison. Thus, the organizational diagram for this essay might look like:

```
Introduction
Characteristic 1
   Subject 1
   Subject 2
Characteristic 2
   Subject 1
   Subject 2
Characteristic 3
   Subject 1
   Subject 2
Conclusion
```

Alternatively, the author might have discussed all three characteristics for Tate and then all three for Knoetze. This would have been diagramed in the following way:

```
Introduction
Subject 1
   Characteristic 1
   Characteristic 2
   Characteristic 3
Subject 2
   Characteristic 1
   Characteristic 2
   Characteristic 3
Conclusion
```

Another comparison–contrast pattern employs a specific type of comparison called an *analogy*. In an analogy, the subject you are describing is likened to someone or something else. For example, we could change the essay in Example 4-8 into an analogy paper by focusing on Tate and again considering the three characteristics. His entrance into the ring could be likened to a theatrical stage entrance:

> Tate came into the ring with all the flair and pomp of a Las Vegas nightclub entertainer. He was preceded by his handlers, carrying signs saying "Tate is Great." When he finally emerged, he was wearing a spangled golden robe . . . .

Likewise, his physical appearance could have been likened to that of a large black panther and his fighting style to that of a cross between a hummingbird and a wasp. An analogy paper, then, might be outlined as:

Introduction
Characteristic 1
    Analogy 1
Characteristic 2
    Analogy 2
Characteristic 3
    Analogy 3
Conclusion

Embedded Patterns

In our discussion of the essay about the Gossamer Albatross (Example 4-4), we mentioned some additional statements that were included in the essay—statements other than those about the two causes for the success of the flight. Those additional statements describe the specifics of the two causes. No paper is pure cause-and-effect, pure description, or pure enumeration. That is, no paper has statements that are all of any one type. In a process paper there will probably be statements that are descriptive and spatial in relationship to one another; in an enumeration paper there will probably be statements that are cause-and-effect in nature. Although all papers should have an identifiable format that resembles one of those we have discussed in this chapter, interspersed throughout that identifiable organizational format there will be different types of statements that give the paper detail, that add meat, so to speak, to the skeleton of the overall organization. A paper containing only statements directly related to the overall organizational pattern would be very short and boring. For example, if we had used only cause-and-effect statements in the Albatross paper, it would have read like this:

> At 8:39 in the morning of June 12, 1979, Bryan Allen flew the Gossamer Albatross across the English Channel, using no propulsion other than his own "power." He was successful for two reasons: (1) because of the unique design of the aircraft, and (2) because of his own personal actions and abilities. These two factors, the man and the machine, had come together to accomplish a task that no one had been able to accomplish previously.

The addition of exemplification, spatial, and time statements makes this essay far more interesting. Good writing characteristically has a recognizable overall pattern but embeds within that pattern other formats. To illustrate this embedding of patterns let us consider the essay in Example 4-9.

Example 4-9

The psychological mechanisms of language understanding have a number of constraints upon their operation. For one thing, they must work quickly enough that they can keep up with speech. A little bit of introspection reveals that the mechanisms just barely keep up. In lectures or when encountering a rapid speaker, the mechanisms often break down with the analysis. The analysis of how the sentence is put together seems to get finished, but a full understanding of the message lags behind. This leads to the feeling that "I understood the words, but I certainly didn't understand what was said."

A second constraint is that the analysis of the sentence must proceed primarily in the same order as the words are spoken. At first, this requirement might seem obvious, but in fact some parts of the analysis cannot really be completed until a majority of the sentence has been heard. In fact, it is sometimes more efficient to analyze sentences backwards, from the last word back to the first. But the size of short-term and sensory memories is simply not sufficient to allow for this.

A final constraint upon the language-analyzing mechanisms is that they must be robust, tolerant of errors and missing information. It must be possible to understand spoken language even when the speaker makes a mistake or when the listener lapses in attentiveness now and then. Language understanding allows these errors, so whatever the language-understanding mechanisms, they must not be overly demanding about receiving perfect linguistic utterances.[8]

In Example 4-9 the basic pattern is that of enumeration. The essay could be outlined in the following way:

Introduction: The psychological mechanisms of language understanding have a number of constraints.
Example 1: For one thing . . . .
Example 2: A second constraint . . . .
Example 3: A final constraint . . . .

Each paragraph deals with one example. Within each paragraph, however, patterns other than enumeration are embedded. The third sentence in paragraph 1, for example, begins a four-sentence exemplification pattern. Paragraphs 2 and 3 contain subpatterns of two and three sentences each. Each paragraph also contains single sentences that are not part of the overall pattern or of a subpattern. Such sentences may perform functions such as restating something, pointing out characteristics of elements previously described, or stating the time or place of an event. In Chapter 7, we will discuss in depth the various functions of some of these statements.

The enumeration format of this paper, like the patterns of all papers, is only a skeleton. Within that format are other patterns of shorter length and single sentences with specific functions. An essay, then, can be viewed as a complex grouping of patterns within patterns.

PLANNING YOUR FORMAT

So far we've discussed four general types of organizational patterns: (1) time, (2) spatial, (3) general-to-specific, and (4) comparison. We've also identified types of statements that usually accompany each pattern. There are, however, two important types of statements we haven't discussed here: introductory and concluding statements. Because the introduction and conclusion of an essay are usually added during the revision phase of composing, we will deal with them in chapter 6.

Most writers state that the beginning and ending of a paper are the parts they usually revise the most. This is because, as we will see in chapter 6, you often don't know how your paper is going to end when you start writing. How, then, can one plan a paper? Or perhaps a more pertinent question would be, "Should a person plan a paper before writing?" The answer to this is yes, but with qualifications.

When you plan your format you should get a feel for the organization you want to use. You should decided whether your paper will have a narrative, cause-and-effect, comparison, or analogy pattern of organization. You can then determine the major parts of the paper by trying to fill in the diagram for that particular pattern.

Let's assume for a moment that someone is planning the cause-and-effect paper about the flight of the Gossamer Albatross presented in Example 4-4. In the planning phase of this paper, the writer would have determined the purpose, the topic, the audience, and the cause-and-effect format. The writer might have outlined the paper in the following fashion.

Introduction
Cause 1: Design of the Albatross, its highly unusual aspects as an
        airplane
Cause 2: Allen's actions and characteristics: he, like the plane,
        was perfect for the task

This outline will serve to give the writer direction. Assuming that the writer has collected adequate information, he or she could begin writing based on this simple organizational plan.

Some writers like to plan their essays in much more detail, identifying some of the subpatterns they will embed in their overall organizational pattern. Doing this with the Gossamer Albatross essay might produce:

Introduction
Cause 1: Design of Albatross
        designed solely to win prize money
        weighed 75 pounds
        stabilizer in front
        wingspan longer than DC-9
        landing gear
        steering controls made of Kelvar
        wings .0005 inches thick
Cause 2: Allen
        ex–bike racer
        ex-skier
        ex–hang glider
        wore running shorts, life jacket, etc.
        ate rolls, bananas, etc.
Conclusion

Some writers make a formal outline of their proposed paper, planning in depth by listing the major components of the format and the detail elements. The major components are usually identified by Roman numerals, the subcomponents by capital letters, Arabic numerals, and lower-case letters, depending on the level of specificity.

I.
  A.
  B.
    1.
    2.
      a.
      b.
II.

A formal outline of the Gossamer Albatross paper might be the following:

I. Design of Albatross
  A. Designed specifically to win prize money
  B. Physical characteristics
    1. Weighed 75 pounds
    2. Wingspan
      a. Longer than DC-9
      b. .0005 inches thick
    3. Landing gear
      a. Made of light alloy
      b. Retractable
    4. Steering controls made of Kelvar
II. Allen
  A. Characteristics contributing to his suitability
    1. Ex–bike racer
    2. Ex–skier
    3. Ex–hang glider
  B. Preparation for Channel attempt
    1. Dress for occasion
      a. Running shoes
      b. Life jacket
    2. Food
      a. Rolls
      b. Bananas

The elements of an outline can also be expressed in sentence form, making the plan even more specific. Here is a sentence outline of the first part of the Albatross paper:

I. The first cause of the Albatross's success was the design.
   A. The plane was developed for no other purpose than to win the prize money.
   B. It had some unique physical characteristics.
      1. It weighed only 75 pounds due to its unique construction.
      2. Its wings were very unusual.
         a. They were longer than those of a DC-9
         b. Their covering was only .0005 inches thick.
      3. The landing gear was also a factor.
         a. It was made of a light metal alloy.
         b. It was retractable and consisted of a small inflated rubber wheel.

The extent to which you plan or outline is a personal choice. An outline can and probably will be changed when you actually start writing. In chapter 6, we will see that writing is a generative act. Your organizational pattern will probably remain fixed, but the detailed statements of events and characteristics that you include in the essay will probably change somewhat from those you identify in your outline.

SUMMARY

Audience and format have a cause-and-effect relationship with one another. When considering your audience, you should also consider the format that would be most appropriate for that audience. Another consideration that goes hand in hand with audience is your purpose for writing. One way of ensuring that you are considering basic purpose along with audience is to use the test frame: "My purpose is to _(purpose)_ to _(audience)_ about/that _(topic)_ ."

The more you know about your audience, the less restricted you are in the writing conventions you use. Based on the criterion of how much is known about the audience, we can identify four general categories of audience: (1) yourself, (2) friends, (3) instructors, and (4) the general public. You will always know quite a bit about the first two categories of audience, but you probably won't know much about the second two categories. With these categories of audience, it is beneficial to obtain information about

the audience that will help you plan your format more efficiently.
Another audience-related consideration is the stance you will take
as a writer. In general, there are four major organizational formats
you can use, each of which has subtypes:

Time
    narration
    process
    cause-and-effect
Spatial
    horizontal
    vertical
    depth
    circular
General to specific
    exemplification
    enumeration
    specific to general
Comparison and contrast
    subject
    characteristic
    analogy

When planning your paper you should identify the overall
organizational pattern and some of the details you will include as
embedded patterns within it. Some writers make a formal outline
of what they are going to write.

Exercises

1. For each of the following essays, identify the type of
organizational format that has been used and the major elements of
the outline for the essay. For example, if the essay is an example of
the exemplification pattern, also pick out the particular examples
used. Check your answers by consulting the outlines provided at
the end of this section.

A

In recent years, certain occupations have lost some of their original
prestige because of an apparent correlation between the salary paid an
individual and the prestige value of the occupation.
    For example, even though teachers' salaries have steadily increased as
the cost of living has increased, teachers are among the lowest paid

professionals. As a result, teaching is looked on as a low-prestige occupation.

Professional athletics, on the other hand, is one of the prestige occupations. This suggests that athletes must be paid a lot, and they are. A baseball player recently signed a five-year contract for $3.5 million.

Medicine and law are prestigious occupations; the ministry is not. Again, the example illustrates the principle: High prestige comes to those who make high salaries.

B

The maintenance of constructive order in American classrooms has always been a problem. This problem appears to be caused by some rather fundamental characteristics of the American heritage.

Americans are, above all, subject to no one. Our heritage teaches us that we are subject only to ourselves and the will of the majority (qualified by many restrictions). It is easy to see the student, suffering under a system set by external authorities, contemplating the injustice of it all and reacting much as our ancestors did when confronted with royal edicts from across the sea.

Americans expect to be able to choose their own ways, to be able to pursue "life, liberty, and . . . happiness" in styles of their choice. Yet the authority of the state sets boundaries and eliminates many options. Mandatory school attendance is an example of such restrictions, and students rebel often at the limitations placed on their ways of pursuing what they feel to be their constitutionally guaranteed rights.

Americans also enjoy a relatively complete freedom to enquire, including access to a variety of materials and experiences. Yet school textbook committees, with the advice of community organizations and individuals, effectively censor materials used in the schools. Is it any wonder that students chafe under the system that limits their right to materials and experiences, when the system guarantees free and open access to such things?

American students often feel the classroom is the ultimate in hypocrisy. Clearly, the guarantees of the American system and the traditions of its heritage apply only to nonclassroom settings. Those who say the classroom is a training ground for democracy know neither the schools nor the system under which they operate.

C

Watching a real chef at work is an education in the culinary arts. His precision suggests a true science; his results suggest the presence of an art.

The true chef first gathers his materials—utensils, raw materials, condiments—about him, along with his recipe folder (to which he never refers).

Once the materials are ready, he proceeds to put the basic ingredients in the largest of his mixing bowls. This is done with a careless abandon, thus contributing to the sense of "art" in the process. However, there is never more than a one percent error.

Then the condiments are added—in what appears as "a dash of this" and "a pinch of that." Again, the absolute accuracy of the measure is astounding, but the artistic flair is preserved through the apparent abandon that he uses when throwing various seasonings into the bowl.

The mixing follows. It is as helter-skelter as the other processes, except even more so. It appears that the mixture will fly all over the room, the strokes are so violent at times. But somehow the material never leaves the bowl, and the mixture is well blended in an amazingly short time.

The science of measure and the art of show combine in any great chef to make superior food and entertainment. More chefs should perform for their customers. With their inspiration, more imaginative activity might take place in the kitchens of America.

D

Today's disco dancer has many things in common with the dancer of the Roaring Twenties. The dancer of the twenties gyrated in incredibly suggestive ways. Today's disco scene is full of gyrations (somewhat different, but still gyrations) that are fully as suggestive. The dances of the twenties gave dancers a chance to strut their plumage, and one certainly finds the same sort of exhibitions on today's dance floors with shirts unbuttoned down to the navel and pants one has to be poured into.

In terms of athletic prowess, both styles of dancing require immense stamina and good coordination. The impact of John Travolta on contemporary disco has been to reveal all the closet athletes. Many of their grandparents were similarly freed to be gymnasts by the advent of the dances of the twenties.

Another similar characteristic in the two ages is the appearance of sheer joy on the dance floor. The dancers of the 1920s smiled a lot; so do today's disco buffs. Somehow, the notion that the dance was a prelude of things to come (a common notion in the 1950s and 1960s) has been replaced by a feeling that dancing is such a fun activity that is a worthy end in itself. The disco dancer of today and the flapper of the twenties are alike in many ways.

E

There are three major reasons why the Broncos did not make the playoffs last year. First, they are in the toughest division in the NFL. The AFC West is the only division with four out of their six teams capable of going to the Super Bowl: Seattle, Oakland, San Diego, and Denver. Hence, the first step in Denver's (or any other AFC West team's) quest for the brass ring is the most difficult—getting past their own division.

Second, Denver was faced with an inordinate number of injuries. For a short while they were without the services of five of the starting offensive eleven and four of the starting defensive squad. Needless to say, this weakened them to the point that they had to play over their heads from Sunday to Sunday just to stay in contention.

Third, the rest of the league finally figured out Denver's style of play. The year they went to the Super Bowl, few NFL teams had ever faced an opponent that relied primarily on defense to provide scoring situations for the offense. Consequently, Denver's aggressive, opportunity-producing defense, coupled with its error-free offense, would often put a game out of reach before opponents could formulate a counterstrategy. This year in particular, that same defense-oriented style of play has been adopted by other NFL teams; this, of course, has nullified the element of surprise Denver previously possessed.

Two of the three reasons for Denver's lack of success last year have recently been remedied. The squad is injury-free once again, and the new offensive/defensive coordinator has initiated a style of play that could again catch all opponents off guard. The one thing Denver can't change is its membership in the toughest division in professional football. However, champions perform best when faced with a challenge, and there is no doubt that Denver is a champion.

---

2. Find ten advertisements that have value-laden words in them. Rewrite those advertisements leaving out or substituting other words for the value words. What effect does this have on the advertisement?

3. Determine the preferences of two of your instructors in the areas of:

   a. paper length
   b. typed vs. untyped assignments
   c. writing conventions to be followed
   d. amount of explanation (Does the instructor want you to write as though he or she understands technical terms or does the instructor want all terms explained?)

Compare the two sets of information.

4. One of the best-known books of poetry is Edgar Lee Masters'
   Spoon River Anthology. In this book are two unusual poems—
   one in which a man named Jonas Keene discusses the suicide of
   Albert Schirding; another in which Albert Schirding discusses
   the suicide of Jonas Keene. This gives the reader a strange and
   unique perspective. Below are two narratives based on these
   poems. Read them and then perform one of the exercises below.

> I'm not sure why Jonas Keene thought his lot a hard one
> because his children were failures. I know of a lot worse than
> that—it is to be a failure while your children are successful.
> You see, I raised a brood of eagles who flew away leaving me a
> crow on an abandoned bough. Desiring to bring honor to my
> name, and thus win my children's admiration, I ran for
> County Superintendent of Schools, investing my life's
> savings to win—I lost—at about the same time that my
> daughter received first prize in Paris for her picture entitled
> "The Old Mill." The feeling that I was not worthy of her
> finished me.
>
> *Albert Schirding*

> Why did Albert Schirding kill himself trying to be County
> Superintendent of Schools? He was blessed with a healthy
> means of life and wonderful children who brought him honor.
> If only one of my boys could have run a newsstand or one of
> my girls married a decent man, I probably wouldn't have
> become ill (as a result of walking in the rain) and refused
> medical aid.
>
> *Jonas Keene*

Activities
   a. As a writer for the local newspaper, you have to write about
      the double suicides. Write both stories separately, depicting
      the differences between the two men.
   b. You are one of the Schirding children writing to your
      brothers and sisters about your father's death.
   c. You are one of the Keene children writing to your brothers
      and sisters about your father's death.
   d. Write a short dramatic dialogue in which Schirding and
      Keene argue their reasons for their suicides.
   e. Make up your own situation.

Answers

Below are the pattern outlines for the five essays in Exercise 1.

A. Exemplification

Introduction: In recent years, certain occupations have lost some of their original prestige because of an apparent correlation between the salary paid an individual and the prestige value of the occupation.
Example 1: For example, even though teachers' salaries . . . .
Example 2: Professional athletics, on the other hand, is . . . .
Example 3: Medicine and law . . . .
Conclusion: Again, the example illustrates the principle . . . .

B. Cause and effect

Introduction: The maintenance of constructive order in American classrooms has always been a problem.
Cause 1: Americans are, above all, subject to no one.
Cause 2: Americans expect to be able to choose . . . .
Cause 3: Americans also enjoy a relatively complete freedom . . . .
Conclusion: American students often feel the classroom to be the ultimate . . . .

C. Process

Introduction: Watching a real chef is an education in the culinary arts.
Step 1: The true chef first gathers . . . .
Step 2: Once the materials are ready, he . . . .
Step 3: Then the condiments are . . . .
Step 4: The mixing follows.
Conclusion: The science of measure and the art of . . .

D. Comparison and contrast

Introduction: Today's disco dancer has many things in common with the dancer of the Roaring Twenties.
Characteristic 1: Gyrating in suggestive ways.
Characteristic 2: Strutting plumage.
Characteristic 3: Athletic prowess.
Characteristic 4: Joy of dancing.
Conclusion: The disco dancer of today and the flapper of the twenties are . . . .

E. Enumeration

Introduction: There are three major reasons why the Broncos did
           not make the playoffs last year.
Example 1: First, they are in the toughest . . .
Example 2: Second, Denver was faced with . . .
Example 3: Third, the rest of the league finally . . .
Conclusion: Two of the three reasons for Denver's . . .

References

1. J. Moffet, *Rhetoric: Theories of Application* (Urbana, Ill.: National Council of Teachers of English, 1967), pp. 114, 115.

2. P. Diederich, *Factors in Judgments of Writing Ability* (Princeton: Educational Testing Service, 1961).

3. W. Irmscher, *The Holt Guide to English* (New York: Holt, Rinehart and Winston, 1972), p. 21.

4. Irmscher, p. 22.

5. Irmscher, p. 22.

6. From "The Most Dangerous Game," by Richard Connell; copyright, 1924, by Richard Connell; copyright renewed, 1952, by Louise Fox Connell; reprinted by permission of Brandt & Brandt Literary Agents, Inc.

7. Reprinted by permision of Farrar, Straus and Giroux, Inc. Excerpt from *Narcissus and Goldman* by Herman Hesse, English translation by Ursual Malinaro. Copyright © 1968 by Farrar, Straus, and Giroux, Inc.

8. P. Lindsay and D. Norman, *Human Information Processing* (New York: Academic Press, 1977), p. 487.

CHAPTER FIVE

COLLECTING INFORMATION

Recall the story of Pat in chapter 1. After she had decided to write a letter to the town newspaper, she sat down at the typewriter filled with determination and purpose and proceeded to type four lines of a letter before coming to an abrupt halt. The reason? Not enough information. How well you can write about a topic is directly related to how much you know about the topic. The more you know, the better you will write.

Most of the time writers collect far more information than they will use. This is true in all forms of composition. For example, the movie *Apocalypse Now* was in production for over five years. And all of this effort was to produce a two-and-one-half-hour feature film.

But how do you know if you have collected enough information to write? You usually find out quickly when you begin to put your ideas on paper as Pat did. If you can't think of anything to say, you probably haven't enough information. As a test, some writers jot down ideas before they begin to write and use the ease (or lack of it) with which those ideas come to mind as an indicator of whether or not they have adequate information. For example, suppose you had

decided to write an essay describing a sports car rally you had
attended, but you weren't sure whether attendance at the event had
provided you with enough facts. Before beginning to write you
might record your thoughts about the rally. This could be done in a
fashion similar to that used in free writing (see chapter 3):
recording random ideas about the topic without worrying about
spelling, organization, or sentence structure. Such a process might
produce the list below:

1. TR7 wins.
2. The sound of thirty sports cars rounding a curve.
3. The winning trophy.
4. Who drives in sports car rallies?
5. Eating dust.
6. Tires blowing out on the Alpha Romero.
7. Cars revving up at the starting bloc.
8. The smell of exhaust and burnt rubber.
9. A $10,000 Porsche.
10. Women drivers.
11. Some older folks
12. A record-winning time.
13. Rebuilding engines.
14. Shifting down around curves.
15. Different flags.
16. No 55-mph speed limits.
17. The gasoline shortage.
18. Roll bars.
19. Rods and pistons.

All these ideas could be put into a descriptive essay about a
sports car rally. If you found that the ideas were easy to think of, it
would indicate that attending the rally had provided you with
enough background information to write an essay. However, if you
could generate only a few ideas and even they were difficult to
produce, it would indicate that you probably needed to collect
more information before you began to write.

Where does one go to gather information on a topic once it has
been determined that more facts and information are needed?
Information is obtained from either **primary sources** or **secondary
sources**. We will consider each type separately.

PRIMARY SOURCES OF INFORMATION

Primary sources are sources of first-hand information. When you
use your own experience as a source of information you are using a
primary or first-hand source; when you interview someone and use

the information given you, you are using primary-source information as well.

We saw in chapter 3 that personal experience can be fruitful in generating possible writing topics. But identifying a topic through personal experience is different from collecting information from personal experience. Recall, for example, the memory free writing in chapter 3 produced by the student who had focused his attention on a strange nighttime visitation from a young boy. That personal experience could have generated the topic "Life after Death: Is There Any Evidence for or Against?" Once the topic was identified through personal experience, the student would still have had to collect information on the topic (assuming that he wasn't an expert or well read on the research that has been done on that topic).

Using personal experience to gather information is a difficult and time-consuming task, yet it is the technique most widely utilized by great authors. If you consider the lives of Hemingway, Fitzgerald, and Twain, for example, you quickly realize that they used personal experience as the basis for most of their writing. Few modern writers have used information obtained from personal experience to better advantage than George Plimpton, the "professional amateur" who does what everyone else only dreams of doing. For example, he has performed briefly as a major-league baseball pitcher, lion tamer, bullfighter, and a percussionist for the New York Philharmonic. He is probably best known for his book *Paper Lion* about his tenure as a quarterback with the Detroit Lions; *Shadow Box*[1] is about his ring encounter with Archie Moore, and he also once joined the Boston Bruins hockey team for an exhibition stint against the Philadelphia Flyers.

Plimpton has based his entire literary career on the art of using personal experience as the source of information. But having experiences does not in itself ensure that the information collected will be useful in writing. That information must first be recorded properly before it can be used as a basis for composing, because no writer can trust his or her memory to store and recall all the facts and incidents that are part of an experience. Time renders memories obscure and sometimes inaccessible. Consequently, when writers use personal experience to collect information, they also make an effort to record their experiences as soon as possible. Commonly this is done by keeping a diary or journal in which information, thoughts, and feelings are recorded at least daily and sometimes twice or three times per day. For example, it is easy to imagine George Plimpton taking time each day to write down the things that happened to him while he was in training with the Detroit Lions. An entry in his nightly diary could have read like this:

Practice today focused on extended warm-up drills especially concentrated on loosening up the hamstring muscles. It seems that there have been an unusual amount of "hammy" pulls in camp this year and the coaches are worried about it. I spend most of the practice working with the quarterbacks and receivers, but while we played catch I couldn't help but keep noticing the linebackers and linemen. Their drills were tantamount to running full speed into the side of the stadium. It's amazing how much punishment the human body can take—at least their human bodies. They (the linebackers and linemen, that is) seem to be a different breed. They don't engage in as much joking and fooling around as some of the other players do. It's almost as though they have to work themselves into such a mental state to endure the punishment they do, that they don't want to break the mood. I sat next to Drooger, the all pro middle linebacker, at lunch. He knew who I was and why I was there, as all the players do, but talking to him was quite a different experience from talking to the other team members. He wasn't rude, just in a different world. He answered all my questions (Yep . . . Nope . . . Yep . . . Yep . . . Nope) but certainly didn't volunteer any information. It was almost as though he felt I was violating some sacred aspect of training camp by being there. I didn't take it personally; simply found it fascinating.

Given that Plimpton did this each day, by the end of training camp he would have had pages upon pages of information from which to write his book.

Some journal entries are far less narrative in form. For example, the Plimpton nightly entries might have looked like:

7:00 am: breakfast as usual
8:00 am: on the practice field
                   warm-ups
                   focused on stretching
                   too many hamstring pulls in camp this year
                   worked with receivers and quarterback again
                   but watched linebackers
                   their drills were brutal
     12:00:   ate with Drooger at lunch
                   not very talkative
                   reinforced my perception of linebackers

The format you use to keep notes on your personal experience is relatively unimportant. You should use the technique that is comfortable for you. The key to note taking is that the notes be understandable to you later and allow you to recall significant facts about your experience.

Although personal experience is perhaps the best way to acquire background information for a paper, many people do not use it, because they don't have the time, money, or energy to do such things as spend two weeks in training camp with a professional football team, fight Archie Moore, or play goalie for the Boston Bruins. There is, however, another way of obtaining first-hand or primary-source information: through the use of interviews.

When you use interviewing as a technique for gathering information you are doing investigative journalism. The word "investigate" comes from the Latin word *investigare*, which means to follow the tracks of. Investigative journalism consists of asking good questions at the right time, tracking down the answers, and being the first to publish a story. Basic to investigative journalism is question asking.

There are many different types of questions, each of which elicits different information and, consequently, is appropriate in different situations. There are six different categories of questions: (1) knowledge questions, (2) comprehension questions, (3) application questions, (4) analysis questions, (5) evaluation questions, and (6) synthesis questions.

A *knowledge question* requires the answerer to recall specific bits of information. In asking such questions, people usually begin in one of the following ways:

"Do you remember . . .?"
"Can you define . . .?"
"List the four . . ."

Such questions are usually easy to answer provided that the individual being asked has a good recollection of the event he or she is being asked about.

Comprehension questions require the interviewee to interpret, compare, contrast, explain, or translate information. Comprehension questions are sometimes more difficult to answer than knowledge questions. Comprehension questions often have the form

"Explain the . . ."
"Describe how you feel about . . ."
"Tell in your own words . . ."

Application questions require an individual to transfer information to a new setting. To answer an application question one must first recall information and then apply it to a new situation. Examples of application questions are:

"Where does it lead you that . . ."
"What would you conclude given that . . ."

Analysis questions require the interviewee to break down a problem into its various parts. When you ask an analysis question you are usually looking for classification, separation, or categorization of information. Example of analysis type questions include:

"What are the causes of . . ."
"What are the consequences of . . ."
"Specify the conditions under which . . ."
"What are the steps in . . ."

Evaluation and *synthesis questions* can also be difficult. To answer an evaluation question a person must evaluate, judge, set criteria, assess, or recommend. Sample evaluation questions are:

"Which of the following do you think are most likely . . .?"
"Describe what you consider to be the value of . . ."

To answer a *synthesis question* a person must put together isolated, seemingly unrelated facts to form a whole. Usually this requires divergent thinking, originality, and imagination. Examples of synthesis questions are:

"What would happen if . . ."
"Describe what it would be like if . . ."

In addition to these six different types, all questions can be either open or closed or primary or secondary. Open questions are broad in nature and allow the respondent a great deal of freedom in determining the amount and kind of information that he or she will give. Some examples of open-ended questions are:

"Tell me about yourself."
"What do you think about the energy crisis?"
"What are your feelings about gun control?"

Such questions allow the interviewee to talk freely. However, the problem with using open-ended questions is that the interviewee might go on and on without really giving you the information you are seeking. This can be avoided by adding some restrictions. For example:

"Tell me about yourself since you've been at college."
"What do you think about the energy crisis as far as using nuclear energy?"
"What are your feelings about gun control as Senate Bill 823 defines it?"

Closed questions limit answer options available to the respondent. With a closed question, the interviewee gives either a brief bit of information or selects the appropriate answer from among those provided in the question. The following questions are closed questions:

"How old are you?"
"Who was the twenty-fifth President of the United States?"
"What is your favorite brand of beer?"
"How would you rate Senator O'Neill on a political continuum: conservative, moderate, liberal, or radical?"

By using closed questions, the interviewer can control the interview more effectively, because the interviewee has less opportunity to wander in his or her responses.

Both open-ended and closed questions can also be either primary or secondary. Primary questions are those in which new topics or new areas are introduced. Secondary questions attempt to elicit more information asked for in a primary question or another secondary question. For example, when the interviewee gives an answer to a question that is vague, incomplete, or superficial, the interviewer can follow up with a secondary question. Secondary questions usually employ phrases such as the following:

"Tell me more about . . ."
"What happened after . . ."
"Explain further your point . . ."

Below is an example of an interview in which secondary questions are used skillfully to obtain detailed information. The interview also has a good distribution of open and closed questions:

Doug: How do you feel about the proposed hike in student fees to offset the athletic department's deficit?

Liz: I think the proposal needs more careful study before it is acted upon by the students.

Doug: Why do you think it needs more study?

Liz: Well, first of all, I'm not too sure if it is wise to hike student fees to support a department if the department hasn't come up with other ways to offset the deficit.

Doug: You feel then that the athletic department hasn't explored all possible methods for raising revenues?

Liz: Yes, most definitely.

Doug: Do you have any other reasons why the proposal needs to be studied more?

Liz: No, not really.

Doug: On this card, there are different ranges of numbers representing the student body. How many students do you think attend athletic events: 100–1000; 1000–5000; 5000–10,000; over 10,000.

Liz: I read in the paper that it was between 1000 and 5000.

Doug: If the athletic department could not find any other means to fund athletics would you be in favor of hiking student fees?

Liz: Yes, to a certain degree.

Doug: What do you mean by "a certain degree"?

As can be inferred from our discussion, question-asking in the context of an interview is a complex and delicate procedure. The type and number of questions you ask is determined by the purpose of the interview and the responses you receive from the interviewee. One of the best ways to ensure that you will ask a variety of appropriate questions is to develop an interview schedule, which is a written account of the questions you wish to ask during an interview. For example, if you were going to interview a state representative to obtain information about current legislation on mandatory busing and the representative's views on that issue, you might make out the following interview schedule:

Interview Schedule

Date_____
Interviewee's Name_____
Age_____District_____Sex_____
Party Affiliation_____
Years in Present Position_____
Years in Politics_____

1. What are your beliefs concerning the justness of mandatory busing?
2. What would happen if busing became mandatory in this state?
3. What do you think is most likely to occur in our state—rejection or acceptance of the mandatory busing bill? Please explain your answer.
4. Can you identify incidents in the past in which your voting record has indicted your support of (or lack of support of) the mandatory busing bill?
5. Describe the necessary components of a successful school desegregation program.
6. What are the causes of the current statewide unrest concerning the busing issue?

The interview schedule allows you to monitor the types of questions you will ask. This will help identify whether you are leaving out important types of questions or are ignoring areas that might be fruitful to investigate. An interview schedule also has the effect of helping you stick to the topic and avoid wasting time discussing something tangential to the topic.

Once appropriate questions have been identified and an interview schedule developed, the interview process itself must be considered. Conducting a good interview is an art. Below are some suggestions for conducting an interview:

1. Make an appointment with the person to be interviewed. Arrange a time and place to hold the interview.
2. Before the interview:
   a. Learn all you can about the person you will be interviewing.
   b. Collect details about the person's occupation and accomplishments.
3. Be on time for the interview.
4. Bring necessary equipment: notepaper, list of questions, several pencils.
5. When conducting the interview:
   a. Be courteous and let the person you are interviewing know you are genuinely interested in what he or she has to say.
   b. Avoid interrupting.
   c. Ask if you may quote the person exactly and carefully record such quotes.
   d. Keep the interviewee on the topic.
   e. Observe the person's facial expressions, mannerisms, and gestures.

   f. Take notes in a manner that will not interfere with the interview.

   g. Listen carefully to discriminate between important and unimportant details. Be sure you understand what the interviewee is telling you before you write it down. If you aren't sure how to spell names, ask the interviewee to spell them for you.

   h. Be sure to get all the necessary information during the interview so you will not have to contact the interviewee a second time.

6. Thank the person. You should also follow up an interview with a thank-you note or call.

7. Recopy and arrange your notes immediately following the interview.

Interviews can generate an enormous amount of information to write about. Perhaps the best example of the type of writing that can be produced from interviews is the collection of stories found in *The Foxfire Book*,[2] which is a collection of essays written by high school students using the interview technique of information gathering. This book was the brainchild of Eliot Wigginton, a high-school teacher. In 1966, Wigginton took a job as a ninth- and tenth-grade English teacher in Rabun Gap, Georgia, which is located in the Appalachians. After experiencing numerous failures at trying to teach his students how to write, Wigginton got the idea of starting a magazine that contained writing produced by his students. When he was met with cries of "What will we write about?" he and the class decided they would focus their attention on the people and rich mountain culture around them. They would go out and interview their fellow inhabitants of the Appalachians and write about the information they obtained from the interviews. They found the inhabitants of the mountain community more than willing to discuss their lives and the common things that made up their days. Consequently, Wigginton's students found themselves writing essays about such topics as:

"Building a Log Cabin"
"White Oak Splits"
"Rope, Straw and Feathers Are to Sleep On"
"Mountain Recipes"
"Weather Signs"
"Home Remedies"
"Hunting Tales"
"Snake Lore"

"Moonshining as an Art"
"Faith Healing"

These essays were eventually put together in *The Foxfire Book*. The students chose the title "Foxfire" because it is a "tiny organism that glows in the dark and is frequently seen in the shaded coves of these mountains."[3] Since the publication of the book, it has become internationally famous. Yet all of the essays were written by high-school students and all the information was obtained via interviews, a very rich source of information.

SECONDARY SOURCES OF INFORMATION

Secondary sources are those from which information is acquired second hand, usually from someone else's written account of an event. The best place to find secondary sources of information is in the library. But before discussing the types of secondary sources you will find in a library, let us mention the occasions on which you might use secondary sources. Generally the use of secondary sources is limited to the writing of research papers or reports, which will be discussed in depth in chapter 10. For many types of writing, you can obtain all necessary information from the prewriting activities in chapter 3 and from primary sources. The decision, of course, whether to use secondary sorces depends on how knowledgable you are about your topic.

The Library

In chapter 3 we discussed using the library to identify writing topics. Now we will consider using the library to gather information from which to write. This does not mean that the topic identification and information-gathering uses of the library are necessarily two separate events. Usually you will begin to collect information while you are using the library to identify and narrow a topic. However, where library use for topic identification ends, use of the library to gather information begins. In this section we will consider some new sources of library information not mentioned in chapter 3 and reconsider some of the sources already cited.

Secondary sources consist of nonfiction material. Some libraries classify nonfiction books by means of the Dewey Decimal System. The categories of the Dewey Decimal System are:

000–099   General works   Encyclopedias, almanacs, hand-
                               books

100–199	Philosophy	Conduct, ethics, psychology
200–299	Religion	Bible, mythology, theology
300–399	Social science	Economics, law, education, commerce, government, folklore
400–499	Language	Languages, grammar, dictionaries
500–599	Science	Mathematics, chemistry, physics, biology, astronomy
600–699	Useful arts	Farming, cooking, sewing, radio, nursing, engineering, television, business, gardening
700–799	Fine arts	Music, painting, drawing, acting, photography, games, sports, amusements
800–899	Literature	Poetry, plays, essays
900–999	History	Biography, travel, geography

If your library does not use the Dewey Decimal system, it probably uses the Library of Congress system. This alternate system uses letters as well as numbers to classify books. It is usually helpful to become as familiar as possible with the classification system your library uses, because such knowledge allows you to locate and scan nonfiction books that might not come to your attention while looking through the card catalog.

In addition to nonfiction books, reference materials are also helpful in gathering information. Reference materials include dictionaries, encyclopedias, almanacs, yearbooks, atlases, pamphlets, booklets, catalogs, and magazines. Some of these we briefly mentioned in Chapter 3; the rest are described here.

The *dictionary* is one of the best general references available. Dictionaries not only help with spelling, pronunciation, and meaning of words, they also give brief information about people, places, foreign terms, and abbreviations. Hence, if you need a date or the meaning of a technical or foreign term, a dictionary is a handy source of information. The *unabridged dictionary* contains over 250,000 words, with a complete history of each word and every definition and use available for each word. Two of the most widely available unabridged dictionaries are *Webster's Third New International Dictionary* and the *Random House Dictionary of the English Language*.

Abridged dictionaries contain about 150,000 words and provide information and definitions, spelling, pronunciation, and usage. In addition, they usually include sections that contain biographical and geographical information. Two abridged dictionaries are the *American Heritage Dictionary of the English Language* and *Webster's New Collegiate Dictionary*.

Besides general dictionaries, there are dictionaries on specific subjects, such as music, geography, art, and science. For example, you can consult the following for information on specific subjects:

Dictionary of Economics
Harvard Dictionary of Music
An Illustrated Dictionary of Art and Archaeology
The Mathematical Dictionary
The Dictionary of Literary Terms
The Oxford Dictionary of English Etymology

Encyclopedias are another commonly used reference source. Encyclopedias contain general articles on a wide variety of topics and are an excellent source of limited but specific information. Encyclopedias are organized alphabetically by subject. There are guide words at the top of each page to aid the reader in locating information; most encyclopedias also have an index that identifies the different topics in each volume. Some encyclopedias publish a yearly supplement (yearbook) that reviews current events and subjects for a particular year. The Encyclopaedia Britannica is probably the most widely used encyclopedia. Some encyclopedias deal only with specific subjects. Two of these are the Encyclopedia of Careers and Vocational Guidance and the Larousse Encyclopedia of Mythology.

Almanacs and yearbooks are published annually. They are useful sources of information about such topics as government, sports, entertainment, and population. The information in an almanac is not arranged in any particular order. Consequently, you have to use both the table of contents and the index to find needed facts. Two popular almanacs are the World Almanac and Book of Facts and the World Book Yearbook of Events.

An atlas is a reference book that contains detailed maps of the world. It also contains statistics about population, climate, and other topics. Some widely used atlases are the Atlas of World History, the International Atlas, and the Times Atlas of World.

Besides the references mentioned above, many college and university libraries have a file cabinet in which they keep an alphabetical listing of pamphlets, booklets, catalogs, handbooks, and clippings about a variety of subjects. This file is called the vertical file. Unfortunately, very few people know that it exists, and consequently it is one of the least-used references in most libraries.

Once you have located the secondary sources that contain facts you might need for your paper, your task is to record the information. When you use secondary sources from the library you must rely on notetaking as your method of recording useful information.

Notes are written records of information you consider important. One critical aspect of notetaking is to record only the important information. But how do you decide what is important? By this time in the writing process you have already identified a purpose, a topic, and an audience. This allows you to be selective in what you take notes on. Not all information, regardless of how interesting it is, should be recorded. Many students make the mistake of trying to record everything, which makes the notetaking part of information collection cumbersome and overwhelming. There are, however, some conventions in notetaking that can help facilitate the process.

Many times you might want to take notes on terminology, especially in a highly technical field. A good technique when taking notes on terms is to divide your notepaper into two unequal parts by drawing a vertical line down the left-hand side of the page about one inch from the margin or edge of the paper. Any terms you want to record are then written to the left of that vertical line and the explanation of the term to the right. Example 5-1 shows a notebook entry in which terms have been recorded.

Example 5-1	
cortex	general name for outside layer of the brain—cortex is the part of the brain that is highly developed in man and developed to lesser extent or not at all in lower animals.
fissure	an indentation in the cortex much like a groove or a crack—the cortex is mapped according to these fissures—that is, the various parts of the cortex as identified by various fissures.
sylvan fissure	prominent fissure running horizontally through cortex that separates the temporal lobe from the other lobes.
lobe	the opposite of a fissure—lobes resemble bulges in the brain—these too are used to map the cortex and identify specific areas.
central fissure	fissure that runs vertically down the middle of the cortex—on one side of this fissure is the frontal lobe—in back of this fissure are the parietal and occipital lobes.

This same procedure is also useful in recording historical information. To preserve and highlight a historical sequence, dates can be written to the left of the vertical line and the description of the event to the right. Example 5-2 shows notes on a sequence of historical events.

Example 5-2

September, 1940	Japanese made triple alliance with Germany and Italy in which parties agreed to cooperate and respect Germany and Italy's leadership in the "New Europe" as well as Japan's leadership in the "New Asia."—Treaty also provided that they would come to the defense of any treaty member who was attacked by a power other than Russia
July, 1941	a large Japanese naval force was sent to attack China's vital supply route from the west. From Indochina, Japan could strike at Burma through Thailand and cut off China's last supply route— could also move through Thailand to attack British naval bases at Singapore—Japan's move to Indochina led to united action by U.S., Great Britain, China—all of Japan's funds in these countries were frozen making it impossible for Japan to purchase war materials.
August 1, 1941	U.S. placed embargo on export of aviation oil and gasoline to Japan—Japan faced with choice: back down and restore relations with U.S., Great Britain, and China or be aggressive

---

Rather than use paper to take notes, some people prefer to use $3 \times 5''$ index cards. The advantage of cards over paper is that information can be easily reshuffled and reorganized after it has been recorded. In using study cards it is sometimes useful to write the date or term to be recorded on the unlined side of the card. It is also helpful to number the cards so that they can be easily put back in order if they are dropped. The information about the date or term is then written on the lined side of the card. Thus, by looking at one side of your cards you can quickly scan the important terms or dates about which information has been recorded.

Recording information is one part of the overall process of gathering information from which to write a paper. Once collected, that information has to be sorted and organized before it becomes truly useful for writing.

ORGANIZING YOUR INFORMATION

Facts and information by themselves do not a paper make. Recall the story in Chapter 1 about Greg. He was able to list pages of facts about his topic, but he knew that Professor Bradley wanted an organization and presentation of those facts that was logical and meaningful.

After collecting information from personal experience, interviews, or secondary sources you will probably have a mountain of facts—certainly more than you will need to write a paper. The next step is to sort and arrange those facts into major ideas or concepts and supporting ideas or details. For example, consider the following list of facts about alcohol. For convenience sake, we've numbered them.

1. the alcohol in beverages is ethanol
2. ethanol is produced by the action of yeast on sugar
3. most alcoholic drinks are made from the sugar in fruits
4. alcohol can be absorbed into one's system without changing form
5. alcohol starts entering the blood within two minutes after it is swallowed and then is carried into the tissue
6. absorption is even faster when the stomach is empty
7. once absorbed it is rapidly carried into the tissue where it is absorbed by the cells
8. in cells it oxidizes immediately
9. large amounts of heat are produced which raises temperature of blood
10. raised temp stimulates heat-control center of brain
11. brain responds by increasing circulation to the skin which causes a rosy skin tone
12. receptors of heat are in the skin; the rush of blood gives a false impression of warmth
13. not all alcohol is oxidized
14. some is released into lungs as vapor
15. this causes breath odor
16. some goes to skin and turns into perspiration
17. some passes to kidneys and leaves the body as urine
18. it usually takes with it large amounts of other bodily fluids
19. vitamin deficiency diseases are common among alcoholics

20. this is because they eat very little during periods of using alcohol
21. this also causes the liver to give up its stored food
22. liver begins to swell as the carbohydrates are replaced by fats
23. this condition is called fatty liver
24. it occurs in 75% of alcoholics
25. when fatty liver shrinks and hardens as fats are used a disease called cirrhosis begins
26. use of alcohol affects stomach
27. causes increase in stomach secretions
28. this leads to swelling of stomach lining called gastritis
29. alcohol is a depressant
30. it is an anesthetic and has numbing effect on the nervous system
31. some people think it is a stimulant
32. this is because its numbing effect on the nerves makes some people less concerned about their behavior
33. brain cortex shows the first effects of alcohol
34. influence on the frontal lobe changes emotional control
35. this leads to a feeling of joy or sadness
36. when it reaches the lower part of left hemisphere speech can be affected
37. this is why people often slur words when they've been drinking
38. when alcohol reaches cerebellum near back of head, muscle action is affected
39. in final stages of drunkenness the cortex stops working; this results in unconsciousness
40. heart action and digestive action slow down, as does respiration
41. the drinker becomes completely helpless

   In its present form this information is relatively useless. For example, if we wanted to translate this information into a general-to-specific paper on alcoholism, where would we begin? What would be the opening general statement? What would be the supporting details?

   For this information to be useful, then, we need to group the facts into categories and then try to label these categories. We performed this same group-and-label activity with brainstorming in Chapter 3. For example, facts 1, 2, and 3 all seem to deal with the chemical makeup of alcohol. Thus, we can clump those three bits of information together and label them " chemical makeup of alcohol and alcoholic drinks":

Chemical makeup of alcohol and alcoholic drinks

1. the alcohol in beverages is ethanol
2. ethanol is produced by the action of yeast on sugar
3. most alcoholic drinks are made from the sugar in fruits

   Facts 5 and 6 seem to deal with how quickly alcohol affects the body. We could label them "alcohol's rapid effect":

Alcohol's rapid effect

5. alcohol starts entering the blood within 2 minutes
6. absorption is even faster when the stomach is empty

Facts 7 through 12 refer to alcohol's affect on the body temperature:

Alcohol's effect on body temperature

7. once absorbed it is rapidly carried into the tissue where it is absorbed by the cells
8. in cells it oxidizes immediately
9. large amounts of heat are produced, which raises the temperature of the blood
10. the raised temperature stimulates heat-control center of the brain
11. brain responds by increasing circulation to the skin, which causes a rosy skin tone
12. receptors of heat are in the skin; the rush of blood gives a false impression of warmth

If we continued to do this, we would eventually have all facts grouped by the major ideas they relate to. This might produce the following:

Chemical makeup of alcohol and alcoholic drinks

1. the alcohol in beverages is ethanol
2. ethanol is produced by the action of yeast on sugar
3. most alcoholic drinks are made from the sugar in fruits

Alcohol's rapid effect

4. after it is swallowed it is carried into the tissue
5. alcohol starts entering the blood within 2 minutes
6. absorption is even faster when the stomach is empty

Alcohol's effect on body temperature

7. once absorbed it is rapidly carried into the tissue where it is absorbed by the cells
8. in cells it oxidizes immediately
9. large amounts of heat are produced, which raises the temperature of the blood
10. the raised temperature stimulates heat control center of the brain
11. brain responds by increasing circulation to the skin causing a rosy skin tone
12. receptors of heat are in the skin; the rush of blood gives a false impression of warmth

Elimination of alcohol from the body

13. all alcohol is not oxidized
14. some is released into lungs as vapor
15. this causes breath odor
16. some goes to skin and turns into perspiration
17. some passes to kidneys and leaves as urine
18. it usually takes with it large amounts of other bodily fluids

Alcohol's effect on the liver

19. vitamin deficiency diseases are common among alcoholics
20. this is because they eat very little during periods of using alcohol
21. this also causes the liver to give up its stored food
22. liver begins to swell as the carbohydrates are replaced by fats
23. this condition is called fatty liver
24. it occurs in 75% of all alcoholics
25. when the fatty liver shrinks and hardens as fats are used a disease called cirrhosis begins

Alcohol's effect on the stomach

26. use of alcohol affects the stomach
27. it causes increase in stomach secretions
28. this leads to swelling of stomach lining called gastritis

Alcohol as a depressant

29. alcohol is a depressant
30. it is an anesthetic and has a numbing effect on the nervous system

31. some people think it is a stimulant
32. this is because its numbing effect on the nerves makes some people less concerned about their behavior

Alcohol's effect on the cortex and cerebellum

33. brain cortex shows the first effects of alcohol
34. influence on the frontal lobe changes emotional control
35. this leads to feeling of joy or sadness
36. when it reaches the lower part of left hemisphere speech can be affected
37. this is why people often slur words when they've been drinking
38. when alcohol reaches cerebellum near back of head muscle, action is affected

Final stages of drunkenness

39. in final stages of drunkenness the cortex stops working, which results in unconsciousness
40. heart action and digestive action slow down as does respiration
41. the drinker becomes completely helpless

Organized in this fashion the information is far more useful. We have identified nine major ideas about alcohol:
1. Chemical makeup of alcohol
2. Alcohol's rapid effect
3. Alcohol's effect on body temperature
4. Elimination of alcohol from the body
5. Alcohol's effect on the liver
6. Alcohol's effect on the stomach
7. Alcohol as a depressant
8. Alcohol's effect on the cortex and cerebellum
9. Final stages of drunkenness

Within each of these major ideas we have also identified supporting details. The next step is that of organizing these major ideas in such a way that they fit into the overall organizational pattern we've identified when planning the essay. Assuming that when planning the paper we determined that we wanted to write a general-to-specific enumeration paper listing the characeristics of alcohol, we might choose to order the major ideas in the following way:

Introduction: Alcohol is a powerful drug that reacts quickly
Example 1: Effect on body temperature
Example 2: Effect on liver
Example 3: Effect on the stomach
Example 4: Depressant effect
Example 5: Effect on cortex
Example 6: Effect during final stages of drunkenness
Conclusion

Note that we've left out the information about the chemical makeup of alcohol and elimination of alcohol from the body. Again, not all information collected and then categorized will be used in a paper.

In Chapter 4 we discussed planning your paper by identifying the overall organizational format (for example: enumeration, process) and filling in some details in outline form for that organizational format. But planning a paper is not a one-step process. When writing, you will probably identify an overall organizational format at the time that you identify a topic, purpose, and audience. But when you collect more information on the topic and organize that information, you will undoubtedly see ways of expanding or changing the organizational format you have already identified. Changing direction as you collect information and begin to write is part of the writing process. A paper will change many times in many different ways before it reaches completion.

SUMMARY

How well and how easily you can write about any topic is directly related to how much information you have about the topic. As a test to see if you have adequate information to begin writing, list facts and information about the topic. If the facts come to you easily, you can conclude that you have adequate background information to begin writing. However, if you find that you can't recall many facts about the topic, you should assume that you need to collect more information before writing.

Information is obtained from either primary or secondary sources. Primary sources are those from which information is received first hand. Two ways of collecting primary-source information are interviews and personal experience. When using personal experience to collect information, you must usually keep a diary or journal to record thoughts and feelings. When conducting an interview, you need to plan appropriate questions to use in the interview.

Secondary sources of information are those that rely on someone else's account of facts. Two secondary sources of information commonly used are nonfiction books and reference sources, both of which can be found in a library. Collecting information from secondary sources is done by reading or skimming the nonfiction books or reference sources pertinent to your topic and then taking notes on important information.

Once information is collected, whether it be from primary or secondary sources, it must be organized. This is accomplished by grouping facts and labeling the groups. The result of this process is a set of main ideas with supporting details. The main ideas can then be placed into the overall organizational format you have identified as suitable for your topic, audience, and purpose.

Exercises

1. Analyze an interview written in a magazine and list the types of questions the interviewer asked. What was the predominant type of question asked: primary-open; primary-closed; secondary-open, or secondary-closed?

2. Decide on an issue on which you and another student would like to gather information through interviewing. One of you will prepare only primary questions and the other mainly secondary questions. Compare your two sets of questions to see how the information obtained will be different.

3. Pick a current issue or event that is important on your campus. Find out who is involved and interview one or more of these people. Compare your interview with others to see how different questions elicited different responses.

4. Identify some selected references in your library that you feel will be useful in your writing. Keep a list of these references for further use. Find out what classification system your library uses.

5. Using a social science or natural science textbook, take two sets of notes on materials in which you will eventually be tested. Use the term method for one set of notes and the sequence method for the other. Discuss which method helped you to remember the material best.

6. Use the group-and-label method to categorize the facts below. After you have finished, check it with our categories. The two may not be exactly the same but you should be able to make some comparisons.

1. Arabs might have invented the first contraceptive centuries ago.
2. with narrow tubes they inserted pebbles into the wombs of their camels.
3. the Arabs wanted to keep the animals from getting pregnant on long trips.
4. this contraceptive device might have been the forerunner of the intrauterine device (IUD).
5. IUD's are used by 50 million women around the world.
6. two million women in the U.S. use IUDs.
7. infection is a problem with IUDs.
8. Early IUDs caused complications.
9. They were made out of glass, ivory, gold, ebony or silkworm gut.
10. in the 1960s antibiotics and new plastics made insertions easier.
11. IUDs proliferated.
12. IUDs cause inflammation of the uterus.
13. they prevent the fertilized eggs from implanting.
14. certain types of IUDs release copper or the hormone progesterone.
15. within the past decade, the incidence of pelvic infections caused by bacteria has reached epidemic proportions.
16. users are 2 to 7 times more susceptible to these infections.
17. infections scar and block the fallopian tubes.
18. the result is a hysterectomy.
19. IUD failure causes ectopic pregnancies.
20. with this pregnancy the fetus grows outside the uterus.
21. some doctors feel the IUD's dangers are being exaggerated.
22. pelvic infections are linked to veneral disease and sexual activity with more than one partner.
23. for women without serious problems, IUDs are preferable to other birth control methods.
24. some physicians still will not recommend IUDs for sexually active women who have not borne children.
25. some physicians advise them for mothers who do not want any more babies.

Answer to Question 6.

A. The origin of the IUD.
   1. Arabs might have invented the first contraceptive centuries ago.
   2. With narrow tubes they inserted pebbles into the wombs of their camels.
   3. The Arabs wanted to keep the animals from getting pregnant on long trips.

    4. This contraceptive might have been the forerunner of the intrauterine device (IUD).

B. Who uses IUDs

    5. IUDs are used by 50 million around the world.

    6. Two million women in the U.S. use an IUD.

C. Early complication of IUDs.

    7. Infection is a problem with IUDs.

    8. Early IUDs caused complications.

    9. They were made out of glass, ivory, gold, ebony, or silkworm gut.

D. A safe IUD.

    10. In the 1960s antibiotics and new plastics made insertions easier.

    11. IUDs proliferated.

E. How IUDs work.

    12. IUDs cause inflammation of the uterus.

    13. They prevent the fertilized eggs from implanting.

    14. Certain types of IUDs release copper or the hormone progesterone.

F. New complications with IUDs.

    15. Within the past decade the incidence of pelvic infections caused by bacteria has reached epidemic proportions.

    16. Users are 2 to 7 times more susceptible to these infections.

    17. Infections scar and block the fallopian tubes.

    18. The result is a hysterectomy.

    19. IUD failure causes ectopic pregnancies.

    20. With this pregnancy the fetus grows outside of the uterus.

G. An opposing view.

    21. Some doctors feel the IUD's dangers are being exaggerated.

    22. Pelvic infections are linked to veneral disease and sexual activity with more than one partner.

    23. For women without serious problems, IUDs are preferable to other birth control methods.

H. One conclusion.

    24. Some physicians still will not recommend IUDs for sexually active women who have not borne children.

    25. Some physicians advise them for mothers who do not want any more babies.

References

1. G. Plimpton, *Paper Lion* (New York: Harper and Row, 1966); *Shadow Box* (Berkeley, Cal.: Putnam Publications, 1973).

2. E. Wigginton, *The Foxfire Book* (New York: Doubleday, 1972).

3. Wigginton, p. 11.

Writing and Revising

CHAPTER SIX

PUTTING THOUGHT TO PAPER

The parts of the writing process set forth in chapters 2 through 5 all take place before you actually begin to write. In chapters 6 through 9 we will consider some of the activities you do during the actual writing of a paper.

We feel there are five parts to the process you go through from the time you begin writing to the time a paper is completed. Those five parts can be grouped into two categories: (1) putting thought to paper and (2) polishing, each of which has subcategories. Our model of what happens once you begin to write can be outlined like this:

A. Putting thought to paper
   1. the spontaneous phase
   2. revising for gaps in logic

B. Polishing
   3. revising to expand and reduce
   4. revising for vocabulary
   5. revising for grammar, usage, and mechanics

As can be seen from this outline, revising (or rewriting) is a major part of the composing process. You begin to revise or rewrite almost immediately after you put your thoughts on paper. What we call writing, then, is actually a blending of two processes—putting down ideas and revising or changing them. The two processes are almost simultaneous. In this chapter we will discuss the putting-thought-to-paper phase of writing. But before doing so, let's obtain a better perspective on the place of revision in the composing process.

REVISION: A PERSPECTIVE

The realization that a composition, to be good, must go through a series of rewrites has been accepted for as long as people have been writing. The importance of revising is well illustrated by this quote from John Kenneth Galbraith, the economist, who says: "There are days when the result [of my writing] is so bad that no fewer than five revisions are required. In contrast, when I'm greatly inspired, only four revisions are needed."[1]

The first drafts of many well-known authors illustrate that Galbraith's reverence for revision is shared by many. Consider Example 6-1, which represents revisions Sinclair Lewis supposedly made on his novel *Babbit*.

Example 6-1

BABBIT

Chapter 1

The tower of ~~a new city~~ *of Zenith* aspired above the morning mist; ~~sheer~~ *austere* towers of steel ~~and~~ *and* cement and ~~silvery~~ limestone, sturdy as cliffs *and* delicate as *shafts of silver* birch trees. ~~They were the promise of strange futures in this American~~ city ~~called Zenith.~~ *delicate as silver rods*

The mist ~~blessed and cursed the hunched~~ *took Friday on the* and fretted *structures* buildings of earler generations: the Post Office with its shingle-tortured mansard and ~~arches that supported nothing;~~ *the red brick minarets of hulking old* houses ~~of minarets and consienately~~ adorned ~~lightning rods;~~ *houses* factories with stingy and sooted windows; ~~dreadful~~ wooden tenements colored like mud. ~~These blotches still made~~ *Mort of Zenith*

was still made up of such grotesqueries, but the
~~up most of the city, but the good~~ clean towers were thrusting them from the

business center, and on the farther hills were shining new houses;

homes—they seemed—for laughter and tranquility.

Over a cement bridge ~~like carven ivory~~ slipped a limousine ~~with sleek~~ *of long*
sleek hood & noiseless engine. These
~~sure lines and soundless engine~~ The four people in evening clothes were

returning from an all-night rehearsal of a ~~Russian~~ Little Theater play, an

artistic adventure ~~considerably~~ illuminated by champagne.[2]

Revising involves adding to, deleting from, and altering what has already been written: "This process of moving toward meaning implies a continual process of revision. Writers have to see what is on the page and then decide to cut, change or keep it."[3]

Another example of editing is that done by William Blake on his poem, "The Tiger" (Example 6-2).

Example 6-2
William Blake: "The Tiger"
(First Draft)

The Tyger
Tyger Tyger burning bright
In the forests of the night
What immortal hand or eye
Dare ~~Could~~ frame they fearful symmetry
Burnt in
~~In what~~ distant deeps or skies
The cruel ~~Burnt~~ the fire of thine eyes
What the hand dare sieze the fire

And what shoulder & what art
Could twist the sinews of they heart
And when thy heart began to beat
What dread hand & what dread feet

~~Could fetch it from the furnace deep~~
~~And in thy horrid ribs dare steep~~
~~In the well of sanguine woe~~
~~In what clay & in what mould~~

~~Were thy eyes of fury roll'd~~
Where   where
~~What~~ the hammer ~~what~~ the chain
In what furnace was thy brain
                                 dread grasp
What the anvil what the ~~arm arm grasp clasp~~
Dare ~~Could~~ its deadly terrors ~~clasp grasp~~ clasp

Tyger Tyger burning bright
In the forests of the night
What immortal hand & eye
       frame
Dare ~~form~~ thy fearful symmetry[4]

Revision, then, is at the heart of writing, yet the *control* of revision must be wedded with the freedom of spontaneity for a good composition to be produced. As the Romantic poet and critic Samuel Taylor Coleridge wrote, "There must be not only a partnership, but a union, an interpenetration of passion and of will, of spontaneous impulses and of voluntary purpose."[5] In this chapter and the following we will discuss specific elements of this necessary blending of spontaneity and control required in writing.

THE SPONTANEOUS PHASE

The poet Percy Bysshe Shelley perhaps described the spontaneous phase of writing best: "When my brain gets heated with thought, it soon boils and throws off images and words faster than I can skim them off."[6]

The spontaneous phase of writing is one in which thoughts are quickly jotted down about the topic and no judgment is made about the correctness of what is being written, the words that are being used, or the overall organization (those judgments are made later). There are some general guidelines you can follow that will help during the spontaneous phase of writing.

1. *Don't attempt to put thought to paper until you are ready.* It was said of John Keats that "he never sits down to write unless he is full of ideas."[7] If you follow the model presented in this text, you can be fairly sure that you will always be full of ideas by the time you begin putting thought to paper. This is because you will have first concentrated on motivation, identified and narrowed your topic, considered the audience for whom your paper is intended,

planned your format, and collected information. Hence, you will have done extensive preparation for your writing that should ensure that you will have something to write about. However, there are times for putting thought to paper that are better than others—times when your mind is more in touch with the topic. During those times, your brain will become "heated with thought" and will "boil over with ideas and images." The key is recognizing those times when they occur.

Most writers do their composing in fits and starts: They write in short spurts, leaving their desks periodically and often running back to their work to record some new ideas on the topic that have darted into their consciousness. You can facilitate the process by screening out thoughts not related to the topic and focusing your attention on the writing process. The important thing is to get a feel for when your mind is starting to boil over with ideas and images and make sure you sit down to write when these times occur.

2. *When writing, don't worry about spelling, punctuation, or sentence structure.* This is an important principle underlying the spontaneous phase. Spontaneity means recording what comes to mind in an unencumbered fashion. Recall again the self 1, self 2 concepts discussed in Chapter 2. Self 2 is our spontaneous side; self 1 is our analytical, judgmental side. If you've given self 2 the proper input for writing, then it should be capable of producing the desired product without much interference from self 1. When writing, self-1 interference usually takes the form of criticism: such thoughts as "How do I punctuate that last sentence? What is the correct way to spell 'psychology'? Should I begin a new paragraph here?" inhibit spontaneity. They are self-1 thoughts and have no place in the spontaneous phase of writing.

The product of spontaneous writing will contain many errors and many things that have to be changed, but this is as it should be. The spontaneous phase produces the first draft of a paper, not a finished product. Once your basic thoughts on the topic are recorded during the spontaneous phase, you will go back over the paper a number of times, adding and deleting ideas and taking care of such details as spelling, punctuation, and grammar.

The key, then, to the spontaneous phase of writing is to keep writing. You should consider your pen or typewriter as nothing more than a recording device that is getting down your thoughts on the subject as quickly as possible, allowing self 2 to do the job for which you have programmed and prepared it.

3. *If you get stuck while writing, leave your work for a while and come back later.* To illustrate this point, consider a description of how one writer worked on a novel:

I did most of the work on the book during the summer of '78. I was through teaching at the university and had no obligations at my office, so I elected to stay home every day and work on the story. Usually I would get up in the morning, make some coffee (a little cream and far too much sugar, my doctor says), and then go to the desk. I would look over what I had written the day before until my mind got into the swing of things again and the words started flowing. I would keep typing (I type faster than I write) as quickly as possible, selecting from the many thoughts that came to me which ones to put down. Most of the time my thoughts came out as fairly well-constructed sentences. Sometimes they were awkward. I never stopped to edit or revise—not even at the word level. If something was misspelled, it stayed misspelled. Invariably I would get to a point where my mind was muddled. I would lose my train of thought completely and would have to stop. The harder I tried to concentrate, the more confused I would become. At these times I would leave my desk and do something else. Sometimes I would play my guitar; at other times I would tease the cat; occasionally (very occasionally) I would wash the stack of dishes that had accumulated next to the sink or cut the grass in the back that was beginning to resemble a hay field. Usually I would find that while doing whatever it was I was doing to get away from my work my thoughts would gradually shift back to the book and my mind would start composing again. It was as though the stopgap I had come to in my writing had been overcome, without any conscious effort on my part, during my diversionary tactics. At these times I would immediately return to my writing with a wealth of new ideas.

This account accurately illustrates the point. When you find yourself at a dead end in your writing, leave it for a short period of time and do somethng else. Your mind, at a subconscious level (self-2 level), will still be working on the paper. When you come back to your writing, you will probably need only to review what you have written to continue where you left off.

As can be inferred from the statements above, the spontaneous phase of putting thought to paper will generate a composition that is far from ready to hand in. There will be some holes in the essay that need filling in; there may be some thoughts not expressed in complete sentences, and the essay may appear disjointed in parts. This is perfectly acceptable, though, for these flaws are corrected in the second phase of putting thought to paper.

REVISING FOR GAPS IN LOGIC

There are three characteristics to consider when revising for gaps in logic: (1) the overall clarity of the essay, (2) paragraphing, and (3) sentence sense.

Clarity of Overall Organization

As was discussed in Chapter 4, every paper should be built on an overall organizational format or pattern. When reading over an essay for gaps in logic, you should make sure you have followed the overall pattern identified when you planned and outlined the paper. For example, suppose that in the planning phase you decided to write a cause-and-effect paper explaining why you believe people are incapable of thinking for themselves in today's world. You collected adequate information, considered your audience and purpose, did some outlining, and came up with the following causes you wanted to cite:

Cause 1. We get much information each day from many sources.
            magazines
            books
            television
Cause 2. We are continually bombarded with propaganda.
            definition of propaganda
Cause 3. We take on the beliefs of the group we belong to.
            we take on beliefs of our country
            we take on beliefs of our race or ethnic group.

This outline might have translated into an essay such as Example 6-3.

Example 6-3

(1) We get new ideas from different sources almost every day. (2) We get them from magazines, books, posters, billboards, radio, and television. (3) Many ideas come from propaganda sources. (4) Propaganda occurs when someone is trying to get us to do something, to buy something, or to believe in something. (6) Some ideas we get come from the groups we belong to. (7) Some people look down on people from other countries simply because they are from a different place. (8) Other people look down on those who belong to different races.

Reading through this essay, we see that all information in the outline has been used. That is one aspect of reading over an essay for overall organization: to make sure you have included all important information.

Even though Example 6-3 contains all previously listed information, it still possesses organizational weaknesses. It doesn't seem to flow; it doesn't make a clear point. It does not demonstrate causes for a specific effect. We can see, then, that it is possible to use all your information but still not make your organizational pattern clear. But why?

In the outline for this paper three causes or reasons illustrating the main idea were identified:

1. We get many ideas each day.
2. Some ideas are purposely aimed at us.
3. We get some ideas from the groups we belong to.

For each of these examples, supporting information and details were identified. When the information was set out in outline form it was easy to see the causes and supporting details, because in outline form we visually mark the causes and supporting details by their placement on the page. When we turn the information in an outline into sentences, however, we lose those visual markers. This is why Example 6-3 doesn't seem to make a point: There is nothing to tell the reader which statements are causes and which are supporting details. To make this essay read more clearly, then, we must somehow indicate the relationship each sentence has with the overall theme.

But where is the overall theme stated? In this essay it is never stated explicitly: The effect of the causes is not made clear. Thus somewhere in the essay we need a clear statement of the effect we are trying to explain. Usually this is placed at the beginning of an essay and is called the topic sentence. The following might serve as a good topic statement for this essay:

Do we really think for ourselves? Probably not, because most of our ideas can be traced to some source outside of us.

We could have said the same thing in one sentence:

Most of us believe we think for ourselves, but virtually all of our thoughts can be traced to some source outside of us.

Regardless of how it is stated, we now have a clearly defined effect to show the causes of, and attention can now be turned to marking the causes. In the essay, those causes are stated in sentences 1, 3, and 6. Because we can't mark these sentences visually, as we can in outline form, we must mark them using words and phrases. This can be accomplished by inserting the following phrases in front of sentences 1, 3, and 6, respectively:

The first reason for our inability to think for ourselves is that . . .
Another contributing factor is that . . .
A final reason for our inability to think for ourselves is that . . .

These phrases clearly indicate to the reader that what comes next is a cause or reason. Adding these to sentences 1, 3, and 6 and inserting a topic sentence gives us the essay in Example 6-4.

Example 6-4

Do we really think for ourselves? Probably not, because most of our ideas can be traced to some source outside of us. The first reason for our inability to think for ourselves is that we get new ideas from different sources almost every day. We get them from magazines, books, posters, billboards, radio, and television. Another contributing factor is that many of our ideas come from propaganda sources. Propaganda means that someone is trying to get us to do something, to buy something, or to believe something. Propaganda can either be concealed or revealed. A final reason for our inability to think for ourselves is that some ideas come from the groups we belong to. Some people look down on people from other countries simply because they are from different places. Other people look down on those who belong to different races.

This essay reads much better than it did before. However, there is still something missing: a statement to conclude or summarize what has been said. Such a statement might be:

For these reasons, we can conclude that people are capable of very little thought that is not controlled by an outside source.

Adding this to the essay gives us a composition that has (1) an introductory topic sentence; (2) clearly marked causes or reasons; and (3) a summary or concluding statement. As a result, the essay is much easier to understand than it was before.

Let's review what we've done in revising this paper for overall organization. First, we added an introductory topic statement. We also added a concluding statement that summed up what we had said. In Chapter 4 we stated that introductions and conclusions are often written last. These elements are most efficiently added during the revising of a paper for gaps in logic. The introduction and conclusion are general statements that tell the reader what you are going to say or have said in the essay, and only after you have written an essay can you effectively summarize what you have said.

Another aspect of revising for gaps in logic is to make sure that each main idea or component of your overall organizational format is identified and easily recognizable. This is done by placing words and phrases in front of those sentences to point out to the reader the relationship those sentences have to the introductory statement.

Once you have made sure that you have a clear overall organizational format that includes an introduction and conclusion, you can concern yourself with paragraphing.

Paragraphing

Dividing an essay into paragraphs is an extension of the process of marking the main ideas. A paragraph is a group of logically related sentences. To illustrate this point, let's reconsider the main ideas we identified about alcohol from our grouping-and-labeling activity at the end of Chapter 5. We suggested in that chapter that those main ideas about alcohol could be presented in an enumeration paper in the following way:

Introduction: Alcohol is a powerful drug that reacts quickly.
  Example 1. Effect on body temperature
  Example 2. Effect on the liver
  Example 3. Effect on the stomach
  Example 4. Depressant effect
  Example 5. Effect on the cortex
  Example 6. Effect during the final stages of drunkenness
Conclusion

If we were to use only the major ideas stated in this outline to write an essay, we might end up with the one in Example 6-5.

Example 6-5

(1) Alcohol is a powerful drug that reacts quickly in the body. (2) One of the first things it does is affect one's body temperature. (3) Alcohol affects the

liver by robbing it of carbohydrates and replacing them with fats. (4) It affects the stomach by causing an increase in secretions, which leads to a swelling of the stomach lining. (5) Alcohol also has a depressant effect, acting as a mild anesthetic and having a numbing effect on the nervous system. (6) Its major effects are on the cortex and cerebellum, which are both profoundly influenced. (7) In the final stages of drunkenness, alcohol almost totally shuts off activity in the cortex and slows down heart action, digestive action, and respiration, rendering the drinker almost totally helpless. (8) Alcohol is, indeed, a very powerful drug.

The ideas expressed in Example 6-5 are all related. Hence, in this essay we have a group of related sentences, which, by our definition, qualifies as a paragraph. But suppose we wanted to add supporting details to the first example of alcohol's powerful effect? That first example (sentence 2) states that alcohol affects body temperature. We could add the following statements about that example:

Once it is absorbed it is rapidly carried into the tissue, where it is taken in by the cells.

There it oxidizes immediately.

Large amounts of heat are produced, causing a rise in the temperature of the blood, which in turn stimulates the heat-control center in the brain.

The brain responds by increasing circulation to the skin, causing a rosy skin tone.

The heat receptors in the skin interpret this rush of blood as increased external temperature, giving the drinker a false impression of warmth.

These sentences all provide explanatory information about the fact that alcohol affects body temperature. Likewise, if we wanted to add supporting information about our fifth example of alcohol's powerful effect (sentence 6), its effect on the cortex and cerebellum, that information might include the following:

Alcohol's influence on the frontal lobe changes emotional control, leading to feelings of joy or sadness.

When it reaches the lower part of the left hemisphere, speech can be affected.

This is why people often slur words when they've been drinking.

When alcohol reaches the cerebellum, near the back of the head, muscle action is affected.

This is why people sometimes stumble or knock things over when they've been drinking.

If we integrate this information with the statements we already have, we would obtain an essay like that in Example 6-6.

Example 6-6

(1) Alcohol is a powerful drug that reacts quickly in the body. (2) One of the first things it does is affect body temperature. (2a) Once it is absorbed it is rapidly carried into the tissue, where it is taken in by the cells. (2b) There it oxidizes immediately. (2c) Large amounts of heat are produced, causing a rise in the temperature of the blood, which in turn stimulates the heat-control center of the brain. (2d) The brain responds by increasing circulation to the skin, causing a rosy skin tone. (2e) The heat receptors in the skin interpret this rush of blood as increased external temperature, giving the drinker a false impression of warmth. (3) Alcohol affects the liver by robbing it of carbohydrates and replacing them with fats. (4) It also affects the stomach, causing an increase in secretions, which leads to a swelling of the stomach lining. (5) Alcohol also has a depressant effect, acting as a mild anesthetic and having a numbing effect on the nervous system. (6) Its major effects are on the cortex and cerebellum, which are both profoundly influenced. (6a) Alcohol's influence on the frontal lobe changes emotional control, leading to feelings of joy or sadness. (6b) When it reaches the lower part of the left hemisphere, speech can be affected. (6c) This is why people often slur words when they've been drinking. (6d) When alcohol reaches the cerebellum, near the back of the head, muscle action is affected. (6e) This is why people sometimes stumble or knock things over when they've been drinking. (7) In the final stages of drunkenness, alcohol almost totally shuts off activity in the cortex and slows down heart action, digestive action, and respiration, rendering the drinker almost totally helpless. (8) Alcohol is, indeed, a very powerful drug.

With this added information, the essay does not seem to be as clear as when it included only statements of the major ideas. This is because in the second version all sentences are not related to each other in the same way. In the first essay, all sentences were examples of the powerful and rapid effects of alcohol. But the second contains sentences that are related to specific examples; they are examples of the examples. Sentences 2a, 2b, 2c, 2d, and 2e relate to sentence 2. They logically go together. Sentences 3, 4, and 5 are general statements of alcohol's effects without added supporting information. They seem to go together. Sentences 6a,

6b, 6c, 6d, and 6e are supporting details about sentence 6, and they go together. Sentence 7 is another example of the introductory generalization (sentence 1) and sentence 8 is the concluding statement. We might group these sentences into categories of logically related statements like this:

Sentence 1

Sentence 2
Sentence 2a
Sentence 2b
Sentence 2c   Group 1
Sentence 2d
Sentence 2e

Sentence 3
Sentence 4   Group 2
Sentence 5

Sentence 6
Sentence 6a
Sentence 6b
Sentence 6c   Group 3
Sentence 6d
Sentence 6e

Sentence 7

Sentence 8

Now we have the sentences organized in such a way that we can form paragraphs fairly easily. We can attach the first sentence—the introductory sentence—to the first group of sentences and form sentences 7 and 8 into a fourth group to give us four groups of sentences or four paragraphs. Rewriting those sentences in paragraph form would produce the essay shown in Example 6-7.

Example 6-7

Alcohol is a powerful drug that acts quickly in the body. One of the first things it does is affect body temperature. Once it is absorbed, it is rapidly carried into the tissue where it is taken in by the cells. There it oxidizes immediately. Large amounts of heat are produced, causing a rise in the temperature of the blood, which in turn stimulates the heat-control center of the brain. The brain responds by increasing circulation to the skin, causing a rosy skin tone. The heat receptors in the skin interpret this rush of blood as increased external termperature, giving the drinker a false impression of warmth.

Another powerful effect that alcohol has is that of robbing the liver of carbohydrates and replacing them with fats. Alcohol can also affect the stomach by causing an increase in secretions, which leads to a swelling of the stomach lining. It is also known to be a depressant, acting as a mild anesthetic and having a numbing effect on the nervous system.

Alcohol also affects the brain. Perhaps the most profound effects of alcohol are on the brain cortex and cerebellum. Alcohol's influence on the frontal lobe changes emotional control, leading to feelings of joy or sadness. When it reaches the lower part of the left hemisphere, speech can be affected. This is why people often slur words when they've been drinking. When alcohol reaches the cerebellum, near the back of the head, muscle action is affected. This is why people sometimes stumble or knock things over when they've been drinking.

In the final stages of drunkenness, alcohol almost totally shuts off the activity in the cortex. It also slows down hearing action and it slows down digestive action. Similarly, it inhibits respiration. All of this renders the drinker almost totally helpless. Alcohol, indeed, is a powerful drug.

Arranging the sentences into paragraphs makes the essay more readable. In a sense, paragraphs perform somewhat the same function that an outine does: When sentences are arranged into paragraphs, the reader is able to see the groupings of ideas. If you study Example 6-7 closely, you will see that in addition to grouping the sentences into paragraphs we have also added some words to the sentence that begins paragraph 2. Those added words are "Another powerful effect that alcohol has is that. . . ." These are transition words that help the reader get from one paragraph to another. They bridge the gap from paragraph 1 to paragraph 2 by telling the reader that "we've finished discussing alcohol's effect on body temperature and now are going to discuss more of the general effects of alcohol." Transitions can be entire sentences, and they can appear at the beginning of a paragraph or at the end. For example, we find a transition sentence at the beginning of paragraph 4: "Alcohol also affects the brain." This sentence cues the reader that we will now discuss another specific effect of alcohol.

When you read over a paper with an eye toward paragraphing, you should try to clump related sentences together. After you put related sentences together, you must add transitional phrases or sentences to aid the reader in making the transition from one paragraph to another.

Sentence Sense

A final consideration when revising an essay for gaps in logic is your use of sentences: You should make sure all your sentences make sense in themselves. The sentence is a basic unit of writing. A sentence is a group of words with a subject and predicate that expresses a complete thought. Most sentences also contain such other parts as direct and indirect objects, predicate nominatives, and predicate adjectives. Technically it is a requirement that all sentences possess a subject and predicate and, probably, one or more of the other parts. When we speak, however, we often leave out parts of sentences. Take, for example, one student's oral account of what she did every morning:

(1) I usually jump out of bed and put some coffee on first thing. (2) Generally can't do a thing before my first cup of coffee. (3) While it's perking, I just kind of stare out the window and watch the world go by. (4) Beautiful this morning. (5) Leaves had just turned. (6) There was a little rain coming down. (7) Kids were going to school. (8) I love to just sit and observe when it's early in the morning.

By definition each of the eight statements should contain a subject and a predicate. In sentence 1 the subject is *I* (the speaker) and the verbs and their complements (there are two predicates in this sentence) are *jump out of bed* and *put some coffee on first thing.* But what about sentence 2? There is an action *(can't do a thing before my first cup of coffee)* but no apparent subject. The subject is not stated but is understood to be "I." When we speak we leave out parts of our sentence, because we know that the listener will fill in the missing parts for us. This is acceptable in spoken language but not in written language. When you leave something out of a sentence in the written language, you are guilty of writing a sentence fragment. The following are some common types of sentence fragments.

Misuses of subordinate clause
  Fragment: I was grateful for his financial assistance. Which
    enabled me to go to college.
  Fragment corrected: I was grateful for his financial assistance,
    which enabled me to go to college.
Misuse of phrase
  Fragment: On the school steps, I saw Alice. Waiting for her
    mother to pick her up.

Fragment corrected: On the school steps, I saw Alice waiting
            for her mother to pick her up.
Omission of verb
   Fragment: After the flood, the barn roof in the yard.
   Fragment corrected: After the flood, the barn roof lay in the
            yard.

There is another important distinction relative to sentences in
which the spoken language is different from the written language.
When we speak, we signify the end of a sentence by dropping our
voice, but when we write we can't do this. In writing, the end of a
sentence is signified by putting a period at the end of the sentence
and capitalizing the first word in the next sentence:

He went to the store. That is where he bought the ring.

Sometimes when writing we forget to mark sentences with a
period and write them one after another without any punctuation,
or we use a comma to separate one sentence from another:

He went to the store, that is where he bought the ring, it was
for his girl friend, Melinda, they plan to get married soon.

This is a run-on sentence.
   We can take many liberties with sentence use in the oral language
that we cannot take in the written language. We can speak in
fragments because we can assume that the person we are speaking
to will fill in the missing information. In the written language,
however, the reader is not there for us to make judgments about. In
the spoken language we don't have to worry about run-on
sentences because we will automatically drop our voice at the end
of a thought (sentence). But when we write, we must mark the end
of a sentence with punctuation. When writing we must be more
aware of our sentence usage than when speaking.
   Because in the spontaneous phase of writing the emphasis is on
getting ideas on paper as quickly as possible, it is likely that the
writing that results will probably contain some fragments and
run-on sentences. Hence, it is a good idea to read over your essay
after the spontaneous phase and correct them. For example,
consider the Example 6-8, which is a produce of the spontaneous
phase of writing:

Example 6-8

The concert was a disaster from the very beginning. (1) Only two songs
having been played in the first set. The rain had already started to fall in a
steady drizzle in Redrocks amphitheater. (2) unofficial attendance

> 12,500. (3) More than had been at the Stones concert two weeks earlier. (4) It soon became obvious to everyone there that they should have canceled the concert before spectators began arriving and this was all happening on a night when a basketball game was being held in nearby McNichols Arena, they usually stagger the scheduling of sporting events and concerts to minimize the traffic congestion in the city but on this particular night they had not. By the end of a half hour the rain was falling in a steady downpour, and people began leaving in droves. Unfortunately the wave of departing spectators abandoning the concert reached their cars at about the same time the basketball game let out. Matters were compounded by the fact that the parking lots for the concert and the arena both empty into the same narrow thoroughfare. The resulting scene was almost humorous. (5) Everyone honking, racing for position in a line that was destined not to move anywhere. The scene remained one of pandemonium until enough patrol cars arrived to sort things out. Gradually the flow of traffic started again but only after people stayed in their cars watching the rain for at least an hour.

For ease of discussion the fragments and run-ons in Example 6-8 have been numbered and underlined. The first three sentence-sense errors are fragments—groups of words punctuated as though they were sentences but that are not. Fragments are usually easily corrected by attaching them to a sentence or by supplying them with a missing subject or verb. The first fragment, "Only two songs having been played . . . ," can be attached to the sentence immediately after it, producing:

> Only two songs had been played in the first set when the rain started to fall in a steady drizzle in Redrocks amphitheater.

The second fragment is missing a verb and the third a subject. These fragments are easily corrected by adding the missing sentence parts:

> The unofficial attendance was 12,500. This was more than had been at the Stones concert two weeks earlier.

The fourth error is a run-on. Four sentences, each capable of standing alone, have been strung together and punctuated as a single sentence. Those four sentences are:

1. It soon became obvious to everyone there that they should have cancelled the concert before spectators began arriving.
2. This was all happening on a night when a basketball game was being held in nearby McNichols Arena.

3. They usually stagger the scheduling of sporting events and concerts to minimize the traffic congestion in the city.
4. On this particular night they had not.

Of course there is nothing inherently wrong with joining independent clauses to produce compound sentences. However joining too many sentences together creates a structure that is so dense with ideas that it becomes difficult to understand. Such is the case with error 4 in Example 6-8. It would be better to divide this sentence into two or three separate sentences:

> It soon became obvious to everyone there that they should have cancelled the concert before spectators began arriving. Unfortunately, this was all happening on a night when a basketball game was being held in nearby McNichols Arena. Usually they stagger the scheduling of sporting events and concerts to minimize the traffic congestion in the city, but on this particular night they had not.

The fifth error is also a fragment; this too can be easily rectified. With all the sentence-sense errors corrected, the essay would appear like that in Example 6-9.

Example 6-9

The concert was a disaster from the very beginning. Only two songs had been played in the first set when the rain started to fall in a steady drizzle in Redrocks amphitheater. The unofficial attendance was 12,500. This was more than had been at the Stones concert two weeks earlier. It soon became obvious to everyone there that they should have canceled the concert before spectators began arriving. Unfortunately, this was all happening on a night when a basketball game was being held in nearby McNichols Arena. Usually they stagger the scheduling of sporting events and concerts to minimize the traffic congestion in the city, but on this particular night they had not. By the end of a half hour the rain was falling in a steady downpour, and people began leaving in droves. Unfortunately, the wave of departing spectators abandoning the concert reached their cars at about the same time the basketball game let out. Matters were compounded by the fact that the parking lots for the concert and the arena both empty into the same narrow thoroughfare. The resulting scene was almost humorous. Everyone was honking and racing for position in a line that was destined not to move anywhere. The scene remained one of pandemonium until enough patrol cars arrived to sort things out. Gradually the flow of traffic started again but only after people stayed in their cars watching the rain for at least an hour.

The process of revising your essay for gaps in logic is one of: (1) adding introductory and concluding statements and marking main ideas with appropriate words and phrases; (2) grouping related sentences into paragraphs and adding transitional words and phrases when necessary; and (3) reading over the essay to make sure that you have written no fragments or run-ons.

Although presented separately in this chapter, these three revising activities are usually done simultaneously—while you group sentences into paragraphs you also correct fragments and run-ons and insert sentences and phrases that clarify your overall organizational pattern.

SUMMARY

Revising and writing are not two separate processes but two parts of the same process. There are five parts to writing and revising, which can be grouped into two major categories:

A. Putting thought to paper
   1. The spontaneous phase
   2. Revising for gaps in logic
B. Polishing
   3. Revising to expand and reduce
   4. Revising for vocabulary
   5. Revising for grammar, usage, and mechanics

The basic purpose of the spontaneous phase is to get ideas down on paper as rapidly as possible. The process can be facilitated by following these guidelines:

1. Don't attempt to put thought to paper until you are ready.
2. When writing, don't worry about spelling, punctuation, or sentence structure.
3. If you get stuck while writing, leave your work for a while and come back to it later.

When revising for gaps in logic, one of the first things to do is make sure you have a clearly stated introduction and conclusion and have marked all major ideas in the essay with appropriate words and phrases. Then sentences should be grouped logically and paragraphs formed. Transitional sentences or phrases should be added to bridge the gaps from one paragraph to another. Finally, you should scan all sentences to make sure you have not included any fragments or run-ons.

Exercises

1. Revise the following paragraph by inserting introductory and concluding statements where necessary. Insert words and phrases that mark the relationship one sentence has with another if you feel they are needed. When you're done, check your answers with those at the end of the chapter.

   One type of health insurance is private or voluntary insurance which may cover hospitalization, physician's fees, or protection from loss of income as a result of illness. Compulsory insurance is furnished by the government for people over sixty-five (Medicare) and for those unable to afford private insurance (Medicaid). Voluntary health insurance plans vary considerably in benefits. Some expire when the beneficiary reaches a given age, others may be canceled at any time, and others may exclude certain important conditions.

2. The following sentences are statements about different yet related major ideas. Group those sentences into paragraphs and provide transition sentences from one paragraph to the next. An introduction should also be attached to the first paragraph. When you're done, check your answers with those at the end of the chapter.

   The major purpose of a newspaper is to provide the reader with news from many sources.

   Some of those sources are local, some are national, and still others are international.

   Thus the newspaper should be the average man's source of information.

   Yet many newspapers are not used to spread knowledge but instead are used as platforms from which biased and self-serving ideas can be force-fed to the public.

   It's very important to judge between fact and opinion in news stories.

   Reporters often state opinions as facts.

   They may also omit news that is favorable to a political opponent and emphasize news that is favorable to a cause or individual they support.

   Cartoons usually exaggerate some physical feature, action, or quality of a person or prominent event.

For example, many political cartoons of President Carter have shown him with a large mouth and an abundance of teeth.

Cartoons such as these are intended to amuse the reading public more than anything else.

However, some cartoons are used as tools to sway public opinion.

An example of such a cartoon might be one that depicts the Internal Revenue Service as a two-headed, many-fanged monster about to devour an undersized, unsuspecting little man labeled John Q. Public.

3. Below is a set of sentences that has been placed out of order. Put the sentences together in some meaningful fashion and then check you answer with that in the back.

1. Within a few years he became not only the nation's most prominent man of writing but also its reigning popular philosopher.

2. However, after a short tenure on the Unitarian pulpit, he resigned because he had lost faith in the principles of Unitarianism.

3. He believed that individuals were able to live life to perfection without control from outside sources such as the government.

4. Essentially, he argued for replacing the control of the government with individual self-discipline.

5. Ralph Waldo Emerson symbolized much that was near to the mind and spirit of his age.

6. But individualism for Emerson did not imply hostility to social reform.

7. He was a descendent of a long line of ministers and attended Harvard to study for the ministry.

8. After a long trip to York, Emerson returned to Massachusetts, where he spent the remainder of his life writing and lecturing.

ANSWERS

1. *There are two main types of health insurance.* One type is private or voluntary insurance, which may cover hospitalization, physician's fees, or protection from loss of income as a

result of illness. *The second type is compulsory insurance,* which is furnished by the government for people over 65 (Medicare) and for those unable to afford private insurance (Medicaid). Voluntary health-insurance plans vary considerably in benefits. Some expire when the beneficiary reaches a given age, others may be cancelled at any time, and others may exclude certain important conditions. *When considering any policy, it is wise to read it carefully, including the fine print.*

2. *The newspaper is an integral part of most American's lives.* The major purpose of a newspaper is to provide the reader with news from many sources. Some of those sources are local, some are national, and still others are international. Thus, the newspaper should be the average man's major source of information. Yet many are not used to spread knowledge but instead are used as platforms from which biased and self-serving ideas are force-fed to the public. *Consequently it is important to become a discriminating consumer of daily news.*

   There are many things you should keep in mind when reading. It is important to judge between fact and opinion in news stories. Reporters often state opinions as facts. They may also omit news that is favorable to a political opponent and emphasize news that is favorable to a cause or individual they support. *It is up to the reader to judge newspaper articles for fairness and accuracy of reporting.*

   Political cartoons are also something to take note of. Cartoons usually exaggerate some physical feature, action, or quality of a person or prominent event. For example, many political cartoons of President Carter have shown him with a large mouth and an abundance of teeth. Cartoons such as these are intended to amuse the reading public more than anything else. However, some cartoons are used as tools to sway public opinion. An example of such a cartoon might be one that depicts the Internal Revenue Service as a two-headed, many-fanged monster about to devour an undersized, unsuspecting little man labeled John Q. Public. *Again, it is up to the reader to judge the accuracy and validity of such portrayals.*

3. Ralph Waldo Emerson symbolized much that was near to the mind and spirit of his age. He was a descendent of a long line of ministers and attended Harvard to study for the ministry. However, after a short tenure on the Unitarian pulpit, he resigned because he had lost faith in the principles of Unitarianism. After a long trip to York, Emerson returned to

Massachusetts, where he spent the remainder of his life writing and lecturing. Within a few years he became not only the nation's most prominent man of writing but also its reigning popular philosopher. He believed that individuals were able to live life to perfection without control from outside sources such as the government. But individualism for Emerson did not imply hostility to social reform. Essentially he argued for replacing the control of the government with individual self-discipline.

References

1. Quoted in D. M. Murray, "Teach the Motivating Force of Revision," paper presented at Rutgers Invitational Seminar on the Teaching of Composition (New Brunswick, N.J.: 1976), p. 2.

2. Reprinted by permission of the Collection of American Literature, Yale University Library.

3. Murray, p. 2.

4. M. H. Abrams et al., eds. *The Norton Anthology of English Literature*, II (New York: W. W. Norton, 1968), p. 621.

5. *Biographia Literaria*, XVIII, rpt. in Abrams et al., p. 617.

6. Records of Shelley, Byron, and the Author, rpt. in Abrams et al., p. 619.

7. *Notes on Keats*, rpt. in Abrams et al., p. 620.

CHAPTER SEVEN

EXPANSION AND REDUCTION

After you have put your thoughts to paper and organized them for logic, the next step is to polish what you have written. The polishing of a paper can be an involved process with many steps. In this chapter we will deal with what is probably the most important of those parts, expansion and reduction. In chapters 8 and 9 we will consider two more aspects of polishing, vocabulary and the mechanics of writing.

Expansion and reduction are key skills in the composing process. *Expansion* is the act of adding ideas to what you have written and consequently increasing the number of words. For example, we could expand on the sentence *It snowed yesterday* by adding ideas about the snow:

> It snowed yesterday, wet heavy snow that broke tree branches and turned the streets into slush.

Adding these ideas to our original sentence increases the number of words from three to sixteen.

Expansion increases the number of words and *reduction*

decreases them. For example, suppose we had written the following sentences:

> I finally bought myself that pair of boots I've been wanting. They are ankle length. They also have a new type of sole made of Mylar.

We could reduce the number of words used to express these ideas by writing:

> I finally bought that pair of ankle-length boots with the Mylar soles that I've been wanting.

This decreases the number of words from twenty-six to seventeen and the number of sentences from four to one.

The purpose of both expansion and reduction is to add emphasis to a written message. When you write, you are trying to convey a message. Usually the overall organizational pattern contains the fundamentals of that message and supporting details. Depending on your purpose for writing and your audience, you might want to emphasize or deemphasize certain fundamentals and supporting details more than others.

When writing, the primary way of emphasizing something is by length. We write more about things we want the reader to pay special attention to. Thus, when reading over an essay with an eye toward expansion and reduction, ask yourself: "Do I want to emphasize this idea by expanding on it, or do I want to deemphasize this idea by reducing it?" The two processes work together to give your essay balance and emphasis. We will discuss expansion first and then reduction, and we will consider some ways of determining which process to use in an essay.

EXPANSION

There are twelve basic ways to expand on an idea in an essay:

1. expansion by time
2. expansion by place
3. expansion by person
4. expansion by thing
5. expansion by reason
6. expansion by result
7. expansion by example

   8. expansion by enumeration
   9. expansion by addition
  10. expansion by transition
  11. expansion by restatement
  12. expansion by summation

Expansion by Time or Place

Expansion by time occurs when you tell more about a time mentioned in a sentence by indicating what happened before, during, or after that time. For example, consider the following sentence:

  Last week was one of the worst weeks in my life.

We could expand this sentence by writing about something that happened before, during, or after that stated time:

  Last week was one of the worst in my life. Before that, things were great.

Or we could have written:

  Last week, before which things were going great, was one of the worst weeks in my life.

We could have expanded by adding a complete sentence or by adding words to the sentence we had already written. When you expand by time you usually use one of the following words: later, earlier, now, then, previously, prior, prior to this, before, then, after, during, during this time.

Expansion by place occurs when you write something about a specific place stated in a sentence or describe another place in reference to the one already mentioned. Commonly, one of the following words or phrases is used to initiate a place expansion: here, there, close by, nearby, at this place, at this location, adjacent to this, amidst, above, below, at the rear of, in front of, next to. For example, we could expand the following sentence, *Seattle is a nice place to live*, by adding the sentence *Near it are the Cascade and Olympic mountain ranges and Puget Sound*. Likewise, we could have added the expansion directly to the sentence:

  Seattle, which is near the Cascade and Olympic mountain ranges and Puget Sound, is a nice place to live.

When you expand by time or place, then, you tell more about a time or place mentioned in the sentence or tell about another time or place related to the one already mentioned. You can expand by time or place, however, when no time or place has been mentioned. To illustrate, consider the sentence *Bill played football.* No time or place is mentioned in this sentence. We could expand on this sentence, however, by specifying when and where Bill played football: *Bill played football during his junior year at Albion College.* Any time you have a statement of an event you can specify the time and place of that event and thus expand on that statement. Time and place expansions can be done in two ways: by telling more about a time or place already mentioned or by specifying the time or place of an event already mentioned.

Expansion by Person or Thing

As is indicated by the name, expansion by person or thing occurs when you tell more about a person or object mentioned in a sentence:

> Phil slipped off his jacket in the annex to the control room and came in wearing a white shirt.

In expanding on the thing, *white shirt,* we might write

> Phil slipped off his jacket in the annex to the control room and came in wearing a white shirt. It has his name embroidered on the pocket and blue trim, and it made him look more like a cowboy than an air traffic controller.

Or we could have expanded on the person, Phil:

> Phil slipped off his jacket in the annex to the control room and came in wearing a white shirt. He was a tall man, broad at the shoulders and narrow at the hips, but with a face that was more boyish than manly.

We can also express person or thing expansions within a sentence rather than by adding a new sentence:

> Phil, a tall, broad-shouldered man with a face that looked more boyish than manly, slipped off his jacket in the annex to the control room and came in wearing a white shirt that had blue trim and his name embroidered on the pocket and made him look more like a cowboy than an air traffic controller.

Generally one of the following pronouns is used to introduce this kind of expansion: who, which, whom, that, this, he, she, it, they, them, everyone. Expansions by person and thing are perhaps the most common and easiest types of expansions to apply.

Expansion by Reason or Result

Result expansions are usually initiated by words such as: consequently, as a result, because of this, resulting in. When you expand by result you state the consequence of an action you have written about. Consider the following sentences, the second of which is a result expansion of the first:

> Inez sat for a moment thinking of the day and how beautiful it had been. As a result, her mind slowly turned to the future and thoughts of success and happiness that today's events had seemed to make more real.

This same result expansion could have been expressed within the first sentence:

> Inez sat for a moment thinking of the day and how beautiful it had been, causing her mind to turn slowly toward the future and thoughts of success and happiness that today's events had seemed to make more real.

When you expand by reason you add the reason for, cause of, or manner or condition under which an event occurred. For example, consider the following sentence:

> The fire had spread ten miles when they reached it, and its rate of expansion had increased.

We could expand this sentence via reason in the following way:

> The fire had spread ten miles when they reached it, and its rate of expansion had increased. This was caused by the fact that the wind had shifted and increased in intensity.

Or we could have performed the expansion within the original sentence:

> The fire had spread ten miles when they reached it, and its rate of expansion had increased, because the wind shifted and increased in intensity.

A reason expansion that concerns manner or condition might be:

The fire had spread ten miles when they reached it, and its rate of expansion had increased. It was moving with a rapidity that frightened all onlookers.

Reason and manner expansions are considered here as one type because it is often impossible to differentiate between ideas that have a reason relationship with one another and those that have a manner relationship. Generally when you expand by reason or manner, words such as these are used: because, because of this, this happened to.

Expansion by Example or Enumeration

When you expand by example you give an example of something stated in a previous sentence:

Morning can be hectic around our house.

To expand the sentence, we might write:

Morning can be hectic around my house. Someone has to feed the two dogs and at the same time put the two cats outside and then find the lizard.

Often such words as "for example," "a case in point," "for instance" are used to form example expansions.

In expansion by enumeration, you give a list of examples rather than a single one and use introductory words that indicate that you are listing the examples:

Mornings can be pretty hectic around my house. First, someone has to feed the two dogs. Second, the cats have to be put out. Finally, someone has to find the lizard.

When you expand via enumeration you commonly use words such as: first, second, third, initially, finally. It is possible to perform example and enumeration expansions within a sentence:

Mornings can be pretty hectic around my house: the dogs must be fed, the cats put out, and the lizard found.

Expansion by Addition or Transition

Expansion by addition and transition are actually the opposite of one another. When you expand by addition you add an idea that is parallel to an idea stated in a previous sentence:

Jack likes candy. He also likes nuts.

Conversely, when you expand via transition you add an idea that is different from the one previously expressed:

Jack likes candy. He doesn't like pastry, however.

Usually one of the following words accompanies an addition expansion: in addition to, furthermore, equally, moreover, and, or; one of the following commonly accompanies a transition expansion: on the other hand, even though, although, however, yet, still, but, nevertheless.

Expansions by addition and transition can often be accomplished within a sentence with the addition of very few words.

Bill likes candy and nuts.
Bill likes candy but not pastry.

Addition and transition expansions often result in compound subjects, verbs, and objects when performed within a sentence.

Expansion by Restatement or Summation

The purpose of expansion by restatement is to clarify something you have written:

Life is the pits. That is, it can sometimes be very difficult.

Often one of the following phrases accompanies a restatement expansion: in other words, that is.

Summation resembles restatement except that it involves restating what was said in a number of sentences rather than in just one sentence. For example, consider the following sentences:

In the mornings I have to feed the dogs. Then it's my job to find the cats, which are usually hiding somewhere in the basement, and put them outside for a while. Finally, I have to feed the lizard his daily portion of insects, which is not the most pleasant task to perform right before breakfast.

These sentences can be expanded by summation by adding:

I've got quite a lot to do around my house each morning.

Usually one of the following words or phrases signals a summation expansion: in short, in summary, in conclusion.

In Chapter 6 we discussed adding introductory and concluding statements to your essay as a part of revising the essay to fill in gaps in logic. A concluding statement is a summation expansion. All of the expansions mentioned thus far can be applied to more than one statement. For example, we could write five sentences describing the vegetation during the prehistoric age and then expand on these five statements via enumeration by writing:

Some of the more common animals that lived off this vegetation were . . . .

Likewise, we could write a number of sentences describing the physical conditions of a large slum area in a major city and then expand on those sentences via reason by writing:

The cause of these inhumane and unlivable conditions is clearly . . . .

There are twelve ways of expanding a sentence. When you read over an essay with an eye toward expansion, you can facilitate the process by asking yourself questions about each sentence. Below is a list of questions designed to help you identify possible expansions:

1. Does this sentence contain the statement of a time I want to tell more about? (Time)
2. Does this sentence contain the statement of an event the time of which I want to designate? (Time)
3. Does this sentence contain the statement of a place I want to tell more about? (Place)
4. Do I want to tell the reader where something mentioned in this sentence is located? (Place)
5. Is there a person mentioned in this sentence that I want to tell more about? (Person)
6. Is there an object or thing mentioned in this sentence that I want to describe in greater detail? (Thing)
7. Is this sentence the statement of an event the reason for which I want to explain? (Reason)

8. Is this sentence the statement of an event the manner of which I want to describe? (Reason)
9. Do I want to describe the result or effects of this statement? (Result)
10. Do I want to give an example of something stated in this sentence? (Example)
11. Do I want to list examples of something stated in this sentence? (Enumeration)
12. Do I want to add a statement equivalent to this sentence? (Addition)
13. Do I want to add a statement that is the opposite of what I said here? (Transition)
14. Do I want to say in different words what I have said in this sentence? (Restatement)
15. Do I want to summarize what I have said in these previous sentences? (Summation)

When you read over your essay you can ask yourself these questions about each sentence. To illustrate, consider the essay in Example 7-1, which has already been revised for gaps in logic and now is ready for expansion.

Example 7-1

(1) My hobby is elite cars—not owning them, of course, just knowing about them.

(2) The most noteworthy of the elite cars of years past was the Bentley. (3) In the 1920s, when diamond heir Woolf Barnato financed their construction, Bentley was *the* name in sporting cars. (4) But today this once-proud auto has lost its uniqueness. (5) Currently, the only Bentleys on the market are in the T-series, which has been in production for more than two decades.

(6) Since 1930, all Bentleys have been produced by Rolls-Royce and have been inferior to the original product. (7) This is because the Rolls-Royce management has made the mistake of trying to make their products similar in appearance. (8) Unfortunately what they have done is to turn the Bentley into a poor copy of its sister car. (9) In fact, the Bentley T-2 and the Rolls-Royce Silver Shadow are almost identical in exterior design. (10) They are different, however, in their comfort. (11) They are also somewhat different in their engine design.

(12) Unfortunately, these differences are not noticed by the car-buying public, and, as a result, we may soon see the demise of this once-proud automobile.

We could expand the essay by considering each sentence in the context of the fifteen expansion-stimulating questions. For example, we might find that our answer to question 7 is *yes* for sentence 1, indicating that we think it appropriate to add a sentence or two explaining the reason for our interest in elite cars. This might be accomplished by adding the sentence:

1a. I acquired this interest from my father, who was a dealer in antique, exotic cars.

We might also decide that it would be worthwhile to answer question 1 (Does this sentence contain the statement of a time I want to tell more about?) as it relates to sentence 2:

2a. Certainly, past years have seen many elegant automobiles.

This process of asking and answering selected questions about each sentence can be continued until the essay is considerably expanded. The questions are an artificial stimulant intended to help you identify expansions. You'll find that after you have gone through the fifteen questions with a few sentences, you will automatically begin to pick out sentences to expand in various ways. For the sample essay in Example 7-1, we might decide to make the following additional expansions:

Expand on sentence 3 by adding a restatement that answers question 14: "Do I want to say in different words what I have said in this sentence?"

Expand on sentence 5 by adding a characteristic statement that answers question 6: "Is there an object or thing mentioned in this sentence that I want to describe in greater detail?"

Expand on sentence 7 by adding a reason statement that answers question 8: "Is this sentence the statement of an event the reason for which I want to explain?"

Add two example expansions to sentence 10 that answer question 10: "Do I want to give an example of something stated in this sentence?"

These expansions and those previously mentioned would produce the essay in Example 7-2.

Example 7-2

(1) My hobby is elite cars—not owning them, of course, just knowing about them. (1a) I acquired this interest from my father, who was a dealer in antique, exotic cars.

(2) The most noteworthy of the elite cars of years past was the Bentley. (2a) Certainly, past years have seen many an elegant automobile. (3) In the 1920s, when diamond heir Woolf Barnato financed their construction, Bentley was *the* name in sporting cars. (3a) In those days, the ultimate in automotive pleasure was embodied in the Bentley. (4) But today this once-proud auto has lost its uniqueness. (5) Currently, the only Bentleys on the market are in the T-series, which has been in production for more than two decades.

(5a) Unfortunately, the T-series leaves much to be desired. (6) Since 1930, all Bentleys have been produced by Rolls-Royce and have been inferior to the original product. (7) This is because the Rolls-Royce management has made the mistake of trying to make their products similar in appearance. (7a) Apparently the motivation for this was to create a family of products that were all similar but had unique characteristics. (8) Unfortunately what they have done is turn the Bentley into a poor copy of its sister car. (9) In fact, the Bentley T-2 and the Rolls-Royce Silver Shadow are almost identical in exterior design. (10) They are different, however, in their comfort. (10a) For example, the Bentley's automatic transition makes for soft, almost imperceptible shifts, whereas the Silver Shadow seems labored in its transfer from one gear to another. (10b) Also, the Bentley's weight advantage over the Shadow makes for a much smoother ride. (11) They are also somewhat different in their engine design.

(12) Unfortunately, these differences are not noticed by the car-buying public, and, as a result, we may soon see the demise of this once-proud automobile.

As can be seen, Example 7-2 is considerably longer than Example 7-1 and meatier in content. Once you have become adept at expanding, one of the easiest aspects of writing will be to turn a short paper into a long paper.

Expansion by Levels

You can expand on the sentences in a paper more than once, producing different levels or layers of expansion. This is accomplished by expanding on expansions. For example, consider the sentence:

The human race cannot continue to grow and prosper and at

the same time ignore its dependent relationship on other forms of life on this planet.

If you had written this sentence and decided to perform an example expansion, you might produce:

> For example, we are dependent on some forms of snakes to keep the insect population down.

If you now wanted to expand on a deeper level, you could perform another expansion, but this time on the expansion you had just written. Doing this, you might decide to perform a transition expansion on the last sentence:

> Yet we continue to encourage uncontrolled development of areas that are vital to the preservation of such reptiles.

You could also perform a third-level expansion by adding a result expansion to this last sentence:

> No doubt this will inevitably yield an enormous insect problem in those same areas in the future.

Thus expanding by levels or layers involves the following steps:

1. Go through your essay performing expansions wherever necessary or desirable.
2. When this first level of expansion is completed, go through the essay again and perform a second set of expansion, but this time limit yourself to expanding only those expansion sentences produced from step 1.
3. Repeat the process as many times as is desirable.

To demonstrate this process consider the following paragraph:

> (1) All learning is a result of some kind of experience that has happened in the past. (2) The simplest kind of learning is the result of experience that involves the motor nerves, those nerves that control our muscles. (3) A person touches a hot stove, jerks his hand back quickly because he feels pain. (4) The next time, the individual will certainly avoid such an incident. (5) We learn through experience by the method of trial and error.

Performing first-level expansions on this paragraph might give us:

I

(1) All learning is a result of some kind of experience that happens in the past. (1a) *Our actions in the present are based on experiences we have already had. (Restatement* expansion of sentence 1). (2) The simplest kind of learning is the result of experiences that involve motor nerves, those nerves that control our muscles. (2a) *Muscles are composed of stringy fibers attached to bones. (Thing* expansion of *muscles* in sentence 2). (3) When a person touches a hot stove, he jerks his hand back quickly because he feels pain. (3a) *The pain generally is intense initially and then fades to a dull sensation in the irritated area. (Thing* expansion of *pain* in sentence 3). (4) The next time the individual will certainly avoid such an incident. (5) We learn through experience by the method of trial and error.

Performing second-level expansion might yield:

II

(1) All learning is a result of some kind of experience that happens in the past. (1a) Our actions in the present are based on experiences we have already had. (1b) *This means that our actions are for the most part determined in all situations. (Result* expansion of sentence 1b). (2) The simplest kind of learning is the result of experiences that involve the motor nerves, those nerves that control our muscles. (2a) Muscles are composed of stringy fibers attached to bones. (2b) *Those fibers are made of large protein molecules produced and synthesized from the food we eat. (Thing* expansion of *fibers* in sentence 2a). (3) When a person touches a hot stove, he jerks his hand back quickly because he feels pain. (3a) The pain generally is intense initially and then fades to a dull sensation in the irritated area. (3b) *However, in cases of severe burns, the intensity of the pain remains high for some time. (Transition* expansion of sentence 3a). (4) The next time the individual will certainly avoid such an incident. (5) We learn through experience by the method of trial and error.

Performing third-level expansions might produce:

III

(1) All learning is a result of some kind of experience that happens in the past. (1a) Our actions in the present are based on experiences we have already had. (1b) This, of course, means that our actions are for the most part determined in all situations. (1c) *Unfortunately, an implication of this*

---

is that we may not have as much free will as we think we do. (Result expansion of sentence 1b). The simplest kind of learning is the result of experiences that involve motor nerves, those nerves that control our muscles. (2a) Muscles are composed of stringy fibers attached to bones. (2b) Those fibers are made of large protein molecules produced and synthesized from the food we eat. (2c) This in itself provides a sound reason for watching one's diet (Result expansion of sentence 2b). When a person touches a hot stove, he jerks his hand back quickly because he feels pain. (3a) The pain generally is intense initially and then fades to a dull sensation in the irritated area. (3b) However, in cases of severe burns, the intensity of the pain remains high for some time. (4) The next time the individual will certainly avoid such an incident. (5) We learn through experience by the method of trial and error.

Some writers use expansion by layers as their basic method of composing. They might begin writing a 400-page novel by writing a five-page short story. They then take the story and decide what part of it they want to expand and how. After the first set of expansions the five-page short story might be a thirty-page story. The writer then determines needed expansions in the thirty-page story; this process of expansion continues until the novel is produced.

The process also generates writing that is logical and well put together, because each added section has an identifiable relationship with some other part in the composition, making the whole easy to read and understand.

Expansion can be a way of emphasizing and clarifying aspects of your paper or as the whole framework around which you write. With it you can start with a sentence and finish with a book.

FORMS OF EXPANSIONS WITHIN SENTENCES

In discussing the twelve different ways of expanding we indicated that the added ideas can be expressed as complete sentences or within the original sentence. Consider the following sentence:

Recently I bought a new car.

We could perform within-sentence expansion on the object (thing) car by writing:

Recently, I bought a new car that was painted with a type of green enamel that makes it seem to glitter.

or we could write:

> Recently I bought a new car with green enamel that makes it seem to glitter.

or:

> Recently I bought a new metallic green car.

In this section we will discuss the various forms that can be used for within-sentence expansion.

Within-sentence expansion can take one of three forms: clauses, phrases, or single words used as modifiers. (If you are uncertain about what a clause or phrase is, you should consult the Grammar Handbook in Part 5 of this book.)

Within-Sentence Expansion Using Subordinate Clauses

A clause is a group of words with a subject and a predicate. Some examples of clauses are:

1. That woman is my mother.
2. I enjoy working in the rain.
3. When I come home at night . . .
4. After he delivers the papers . . .

Clauses 1 and 2 make sense by themselves, but clauses 3 and 4 are incomplete as they are written. Something else has to be added to them in order for them to be understandable:

> When I come home at night, I eat supper and then watch television.

When a clause makes sense by itself (can stand alone), it is called an independent or main clause. But when a clause needs something else to go with it, it is called a dependent or subordinate clause. A dependent clause must be attached to an independent clause, as shown in the example above. A very common way of performing within-sentence expansions is to use a subordinate clause to express the expansion. Below we've given examples of expansions expressed as sentences (between-sentence expansions) and as clauses (clausal within-sentence expansions) for each of the twelve types of expansions:

1. Time

Original Sentence Yesterday was a good day.
Between-sentence expansion I got a lot accomplished.
Within-sentence expansion (clausal) Yesterday was a good day, during which I got a lot accomplished.

2. Place

Original	Washington is a nice place to live.
BSE	It is known for its lakes and mountain ranges.
WSE (clausal)	Washington, which is known for its lakes and mountain ranges, is a nice place to live.

3. Person

Original	Mark is a friend of mine.
BSE	He plays quarterback on the football team.
WSE (clausal)	Mark, who plays quarterback on the football team, is a friend of mine.

4. Thing

Original	Phil bought a new Camaro.
BSE	It has a white leather interior.
WSE (clausal)	Phil bought a new Camaro that has a white leather interior.

5. Reason

Original	He washed his car.
BSE	This was done because he had to attend a wedding.
WSE (clausal)	He washed his car because he had to attend a wedding.

6. Result

Original	The team played well and had no injuries during the season.
BSE	This resulted in their first undefeated season.
WSE (clausal)	The team played well and had no injuries during the season, which resulted in their first undefeated season.

7. Example

Original	Life can get hectic around our house.
BSE	An example of this is the chaos in the morning.
WSE (clausal)	Life can get hectic around our house, an

example of which is the chaos in the morning.

8. Enumeration

Original	Many things happened on our trip across country.
BSE	First we got a flat tire. Then we were arrested. Finally, we ran out of money.
WSE (clausal)	Many things happened on our trip across country: (1) we got a flat tire; (2) we were arrested; (3) we ran out of money.

9. Addition

Original	Jack is a friend of mine.
BSE	Furthermore, he is a nice person.
WSE (clausal)	Jack is a friend of mine, and he is a nice person.

10. Transition

Original	He is handsome.
BSE	However, he is not very bright.
WSE (clausal)	He is handsome, but he is not very bright.

11. Restatement

Original	Life can be the pits sometimes.
BSE	It can be very difficult.
WSE (clausal)	Life can be the pits sometimes: It can be very difficult.

12. Summation

Original	Time is of the essence. If we don't get the job done by five o'clock we won't get paid.
BSE	In conclusion, we've got to hustle.
WSE (clausal)	Time is of the essence. If we don't get the job done by five o'clock we won't get paid, which means we've got to hustle.

As the above examples indicate, all twelve types of expansion can be produced by using either a sentence or a clause. Note, however, that with transition and addition expansions, independent clauses rather than dependent clauses were used, because the addition of an equal idea to one already stated requires the use of the same form (an independent clause) as the original idea.

The sentences above are not the only ways that clausal within-sentence expansions can be performed. They illustrate just a few of the ways the expanded ideas could have been expressed via clauses. One change that could have been made to almost all of the within-sentence expansions involves placement of clauses. For example, in the sentence *He washed his car because he had to attend a wedding*, the expansion could have been placed at the beginning.

Because he had to attend a wedding, he washed his car.

This change of placement is not possible for all the examples given; however, with many of them it is. Experimenting with different locations for your expansions can give your sentences a unique style.

Within-Sentence Expansions Using Phrases

Another way of performing a within-sentence expansion is through the use of phrases. A phrase, like a clause, is a group of related words, but a phrase does not contain a subject and predicate. Generally, phrasal within-sentence expansions employ one of four types of phrases: (1) prepositional phrases, (2) participial phrases, (3) infinitive phrases, and (4) verb phrases.

A *prepositional phrase* is a group of related words introduced by a preposition (for example, into the store, around the corner, at twelve o'clock). Prepositional phrases are most often used for time and place expansions.

A *participial phrase* is a group of words introduced by a verb that ends in *ing, d, ed, n* or *en*. In the following sentence, the words *watching television* are a participial phrase.

The boy did his homework while watching television.

This participial phrase might have been a time expansion on the basic sentence *The boy did his homework*.

An *infinitive phrase* always begins with the word *to* immediately followed by a verb: "to run," "to sing," "to laugh." Infinitive phrases are commonly used for result and reason within-sentence expansions:

He cried to express his emotions.

A *verb phrase* begins with a verb, but one that is not a participle or infinitive. Some verb phrases are: "falls quickly," "yells loudly," "happens to me." We have listed the twelve different

types of expansions and given an example of a between-sentence
expansion and phrasal within-sentence expansion for each:

1. Time

Original	Bill finally made the team.
BSE	This was accomplished only after a great deal of work on his part.
WSE (phrasal)	Bill finally made the team after a great deal of work.

2. Place

Original	Seattle is a good place to live.
BSE	It is near the Canadian border.
WSE (phrasal)	Seattle, near the Canadian border, is a good place to live.

3. Person

Original	That man is the one who did it.
BSE	He is wearing a brown coat.
WSE (phrasal)	That man wearing a brown coat is the one who did it.

4. Thing

Original	Phil bought a new Camaro.
BSE	It has leather upholstery.
WSE (phrasal)	Phil bought a new Camaro with leather upholstery.

5. Reason

Original	He washed his car on Saturday.
BSE	This was done because he wanted to impress his girlfriend.
WSE (phrasal)	He washed his car Saturday to impress his girlfriend.

6. Result

Original	The plane hit the ground with tremendous force.
BSE	This caused an enormous explosion.
WSE (phrasal)	The plane hit the ground with a tremendous force, causing an enormous explosion.

7. Example

Original	Some things are difficult to do in the snow.
BSE	For example, playing outdoor basketball is

| | almost impossible when there's snow on the ground. |
| WSE *(phrasal)* | Some things, such as playing outdoor basketball, are difficult to do in the snow. |

8. Enumeration

Original	Many things happened on our trip across country.
BSE	First we had a blow out. Then we ran out of gas. Finally we ran out of money.
WSE *(phrasal)*	Many things happened on our trip across country: (1) getting a blow out; (2) running out of gas; (3) running out of money.

9. Addition

Original	Jack ran a ten-mile race Saturday.
BSE	He also rode his bike twenty miles that same day.
WSE *(phrasal)*	Jack ran a ten-mile race Saturday and rode his bike twenty miles that same day.

10. Transition

Original	He remained after school each day.
BSE	However, he begrudged every minute of it.
WSE *(phrasal)*	He remained after school each day but begrudged every minute of it.

11. Restatement

Original	He prowls each night by the light of the moon.
BSE	That is to say, he walks in his sleep.
WSE *(phrasal)*	He prowls each night, or walks in his sleep, by the light of the moon.

12. Summation

Original	The car I recently bought is the wrong color, has no power, and needs $400 worth of work.
BSE	In summary, it leaves much to be desired.
WSE *(phrasal)*	The car I recently bought is the wrong color, has no power, and needs $400 worth of work, leaving much to be desired.

Any expansion that can be performed between sentences can also be performed using phrases within sentences.

Changing the position of your expansion can have the effect of changing the style of your writing. So can changing the form of your expansion. That is, in one sentence you might expand using a clause and in the next sentence use a phrase to vary your style. Consider the following sentences:

> I once toured a submarine. I was shocked most by the lack of space. You are not only confined horizontally, but you are also confined vertically.

We could expand these sentences by adding the following clausal within-sentence expansions:

> I once toured a submarine that was anchored at the Fenton Docks near my home. I was shocked most by the lack of space, which is always at a premium on such a vessel. You are not only confined horizontally, which has a drastic effect on your sense of slimness; you are also confined vertically, which gives you a sense of being taller than normal.

Rather than use clausal expansion four times, we could vary the style of these sentences by using a mixture of clausal and phrasal expansions:

> I once toured a submarine anchored at the Fenton Docks near my home. I was shocked most by the lack of space, which is always at a premium on such a vessel. You are not only confined horizontally, with a drastic effect on one's sense of slimness; you are also confined vertically, giving you a sense of being taller than normal.

Style in writing is a subtle quality affected by seemingly minor changes that taken as a whole have a profound effect on one's writing.

Within-Sentence Expansions Using Single-Word Modifiers

Single-word within-sentence expansions are accomplished by adding a single-word modifier in an existing sentence. Most commonly, time, place, person, thing, reason, example, enumeration, and addition expansions are the ones done by single-word within-sentence expansions. Below we've given examples of each of these types:

1. Time

Original	Bill finally completed a marathon.
BSE	He did it on Saturday.
WSE (single word)	Bill finally completed a marathon Saturday.

2. Place

Original	Jack is not used to the cold Colorado weather.
BSE	He is from California.
WSE (single word)	Jack, a Californian, is not used to the cold Colorado weather.

3. Person

Original	He gave the letter to the gentleman in the blue suit.
BSE	The gentleman was wearing glasses.
WSE (single word)	He gave the letter to the bespectacled gentleman in the blue suit.

4. Thing

Original	Phil bought a new Camaro.
BSE	It was painted bright orange.
WSE (single word)	Phil bought a new, bright orange Camaro.

5. Reason

Original	He tossed the package containing the money over the side of the boat.
BSE	He did this without realizing what he was doing.
WSE (single word)	He inadvertently tossed the package containing the money over the side of the boat.

6. Example

Original	Prehistoric herbivores died out with the onslaught of the Ice Age.
BSE	One type of herbivore was the triceratops.
WSE (single word)	Prehistoric herbivores such as the triceratops died out with the onslaught of the Ice Age.

7. Enumeration

Original	Most large sea creatures are mammals.
BSE	Whales are one example. Sea lions are another. Dolphins are a third.
WSE (single word)	Most large sea creatures are mammals: whales, sea lions, dolphins.

8. Addition

Original	Bill likes food high in carbohydrates.
BSE	He also likes cigarettes.
WSE (single word)	Bill likes food high in carbohydrates and cigarettes.

The process of adding expansions is one of reading over an essay and expanding on it wherever appropriate. When an added idea comes to mind, decide whether you want to add that idea as a sentence, a clause, a phrase, or a single word. This process will increase the length of an essay and also improve the style of the writing. But expansion is only one method for improving the style of your writing. There is another similar process called reduction.

REDUCTION

When you expand, you add ideas to what you have already written; when you reduce, you express your ideas in fewer words. For example, consider the following set of sentences:

John is my friend. He is captain of the football team. He is a quarterback. He is really a good quarterback, too.

This sounds like something we might expect a child to write or say. But let's reduce the number of words we've used to express the ideas in these sentences by combining all the ideas into one sentence:

My friend John, who is captain of the football team, is a fine quarterback.

This sentence expresses the same thoughts as the previous set of sentences, but in fewer sentences and fewer words. As a consequence, the writing sounds more mature. In the original sentences all ideas were expressed as independent clauses, but when the sentences were combined, only one idea was expressed as an independent clause: John is a quarterback. The other ideas (John is my friend; John is captain of the football team; John is a good quarterback.) were all reduced from independent clauses to lesser structures: dependent clauses, phrases, and single-word modifiers, and then attached to the independent clause. When you reduce within an essay, you look for sentences that can be reduced to subordinate clauses, phrases, and single-word modifiers and attach them to other sentences.

Generally any reducible sentence has two characteristics: (1) it repeats words from a previous sentence, and (2) it has a relationship with a previous sentence that can be classified in the same twelve ways as the types of expansions. We'll briefly consider each characteristic of reducible sentences.

Characteristic 1. Repeated Words

To illustrate this first characteristic let's reconsider the four original sentences about the quarterback, John:

1. John is my friend.
2. He is captain of the football team.
3. He is quarterback.
4. He is a good quarterback.

Looking over these sentences we see that *John* (or the pronoun *he*) appears in each sentence. This cues us to a possible reduction. When a concept is repeated in two or more sentences, those sentences can probably be reduced to one sentence by stating the concept once and putting everything that is said about that concept into one sentence. In these sentences four things are said about John:

> John:
>   is my friend
>   is captain of the football team
>   is a quarterback
>   is a good quarterback

Once the repeated concept and what is said about it is identified, you must designate one statement about the concept as the independent clause and express the others as dependent clauses, phrases, and single-word modifiers. For example, if you decided to pick *John is my friend* as the independent clause and wanted to reduce and attach the other ideas to this clause, you would write:

John, who is a good quarterback and captain of the football team, is my friend.

If you selected *John is the quarterback* as the independent clause, you would write:

My friend John, the captain of the football team, is a good quarterback.

When you have identified a repeated concept and what is said about it, you should try out different clauses to use as the independent clause to vary the style of your writing. Thus, one way to perform reductions in an essay is to:

1. look for a word or concept that is repeated in two or more sentences
2. identify what is said about that concept in those sentences
3. pick one sentence to keep the same or state as a new independent clause
4. reduce what is said in the other sentences to subordinate clauses, phrases, and single-word modifiers and attach them to the selected independent clause

Characteristic 2. Relationship with Previous Sentence

In the expansion section of this chapter we saw that there are twelve types of relationship one sentence can have with another. When you reduce a sentence to a clause, phrase, or single-word modifier and then attach it to another sentence, you can do so only if the two original sentences have one of those twelve types of relationships with each other. For example, consider the following two sentences:

In the late afternoon I usually jog from five to ten miles. Afterwards I lie down and rest for about twenty minutes.

We could reduce the second sentence and attach it to the first in the following way:

In the afternoon I usually jog from five to ten miles and then rest for about twenty minutes.

This second sentence has a time relationship with the first. If one sentence has no relationship with another, reduction and attachment are impossible or at least illogical:

> Mary has brown eyes.
> The United Nations met this Saturday.
> *Mary, who the United Nations met this Saturday, has brown eyes.[1]

Thus the second characteristic of reducible sentences is that they have an identifiable relationship with another sentence—a relationship that can be classified in one of the twelve ways that expansions are classified. This gives us a second technique for reduction:

1. Look for sentences that have one of the twelve characteristics described earlier in this chapter for expansions.
2. Reduce the identified sentence to a dependent clause, a phrase, or a set of single-word modifiers.
3. Attach the reduced structure to the sentence with which it has a relationship.

Reduction by Deletion

Consider the sentence *She is the woman who is best suited for the job.* We could delete the words who *is* and still have a sentence that conveys the same message:

> She is the woman best suited for the job.

Frequently writers use words whose primary purpose is to repeat concepts already stated. For example, in the sentence above the function of the relative pronoun *who* is to repeat the concept *woman*, which has been stated twice prior to he use of *who* (*she* and *woman* both refer to the same concept). When repeated concepts are obvious to the reader it is considered characteristic of good writing to delete the words that express them. To illustrate this, consider Example 7-3.

Example 7-3

Grammar is the study of language. Supposedly every grammar is divided into three parts: phonology, morphology, and syntax. Phonology is the study of the sound system of a language, morphology is the study of the smallest units of meaning within a language, and syntax is the study of the structure of a language. In high school what we were taught by our teachers was basically the syntax of the English language. Syntax is what you study when you do such things as diagram a sentence and identify the subject, predicate and complement of a sentence. Yet we didn't receive any instruction on the sound system of the English language or the smallest units of meaning within the English language. Consequently I never heard of such phonological elements as phonemes, allophones, fricatives, or nasals until I took an introductory course in linguistics at college. I find what I am learning now is infinitely more interesting than what I learned about language in high school. I feel that high-school students should be given a choice about the type of grammar they want to learn. Those people who want to learn how to diagram a sentence should be allowed to do so, but those who want to learn other aspects of the language should also have the freedom to pursue their interests about language. It would certainly enhance a person's preparation for college if such courses were given at the high-school level.

A small but significant proportion of the words in this essay can be left out without destroying the basic message. In Example 7-4 we've crossed out some of those words. Read through the essay leaving out the crossed-out words. It should sound better to you than the essay in Example 7-3.

Example 7-4

Grammar is the study of language. ~~Supposedly~~ every grammar is divided into three parts: phonology, morphology, and syntax. Phonology is the study of the sound system of a language. Morphology is the study of the smallest units of meaning ~~within a language~~, and syntax is the study of ~~the~~ structure ~~of a language~~. In high school what we were taught ~~by our teachers~~ was ~~basically the~~ syntax ~~of the English language~~. Syntax is what you study when you do such things as diagram a sentence and identify the subject, predicate, and complement ~~of a sentence~~. Yet we didn't receive any instruction on the sound system of the ~~English~~ language or the smallest units of meaning ~~within the English language~~. Consequently I never heard of such phonological elements as phonemes, allophones, fricatives, or nasals until I took an introductory course in linguistics ~~at college~~. ~~I find~~ what I am learning now is infinitely more interesting than what I learned ~~about language~~ in high school. I feel that high-school students should be given a choice about the type of grammar they ~~want to~~ learn. Those people who want to learn ~~how~~ to diagram a sentence should be allowed to ~~do so~~, but those who want to learn other aspects of ~~the~~

language should ~~also~~ have the freedom to pursue their interests ~~about~~ ~~language.~~ It would certainly enhance a person's preparation for college~~if~~ ~~such courses were given at the high-school level.~~

Given the writer's desire to reduce what has been written, a good polishing technique is to read through an essay crossing out all words and phrases that are obvious to the reader given the context of the essay. Most writers have a reluctance to do this, likening the deletion of a word or phrase to the severing of a finger. In the long run, however, streamlining an essay will make it more comprehensible to the reader and consequently more enjoyable.

There are three basic ways of performing reduction within an essay. The first two ways both involve attaching subordinate clauses, phrases, and single-word modifiers to independent clauses. But this is precisely the result that was accomplished by within-sentence expansion. That process also has the effect of adding clauses, phrases, and single-word modifiers to independent clauses. Reduction and within-sentence expansion do precisely the same things to independent clauses, but they have quite different effects on the overall essay.

Consider for a moment the following sentences:

Mary likes to run. She does this to improve her health. She does most of her jogging at the track. It's at Jefferson High School.

Let us first expand on the ideas within these sentences using within-sentence expansion:

Mary, a tall, thin blonde, likes to run. She does this to improve her health, which at times is not good. She does most of her jogging at the track rather than around the park. The track is at Jefferson High School, a few blocks from her house.

Now let's take the original five sentences and reduce some of them:

Mary likes to run at the track at Jefferson High School. She does this to improve her health.

Both processes have increased the number of ideas expressed per sentence. This can be seen by calculating the average number of words used per sentence. In the original set of sentences there were twenty-five words and four sentences, or, on the average, 6.25 words per sentence. In the expanded sentences there were forty-eight words and four sentences, or twelve words per sentence. In the reduced sentences there are eighteen words and two sentences, or about nine words per sentence. Both expansion and reduction, then, result in about the same number of ideas per sentence, but expansion does something in addition to this. It also increases the overall number of ideas. This is quite obvious by just looking at the length of the expanded and reduced passages. The expanded sentences have a total of forty-eight words, the reduced sentences a total of nineteen. When you reduce, you pack more ideas into each sentence, but you do not increase the total number of ideas; when you expand, you also pack more ideas into each sentence, but you also increase the total number of ideas.

REDUCTION VS. EXPANSION

As we have seen, both expansion and reduction increase the number of words per sentence; expansion also increases the total number of words in an essay. Reduction, on the other hand, decreases the total number of words. How then do you know which one to perform when revising for expansion and reduction? There are actually two decisions to make when considering expansion and reduction: (1) whether to use expansion or reduction, and (2) whether to use within-sentence expansion or between-sentence expansion (given that you've decided to expand at all).

As was mentioned in the first part of this chapter, the decision to expand or reduce is decided on the basis of emphasis. If you want to emphasize something, you should expand it. If you want to deemphasize something, you should reduce it.

For a moment let's look at the similarities and differences between the two types of expansions, within- and between-sentence. To do this, we'll again use the sentences about Mary:

I

Mary likes to run. She does this to improve her health. She does most of her jogging at the track. It's at Jefferson High School.

In the last section, we saw that we could add ideas to each sentence using within-sentence expansion:

II

Mary, a tall, thin blonde, likes to run. She does this to improve her health, which at times is not good. She does most of her jogging at the track rather than around the park. The track is at Jefferson High School, a few blocks from her house.

In the first sentence we have added the ideas that Mary is tall, thin, and blonde, which can all be considered *person* expansions. In the second sentence we have added the idea that Mary's health is at times not good; this can be considered an expansion of the *thing* health. In the third sentence we have added the idea that her jogging could have been done in the park, a *transitional* expansion. And in the final sentence, we have added the idea that Jefferson High School is a few blocks from Mary's house, a *place* expansion. Let us now add these same ideas using between-sentence expansion rather than within-sentence expansion:

III

Mary is a tall, thin blonde. She likes to run. She does this to improve her health. It's not so good at times. She does most of her jogging at the track. She could do it around the park, however. The track is at Jefferson High School. It's a few blocks from her house.

In this paragraph, the same ideas have been added but with different results. Between-sentence expansion, unlike within-sentence expansion and reduction, does not increase the number of ideas per sentence; it simply increases the number of ideas in the essay. In itself, increasing the number of ideas in an essay is a good trait, but it is not sufficient to improve the writing style: The style of paragraph III is obviously inferior to that of paragraph II. There must be a balance between increasing the number of ideas and increasing the number of ideas per sentence.

A good way to measure this balance is to monitor the average number of words per sentence: Count the words you have written and divide by the number of sentences to obtain a Sentence Complexity Index. In the original four sentences about Mary (paragraph I), that index was twenty-five divided by four, which gave us 6.25. For the sentences about Mary that were expanded using within-sentence expansion (paragraph II), the index was forty-eight divided by four, or 12.00. Finally, for the sentences that were expanded using between-sentence expansion (paragraph III), the index was fifty-four divided by eight, or 6.85. This index illustrates how many ideas you are packing into each sentence. The higher the index, the more ideas you are using per sentence. In general, for college or university level writing, that index should be around 15.00. You should be averaging about fifteen words per sentence in your essays.

The Sentence Complexity Index provides a useful tool in helping you decide whether to use within- or between-sentence expansion. If that index falls below 15.00, you should rely primarily on within-sentence expansion; if the index is above 15.00 you can use either within- or between-sentence expansion. But the index may become too high. Consider the situation in which a writer has used a great deal of reduction and within-sentence expansion, both of which increase the number of ideas per sentence and consequently increases the Sentence Complexity Index. Doing this with the original four sentences about Mary might yield something like:

> Mary, a tall, thin blonde, likes to run to improve her health, which at times is not good, at the track at Jefferson High School, a few blocks from her house, rather than around the park.

If we calculate our index on this sentence we find that we have 35 words and one sentence, giving us an index of 35.00. This is quite high, and the sentence is almost incomprehensible. Generally, if your Sentence Complexity Index is above 25.00, you should start to rely heavily on between-sentence expansion rather than within-sentence expansion.

There is one caution that must be mentioned in connection with the Sentence Complexity Index. It is just a tool. The range of 15.00 to 25.00 is not absolute. There are writing situations in which the index might be below 15.00 or above 25.00 and your essay would still be good. The good writer is one who can use all the tools effectively. Hence, your writing will reach maximum effectiveness if you can utilize reduction, within-sentence expansion, and between-sentence expansion. Perhaps you might write in such a way that some paragraphs have a Sentence Complexity Index below 15.00 and some have an index above 25.00, giving your composition a great deal of variety of sentence style and structure.

The keys to dealing with reduction and expansion are knowledge and control. Knowing how to reduce and expand gives you control over what and how you write. The Sentence Complexity Index and your own intuition and feel for writing guide you in making decisions about when to use reduction and when to use expansion.

SUMMARY

After you have put thought to paper, the first step in polishing an essay is to expand and reduce it. Expansion adds ideas to what you have already written; reduction expresses the same ideas in fewer sentences and words. There are twelve ways to expand on an idea. They are:

1. expand by time
2. expand by place
3. expand by person
4. expand by thing
5. expand by reason
6. expand by result
7. expand by example
8. expand by enumeration
9. expand by addition
10. expand by transition
11. expand by restatement
12. expand by summation

These twelve types of expansion can be performed between sentences by adding sentences or within sentences by adding clauses, phrases, and single-word modifiers.

Reduction is very similar to within-sentence expansion in its effect on sentences. Both reduction and within-sentence expansion increase the number of ideas per sentence. Reduction does not increase the total number of ideas in an essay; however, within-sentence expansion does. A key factor in reducing is to look for reducible sentences; which are sentences that (1) repeat words and concepts from previous sentences; (2) have a relationship with a previous sentence that can be classified by one of the twelve categories use for expansion; and (3) include unnecessary words.

The decision of whether to expand or reduce when polishing an essay is made on the basis of emphasis. Ideas you want to emphasize are expanded; ideas you want to deemphasize are reduced. The decision whether to use within- or between-sentence expansion is made on the basis of sentence complexity. Ideally, a balance is sought between sentences that express many ideas and sentences that express only a few ideas. The Sentence Complexity Index, which is calculated by dividing the total number of words by the total number of sentences, can be used to monitor this balance. A general rule of thumb is that the calculated index for a given essay should fall between 15.00 and 25.00. An index below 15.00 indicates that within-sentence expansion should be used; an index above 25.00 indicates that between-sentence expansion should be used.

Exercises

1. The following paragraph is short, choppy, and in need of expansion. After each sentence a specific type of expansion to be performed on that sentence has been indicated. Rewrite the paragraph performing all requested expansion, but limit yourself to *within-sentence expansion only*. When you are finished, check your rewritten paragraph with that at the end of this chapter.

   The boy pressed his head deep into the straw pillow (Perform a *thing* expansion of *pillow*.) It gave him the same feeling he got when he rubbed his face against the sheets that hung on the clothesline every Monday. (Perform a *time* expansion on Monday.) In a matter of moments he found himself pulling the covers over his head. (Perform a *reason* expansion.) In spite of his efforts to stay awake and guard himself from the dangers of the night, sleep gradually overcame him. (Perform a *reason* expansion.)

2. Go back to the paragraph in exercise 1 above and perform the same expansions, but this time use between-sentence expansions only. Compare the results with those generated from exercise 1. Also compare your answer with that at the end of the chapter. Does one type of expansion produce a different style of writing from the other?

3. Reduce the following paragraph and check your answer with that at the end of the chapter.

   The behavioral connection among sex, aggression, and dominance is born out in a variety of studies. The neurological connection is also borne out in such studies. The mating rituals of great cats are barely distinguishable, in their early stages, from fighting. The mating rituals of other animals in the early stages are also similar to fighting. The use of sex to establish dominance is sometimes evident in human heterosexual and homosexual practices. Sex is also used to maintain dominance once it is established. It is a human activity with complex motivations. It also has grave consequences. Certainly it will continue to puzzle and drive man for some time to come.

4. *Sentence combining.* Below is a sentence-combining exercise consisting of five sets of sentences. Combine each set into a single sentence and then write all five sentences as a

paragraph. Check your paragraph with that in the answer section.

A. Tuning is a function of something.
   The tuning is for television.
   The tuning is for radio.
   The tuning is actual.
   The function is of time.
B. Each channel has a band of something.
   The band is frequencies.
   The band is specific.
   The frequencies are measured in megahertz.
   The frequencies are measured in millions of cycles.
   The cycles are per seconds.
C. The device separates each second.
   The device is for tuning.
   The device is quartz.
   The separation is into millionths of parts.
   The millionths are many.
   The parts are equal.
   The separation is to tune the channel.
   The tuning is exact.
D. The correctness of the device prevents the set from straying.
   The circuitry prevents the set from straying.
   The circuitry is frequency control.
   The circuitry is automatic.
   The straying is off the channel.
   The set is radio.
   The set is television.
E. An advantage of this device is the fact that something.
   The advantage is distinct.
   The device is called a key point tuner.
   It lets the viewer tune from any channel to another.
   It lets the listener tune from any channel to another.
   The tuning is direct.
   The viewer skips those channels in between.
   The listener skips those channels in between.

ANSWERS

1. The boy pressed his head deep into the straw pillow, *which was cold but smooth and fresh smelling.* It gave him the same feelings he got when he rubbed his face against the sheets that

hung on the clothesline every Monday, *a day his mom devoted to washing and cleaning.* In a matter of moments he found himself pulling the covers over his head *to hide from the sounds of the night, sounds that reminded him of what he had thought were long-forgotten ghost stories.* In spite of his efforts to stay awake and guard himself from the dangers of the night, sleep overcame him, *because the day had drained all of his strength and put a limit on the length of time he could maintain his vigil.*

2. The boy pressed his head deep into the straw pillow. *It was cold but smooth and fresh smelling.* It gave him the same feelings he got when he rubbed his face against the sheets that hung on the clothesline every Monday. *That was the day his mom traditionally devoted to washing and cleaning.* In a matter of moments he found himself pulling the covers over his head. *He did this to hide from the sounds of the night, sounds that reminded him of what he had thought were long-forgotten ghost stories.* In spite of his efforts to stay awake and guard himself from the dangers of the night, sleep overcame him. *This was because the day had drained all of his strength and put a limit on the length of time he could maintain his vigil.*

3. The behavioral as well as neurological connection among sex, aggression, and dominance is borne out in a variety of studies. The mating rituals of great cats and many other animals are barely distinguishable from their early stages of fighting. The use of sex to establish and maintain dominance is sometimes evident in human heterosexual and homosexual practices. Sex is a human activity with complex motivation and grave consequences—an activity that will certainly continue to puzzle and drive man for some time to come.

4. Radio and television tuning is actually a function of time. Each channel has a specific band of frequencies, measured in megahertz and millions of cycles per second. The tuning and quartz device separates each second into many millionths of equal parts to tune exactly the desired channel. The correctness of the device and the automatic or frequency-control circuitry prevent the radio or television from straying off the channel. A distinct advantage of this device, called a key-point tuner, is the fact that it lets the viewer or listener tune directly from any channel to another, skipping those channels in between.

NOTE

1. An asterisk before a sentence indicates a nonsense sentence.

CHAPTER EIGHT

VOCABULARY

The second step in polishing a paper is to revise it for vocabulary. "Vocabulary" is a term used frequently in discussions of composing techniques. It is also a word that is often left undefined or poorly defined. In the first part of this chapter, we will define "vocabulary"; in the second section we will discuss vocabulary-revision techniques. Finally, we will consider sources of vocabulary.

VOCABULARY DEFINED

What exactly is meant by using good vocabulary? Consider the following paragraph:

(1) The fire began small. (2) Then it became a big fire. (3) It was such a big fire that many people had to come and fight the fire. (4) Some of the people lost their lives in the fire.

Most people would agree that this is an immature paragraph. But what makes it immature? For the moment we will ignore its need for expansion and reduction and focus instead on the essay's immature vocabulary.

One of the major reasons for the vocabulary immaturity of the paragraph is that the same words have been used repeatedly: *fire* is used five times, and *people* and *big* are used twice each. Consider the effects on the vocabulary level of the essay if we replace some of these overused words with synonyms or pronouns:

(1) The fire began small. (2) Then it became a big blaze. (3) It was such a *large* fire that many people had to come and fight *it*. (4) Some of the *workers* lost their lives in the *holocaust*.

The paragraph has been transformed from something we might expect a five-year-old to say into something we could envision an adult uttering, simply by replacing overused words. The more you use different words to express the same concepts, the more mature the vocabulary level of your essay will be.

By redundancy of concepts we mean ideas that are stated over and over again in a paper. Repetition in itself is not a negative characteristic. Without reiteration of concepts, a reader would not be able to understand what you were saying. By definition, a coherent paragraph or essay is a collection of related ideas. Hence its sentences will be about the same things. If you're writing about people fighting a fire you will repeatedly refer to *fire* and *people*. Repetition of ideas, then, is the cohesive force underlying writing. However, repetition of words to express those concepts is a negative characteristic. The skilled writer is one who can use different words to express reiterated concepts.

One characteristic of good vocabulary is: the use of different words to express repetitive concepts. If you concentrate on decreasing the number of repeated words, you will increase the vocabulary level of your essay. This is not the only way of improving your vocabulary. There is a second aspect to be considered. To illustrate this, let's make some further changes in our sample paragraph. Those changes are:

a. replace the word *began* in sentence 1 with the word *started*.
b. replace the word *became* in sentence 2 with the words *developed into*.
c. replace the word *big* in sentence 2 with the word *huge*.
d. replace the word *large* in sentence 3 with the word *monumental*.
e. replace *many* in sentence 3 with *a multitude of*.
f. replace *fight* in sentence 3 with *battle*.
g. replace *some* in sentence 4 with *a small fraction of*.
h. replace *workers* in sentence 4 with *firefighters*.

Performing these substitutions would produce:

> (1) The fire started small. (2) Then it developed into a huge blaze. (3) It became such a monumental fire that a multitude of people had to come and battle it. (4) A small fraction of the firefighters lost their lives in the holocaust.

The result of performing these substitutions has again been a raising of the vocabulary level of the paragraph. Of course, this paragraph is contrived, and the vocabulary inserted in this last version is probably too sophisticated for the message and tone of the paragraph. But what was done to produce this change in vocabulary? If you look back at the eight substitutions that were made you will find that all the substituted words are more sophisticated or complex than the words they replace. It is generally considered more sophisticated or mature to use infrequently utilized words than to use very common words. A second consideration, then, when revising a paper for vocabulary is the use of more technical or sophisticated words when appropriate. The last part of this definition, *when appropriate*, is very important. The vocabulary in some essays should be technical and sophisticated, but in some it should be quite simple.

The final consideration in vocabulary revision deals with precision of word and phrase usage: whether you have properly used the words and phrases in your composition. In the English language there are many words and phrases that look and sound almost identical but differ in meaning. The third part of revising an essay for vocabulary, then, is to consider the precision of meaning of the words and phrases used.

In the following section we will consider revision techniques for these three components of vocabulary.

Revision to Eliminate Repeated Words

To illustrate this revision technique we will use the following essay:

---

1. Of all the things I own the one I like the best is my car. 2. It is a 1957 Chevy Belair two-door, two-toned, with a sun roof. 3. My car has a new, expensive, round vent on the hood rising up just in back of the emblem that gives the car the look of moving even when it is standing still. 4. Its interior is one of the car's best features. 5. The interior has white leather upholstery

with powder blue trim. 6. The buttons on the upholstery are sewed into the seats and backrests, giving it a new, expensive, cushiony look. 7. The dash is made of the newest acrylic plastic, which is treated to ward off the sun's rays and keep down the level of heat when the car has been in the sun for a long time. 8. The car has an expensive racing steering wheel that is smaller than normal and leather covered with a new wooden turning knob. 9. It also has all of the newest gadgets on the dash. 10. It has a tach that shows rpm's, an oil pressure meter, a water temperature meter, and a brake fluid meter. 11. The wheels on the car are bigger than normal, with white lettering that sticks out and chrome spoked wheel rims. 12. The car's sleek design cuts down on wind resistance and gives it really good mileage. 13. All in all my car is one of the best things I've ever owned.

The Sentence Complexity Index for this essay is 18.38. Let's consider this an indication that no further expansion or reduction is necessary and go on to revise the essay for vocabulary. We'll start by identifying and circling repeated words.

1. Of all the things I own the one I like the best is my car. 2. It is a 1957 Chevy Belair two-door, two toned, with a sun roof. 3. My car has a new, expensive, round vent on the hood rising up just in back of the emblem that gives the car the look of moving even when it is standing still. 4. Its interior is one of the car's best features. 5. The interior has white leather upholstery with powder blue trim. 6. The buttons on the upholstery are sewed into the seats and backrests, giving it a new, expensive, cushiony look 7. The dash is made of the newest acrylic plastic, which is treated to ward off the sun's rays and keep down the level of heat when the car has been in the sun for a long time. 8. The car has an expensive racing steering wheel that is smaller than normal and leather covered with a new wooden turning knob. 9. It also has all of the newest gadgets on the dash 10. It has a tach that shows rpms, an oil pressure meter, a water temperature meter, and a brake fluid meter 11. The wheels on the car are bigger than normal with white lettering that sticks out and chrome spoked wheel rims. 12. The car's sleek design cuts down on wind resistance and gives it really good mileage. 13. All in all my car is one of the best things I've ever owned

We have circled almost forty words in this essay representing repeated words. There are some repeated words that we haven't circled, such as *his*, *an*, *the*, and others, because such words, often called function words, must be used over and over again. Below is a list of some of those function words that should be ignored:

Articles a, an, the
Demonstratives this, that, these, those
Personal pronouns I, you, he, she, it, we, they, me, him, my, your,
                    his, her, its, our, their, mine, yours, hers, ours,
                    theirs, who, whom, which, that
Forms of the verb **be** am, are, is, was, were, be, being, been
Auxiliary verbs do, does, did, doing
                  have, has, had, having
                  can, could, may, might, will, would, shall, should
Reflexive pronouns myself, itself, yourself, himself, herself, itself,
                    ourselves
Coordinate conjunctions and, but, or, nor
Negative markers no, not
Common prepositions of, on, to, at, by, for, from, in, with, above,
                    about, across, after, against, around, before,
                    behind, below, beneath, beside, between,
                    beyond, down, during, except, following,
                    like, near, off, out, over, through, toward,
                    under, until, without

Once you've circled the repeated words in an essay the next step
is to look for those words you've repeated the most. Doing this with
our sample essay, we see that we have repeated:

car	9 times
new	5 times
best	3 times
expensive	3 times
sun	3 times
meter	3 times
wheel	3 times
all	3 times
two	2 times
one	2 times
interior	2 times
upholstery	2 times
look	2 times
leather	2 times
dash	2 times
normal	2 times
white	2 times
own	2 times

This procedure clearly shows that we have used the word *car* to excess. We have also used *new* frequently. The next step is to replace some of our uses of *car* and *new* with other terms that mean about the same thing. Of course, we might want to change some of the other words that have been repeated. A good rule of thumb is to try to change or delete as many repeated words as possible. To illustrate, let us change and delete some of the repeated words in our sample essay:

---

1. Of all the things I own the one I like the best is my car. 2. It is a 1957 Chevy Belair, two-door, two-toned, with a sun roof. 3. *It* has a new, expensive, round vent on the hood, rising up just in back of the emblem, that gives the look of moving even when *it* is standing still. 4. *The* interior is one of *its most appealing* features. 5. *It* has white leather upholstery with powder blue trim. 6. The buttons on the upholstery are sewed into the seats and backrests giving it a *luxurious,* cushiony *appearance.* 7. The dash is made of acrylic plastic, which is treated to ward off the sun's rays and keep down the level of heat when the car has been in the *sunlight* for a long time. 8. The *automobile* has a racing steering wheel that is smaller than normal and leather covered with a wooden turning knob. 9. It also has all of the *most modern* gadgets on the dash. 10. It has a tach that shows rpm's, an oil pressure meter, and water temperature and brake fluid *gauges.* 11. The wheels are bigger than normal, with white lettering that sticks out and chrome spoked rims. 12. The *automobile's* sleek design cuts down on wind resistance and gives it good mileage. 13. In all my car is one of *my nicest possessions.*

If you compare this version of the essay with its original form, you will find that this one flows much better and is a notch above the other in vocabulary quality. To accomplish this, the following deletions were performed:

the car	sentence 3
new	sentence 6
newest	sentence 7
expensive	sentence 8
new	sentence 8
meter	sentence 10
on the car	sentence 11
wheel	sentence 11
really	sentence 12
all	sentence 13

Although it is a useful technique, deletion cannot be used as frequently as substitution when revising an essay for vocabulary. In the sample essay above, the following substitutions were made:

it	for	my car	sentence 3
the car	for	it	sentence 3
the	for	it	sentence 4
its	for	car's	sentence 4
most appealing	for	best	sentence 4
it	for	the interior	sentence 5
luxurious	for	expensive	sentence 6
appearance	for	look	sentence 6
sunlight	for	sun	sentence 7
automobile	for	car	sentence 8
most modern	for	newest	sentence 9
gauges	for	meters	sentence 10
automobile's	for	car's	sentence 12
my nicest possessions	for	best things I've ever owned	sentence 13

Thus one process to follow when revising an essay for vocabulary is to:

1. identify the repeated words (excluding some common function words) in your essay.
2. identify which words have been repeated most frequently.
3. substitute different words for those repeated words wherever you feel a substitution would be an improvement and delete some repeated words.

This process will ensure that you don't overuse any words. Using different words for reiterated concepts, however, is not the only aspect of vocabulary quality in writing.

Revising To Use More Technical or Sophisticated Words

Decreasing the number of repeated words used does not in itself make the vocabulary level of your essay acceptable. You must also be concerned with the sophistication and technicality of the words you use. Certain words are considered more sophisticated than others. For example, consider the following:

house
home
dwelling
household
domicile

All of these words relate to the same concept and in many cases can be used as synonyms. However, the last three are more sophisticated than the first two. When you are revising an essay for vocabulary, increasing the level of sophistication of the words you have used is an excellent way of dressing up and polishing a composition. This might include the use of more technical terms. For example, in a science class you would certainly want to use such terms as nucleus, neutron, proton, and electron when discussing the atom rather than such phrases as "the positive part of the center of an atom" or "the part of the atom that rotates around the center."

But more complex is not always better. Take, for example, the following sentence:

John commutated to the haberdashery to coemptionate some comestibles.

The vocabulary level of this sentence is certainly sophisticated in that infrequently used words have been selected. Unfortunately those words are so sophisticated that few people would understand that this sentence conveys the message, "John went to the store to buy some food." Judgment, then, has to be used in this part of vocabulary revision. You must take into consideration your audience and your purpose for writing.

The revising process for this aspect of vocabulary in itself is quite simple. It consists in reading over your essay and asking yourself, "Is there a *better* word or phrase I might use in place of this one?" This often produces some dramatic results in a composition. Utilizing this process with our sample essay might yield the following:

1. Of all the things I own the one I *favor most* is my car. 2. It is a 1957 *Chevrolet* Belair, two-door, two-toned with a sun roof. 3. It has a new, expensive, *cylindrical* vent on the hood, *protruding upward* just in back of

the emblem, that gives the *impression* of *motion* even when the car is standing still. 4. The interior is one of its most appealing features. 5. It has white leather upholstery with powder blue trim. 6. The buttons on the upholstery are *embedded in* the seats and backrests, giving it a luxurious, *padded* appearance. 7. The *dashboard consists of* acrylic *resin* that is treated to *repel* the sun's rays and *minimize* the level of heat when the car has been in the sunlight for an *extended period of* time. 8. The automobile has a racing steering wheel that is *undersized* and leather covered with a wooden turning knob. 9. It also has all of the most modern *instruments* on the *dashboard*. 10. It has *a tachometer* that *registers* rpm's, an oil-pressure meter, and water temperature and brake fluid gauges. 11. The wheels are *oversized* with *raised* white lettering and chrome spoked rims. 12. The car's *aerodynamic* design *reduces* wind resistance and *effects excellent* mileage. 13. My car is one of my nicest possessions.

The changes that were made in the previous essay to produce this one are:

favor	for	like	sentence 1
most	for	best	sentence 1
Chevrolet	for	Chevy	sentence 2
cylindrical	for	round	sentence 3
protruding up	for	rising up	sentence 3
impression	for	look of	sentence 3
motion	for	moving	sentence 3
embedded in	for	sewed in	sentence 6
padded	for	cushiony	sentence 6
dashboard	for	dash	sentence 7
resin	for	plastic	sentence 7
repel	for	ward off	sentence 7
minimize	for	keep down	sentence 7
extended period	for	long	sentence 7
undersized	for	smaller than normal	sentence 8
instruments	for	gadgets	sentence 9
dashboard	for	dash	sentence 9
tachometer	for	tach	sentence 10
registers	for	shows	sentence 10
oversized	for	bigger than normal	sentence 11
raised	for	sticks out	sentence 11
aerodynamic	for	sleek	sentence 12
reduces	for	cuts down on	sentence 12
effects	for	gives	sentence 12
excellent	for	good	sentence 12

These changes have produced a vocabulary level that is more acceptable for college-level writing than that of the previous essays.

Revising for Precision of Usage

The final consideration when revising an essay for vocabulary is the precision of meaning of the words and phrases used. The process of revising an essay for precision of vocabulary is approximately the same as revising to use more technical and sophisticated words. You read through the paper asking yourself: "Does this word or phrase mean precisely what I intend it to mean?" Of course this means that you must have a fairly thorough knowledge of the words and phrases in the English language that are commonly confused.

To illustrate some typical errors of precision, consider the following sentences:

1. He was kind of a philanthropist.
2. Even in her hour of mourning, she was not let alone by the curious onlookers.
3. With regards to the time limit you have given me, I must now ask for an extension.
4. The award he received was muchly deserved.
5. He expressed his thoughts out loud.

Each of these sentences contains an error in vocabulary precision. Words and phrases have been used that are technically inappropriate in their present contexts. In sentence 1, for instance, the use of the phrase "kind of" is a precision error. Technically "somewhat of" should have been used: "He was somewhat of a philanthropist." The phrase "kind of" is informal and is usually avoided in the written language. In the second sentence, the word "let" is inappropriate. The verb *let* should not be substituted for the verb *leave*. Thus, sentence 2 should have read, "Even in her hour of mourning she was not left alone by the curious onlookers." In the third sentence "regards" is imprecisely used. The word "regards" means "big wishes." The appropriate phrase to use in this sentence is "with regard to": "With regard to the time limit you have given me, I must now ask for an extension." In sentence 4 "muchly" is incorrect. There is no such word as "muchly." The word *much* can be used as an adjective or an adverb; thus the *ly* is unnecessary: "The award he received was much deserved." In the last sentence "out loud" is used improperly. "Aloud" is the word that should be used in formal situations: "He expressed his thoughts aloud."

If you find any of these precision errors difficult to identify or understand it is because they are commonly made in the spoken language. Someday many of them may be considered acceptable in writing, but until then you should carefully check anything you write to make sure you have not included words or phrases that would be considered precision errors. In Part 5 of this text we have listed many of the common precision errors under the section "Commonly Confused Terms." It is a good idea to read over that section to become familiar with these errors and better able to identify them in your own writing.

Revising an essay for vocabulary is always a matter of substituting one word or phrase for another. The substitution might be done (1) to reduce the number of repeated words, (2) to utilize more sophisticated or technical terms, or (3) to use words and phrases that are more precise in meaning. To revise vocabulary the writer must have a ready store of words to use as substitutes. In the next section we discuss some sources of such words.

SOURCES OF VOCABULARY

Vocabulary words useful as substitutes in an essay can come from internal sources (your memory) or from external sources. We'll consider external sources first and then discuss ways of improving vocabulary storage internally.

External Sources of New Vocabulary

There are two primary external sources of vocabulary words: dictionaries and the thesaurus. In chapters 3 and 5 we listed a number of different types of dictionaries, many of which are specific to certain academic areas. These are particularly useful when you revise a paper with the intent of using more technical terminology. Similarly, general dictionaries can supply you with more sophisticated vocabulary. You can use the dictionary to look up words you want to find substitutes for and then select an appropriate synonym from those given in the definition of the word. A better source for obtaining substitute words in this fashion, though, is a thesaurus.

A thesaurus is a book in which words are grouped by synonyms. The most famous and widely used is *Roget's International Thesaurus*. It contains over 1,000 categories and 50,000 words. It is one of the most powerful revision tools for writing ever developed. With it you can easily and quickly find words to substitute for overused words. Suppose, for example, that in an essay you had used the word *country* a number of times and wanted to find a word or phrase to use in place of it. If you looked up *country* in a thesaurus you would find the following words and phrases listed with it:

country, lane, nation, state, polity, body politic, republic, commonwealth, kingdom, empire, empery, realm, dominion, domain, principality, principate, duchy, dukedom, city state, free city, province, territory, colony, settlement

Depending on the context in which the word was used and your purpose and audience, some of these words could readily be used as replacements for the word *country*.

The thesaurus and various dictionaries are handy source books to use when revising an essay for vocabulary. Your speaking vocabulary, an internal source of vocabulary, is another source of substitutions.

Internal Sources of New Vocabulary

Having a large speaking vocabulary or internal source of new words is the ideal tool for vocabulary revision. A large speaking vocabulary does not come easily. It takes systematic study and a great deal of effort to expand your vocabulary. There are two basic ways of expanding your vocabulary: (1) through a knowledge of affixes, and (2) through the addition of new words. We'll consider affixes first and then discuss ways of adding new terms to your vocabulary.

The word *affix* is a general name for a prefix or a suffix. You can expand your vocabulary using affixes by forming *derivatives* of words you already know. For example, if you know what the word *extension* means and the affix *hyper*, you then will know what the word *hyperextension* means.

The use of foreign words in our language is most evident when you study affixes. The word *translation*, for example, combines the

Latin prefix *trans* (across) with the Latin particle *latus* (carried) and the typical noun suffix -*ion*.

A knowledge of affixes is a quick and effective way of expanding your vocabulary. Prefixes are the most numerous type of affix and the ones with the greatest flexibility. Below are some of the more common Latin, Greek, and Anglo-Saxon prefixes, their meanings, and an example of a word in which each prefix appears.

Latin prefixes

ab-, abs-, a-	from, away	abstain
ad-	to, toward	adjoin
ante-	before	antecedent
bene-	well, good	benefactor
bi-	two	bimodal
circum-	around, about	circumnavigate
con-	with	concurrent
contra-	against	contradistinction
de-	down	depress
dis-	apart, opposite of	dislike
ex-	out, from	excavate
extra-	beyond	extracurricular
in-, il-, im-, ir-	not	inept, illicit, immature, irrational
in-, im-	in	infringe, impede
inter-	between	intercede
intra-	within	intramural
intro-	within	introspection
juxta-	near	juxtapose
non-	not, opposite from	nonviolent
per-	through	perforate
post-	after	postmortem
pre-	before	predetermine
re-	again, back	reclaim, recoil
retro-	backward	retroflex
semi-	half, partly	semiskilled
sub-	under	submarine
super-	over	supersonic
trans-	across	transcontinental
ultra-	beyond, extremely	ultraconservative

Greek prefixes

a-, an-	not	amorphous, anhydrous
ambi-, amphi-	around, both	ambidextrous, amphibious

ana-	back, opposite	anaphase
anti-	against	antiwar
cata-	down	cataclysm
dia-	through	diatribe
dys-	bad	dysfunction
epi-	upon	epigram
eu-	good	euphemism
hyper-	beyond, excess	hyperactive
hypo-	under	hypotension
meta-	beyond	metaphysics
	denoting change	metamorphosis
para-	side by side, near	paraphrase
peri-	around	perimeter
prot-	first	prototype
syn-, sym-	together	synchronize, symphony

Anglo-Saxon prefixes

a-	in, on, of	ashore, akin
be-	near, about	beside
for-	off, to the uttermost	forswear, forbear
mis-	wrong, bad	misunderstand
out-	beyond, more than	outlaw
over-	too much	overcompensate
un-	not	unbeaten
with-	against	withstand

A knowledge of these prefixes can help you not only expand your vocabulary by forming derivatives but also understand words you encounter when reading. For example, below are some fairly infrequently used words whose meanings you might guess simply by knowing the meaning of the prefixes they contain.

1. *ab, a, abs*— "from," "away," "off"

abdicate—formally remove oneself from, relinquish, surrender
abhor—shrink from, detest, loathe
abrasion—scraping or wearing away of the skin by friction
abscond—steal off and hide, depart secretly
absolve—set free from some duty or responsibility
averse—opposed, unwilling
avert—turn away, ward off, prevent
avocation—hobby, occupation away from one's customary occupation

2. un— "not," "lack of," "do the opposite of," "remove or release from"

unabridged—complete, not made shorter
unbiased—not prejudiced in favor of or against, fair
unconcern—lack of anxiety, interest, indifference
undeceive—free from deception or mistaken ideas, set straight
unnerve—cause to lose self-control, upset

3. *ante*— "before," and *post*— "after"

antecedents—ancestors, forefathers
antedate—assign a date before the true date
anteroom—waiting room
postmortem—thorough examination of a body after death

4. *bi*— "two," and *semi*— "half," "partly"

bicameral—consisting of two chambers or legislative houses
biennial—occurring every two years
semiannual—occurring every half year or twice a year
bilateral—having two sides
bilingual—speaking two languages equally well
bipartisan—representing two political parties
semiconscious—half conscious, not fully conscious
semidetached—partly detached, sharing a wall with an adjoining building

5. *extra*— "beyond," and *intra*— "within"

extraneous—foreign, coming from or existing outside
extracurricular—outside the regular curriculum or course of study
intraparty—within a party
intrastate—within a state
intravenous—within or by way of the veins

The word *prefix* denotes something that is attached to the beginning of words (*pre* means "before"). *Suffixes* are attached to the endings of words. Suffixes, in general, do not change the meaning of words as prefixes do. Usually the role of a suffix is to change the part of speech of a word. For example, using the suffix —*ate* we can change the noun *affection* into the adjective *affectionate.* Below is a list of the common suffixes and the parts of speech they signify.

> Suffixes marking nouns: -acy, -age, -an, -ance, -ancy, -ant, -ar, -ard, -ary, -ate, -cy, -dom, -ee, -eer, -ence, -ency, -ent, -er, -ery, -ess, -ette, -hood, -ice, -ie, -ier, -ite, -ism, -ist, -ity, -ive, -kin, -let, -ment, -mony, -ness, -or, -ory, -ship, -ster, -teen, -tion, -tude, -ty, -ure, -y, -yer

> Suffixes marking verbs: -ate, -en, -fy, -ify, -ise, -ize

> Suffixes marking adjectives: -able, -ac, -aceous, -al, -am, -ar, -ary, -ate, -ble, -ent, -er, -ern, -escent, -ful, -ible, -ic, -ical, -id, -ile, -ine, -ish, -less, -like,- ly, -ory, -ose, -ous, -some, -ty, -ulent, -wise, -y

> Suffixes marking adverbs: -ally, -fold, -like, -ly, -ward, -ways, -wise

Affixes can expand your vocabulary by helping you get more mileage out of the words you already know. Another way of expanding your vocabulary is to add new words to your speaking vocabulary. In her book *Errors and Expectations*, the late Mina Shaughnessy states that there are eight basic categories of words to which college students should pay special attention. Those are:

1. Words that allude to events, places, and people that are assumed to be commonly, if but vaguely, known (Gandhi, the French Revolution, the Nile).
2. Words that serve as formal equivalents to concepts already familiar to the student in different words (*atheist* is the equivalent of "someone who doesn't believe in God").
3. Words that serve to identify complex historical movements (Renaissance, Marxism, evolution).
4. Words that, although part of the nomenclature of certain fields, are also used in the wider culture with variant meanings (in literature, for example, such terms as *fiction, drama,* or *novel*).
5. Words that are intended to initiate highly specific academic activities (define, compare, generalize, document, illustrate, prove, summarize, interpret).
6. Words that are used in deliberately ambiguous ways in order to enrich or refine meaning (irony, figures of speech, etc.).
7. Words that indicate relationships such as addition, negation, condition, or causation (moreover, therefore, however).
8. Words that represent Latin- or Greek-based synonyms for

familiar words (*initiate* or *commence* for *begin*) and that tend to give an academic flavor to the writing and speech of teachers.[1]

There are a number of ways you can learn new words in each of these categories. One of the most effective is to keep a vocabulary notebook. This technique is very practical, especially because in college classes you are confronted with hundreds of new words all the time. For example, in one psychology book, a student might find the following unfamiliar words all on a single page: legacy, neural, modalities, empirical, apperception, milieu, therapeutics.

A good way to use a vocabulary notebook is to divide each subject area (psychology, history, accounting) into eight categories—one for each of Shaughnessy's eight types of words. Then when you come across a word you don't know while reading in a particular content area, you can find its meaning (using context or the dictionary) and place it in the appropriate category for that subject area. If you read over the words in your vocabulary notebook two or three times each week they will quickly become part of your speaking vocabulary and become usable in your writing.

SUMMARY

The second aspect of polishing a paper is to revise it for vocabulary. Good vocabulary in an essay means:

1. the use of different words to express repetitive concepts
2. the use of technical and sophisticated words when approrpiate
3. precision of meaning

Overly used words can be identified by circling all repeated words (with the exception of some commonly used function words) in an essay. Different words can then be substituted for those words. At the same time or immediately following, you can scan the vocabulary in your essay asking: "Is there a better word or phrase I might want to use in place of this one?" Given a *yes* answer to this question, you can then substitute more technical or sophisticated terms. Attention can then be turned to the precision of meaning of the words and phrases used.

All of these vocabulary revision techniques require a source of terms and phrases that can function as substitutes. The dictionary and the thesaurus are very useful *external* sources of such words. To use *internal* sources for such words requires that you expand your speaking vocabulary. This can be accomplished by a knowledge and use of various affixes and by the selective learning of new words and phrases. To increase awareness of common precision errors it is recommended that you read the section entitled "Commonly Confused Terms" in Part 5 of this text.

Exercises

1. The following paragraph has some frequently repeated words and some words and phrases that are inappropriate for formal writing. Rewrite the paragraph making the necessary vocabulary changes and then check your revision with that in the answer section.

> For a bunch of years the RDB Corporation has been looking for a person able to run the company's daily operations. Just in the last few weeks that looking has centered on a person named Hamilton Lyman, Jr., one of the bosses at IT and L. People say that Lyman wants to get a boss's position that has possibilities of advancement rather than the go-nowhere job he has now. From the first interviews with Lyman it seems that his desire and ability are both high.

2. Identify at least ten words in which each of the following prefixes is used. Use the dictionary if necessary.

    ante-
    dis-
    juxta-
    retro-
    hypo-
    meta-
    peri-
    mis-
    over-
    ultra-

3. *Saying what you mean:* The basic meanings of the following words in the following groups are similar, but each term has a specific implication. Using a dictionary if you have to, give the precise meaning of each word.

A. The following words have something to do with the highest point attainable:
   a. apex
   b. acme
   c. climax
   d. zenith
   e. pinnacle

B. The following words have something to do with saying something in a brief way:
   a. concise
   b. terse
   c. pithy
   d. laconic
   e. summary

C. The following words have something to do with the imitation of something or someone:
   a. caricature
   b. counterfeit
   c. parody
   d. burlesque
   e. forgery

D. The following words have something to do with being inactive:
   a. indolent
   b. inert
   c. idle
   d. lethargic
   e. languid

E. The following words have something to do with the ability to achieve in a given field:
   a. proficiency
   b. efficiency
   c. dexterity
   d. deftness
   e. aptitude

4. Fewer and better words: The following sentences can be stated much more concisely with the help of the words listed below. Rewrite each sentence, using the appropriate word for compactness.

profane	obtrudes	sequel	imminent
implied	ambiguous	anonymous	harassed
resilient	discreet	gorging	unscrupulous
chronological	glutted	introspection	interspersed
dilapidated	retaliation	sacrilegious	hypothetical

a. The officer was filled to excess with power.
b. It was distasteful to see the boy eat in a gluttonous manner.
c. The city council was persistently vexed by the town's petty demands.
d. Tom has the habit of thrusting his opinions upon others without any invitation.
e. Some people use the word "liberty" in an unworthy way.
f. It is natural to want to pay back an injury someone has inflicted on us.

g. The coach hinted that I had been chosen, although he did not put it in so many words.
h. Many of us admire Gail for her ability to regain a cheerful outlook no matter how low her spirits have dropped.
i. This story is a continuation of the one that appeared last month.
j. To scrutinize one's own thoughts and feelings occasionally is wholesome.
k. On the first page all of the events are arranged according to the time when they took place.
l. The work bears no author's name.
m. This statement can be interpreted in many different ways.
n. Everyone felt that the crisis was likely to come very soon.
o. Apt quotations were used at intervals throughout his speech.
p. The teacher considered the remark disrespectful of something which is sacred.
q. The man disregards all principles of right and wrong in his business dealings.
r. The manager found the apartment shabby and in need of repairs.
s. The case which I am describing is merely an imaginary one which I am assuming tentatively.
t. Politicians must use good judgment both in their actions and in their speech.

5. *Choosing the right word:* Choose the correct word for each sentence. Check your answers with ours to see if you understand the troublesome words.
a. The convict was able to _____ the police only a short time. (allude, elude)
b. A pilot's instructions must be _____. (explicit, implicit)
c. My daughter has an _____ vocabulary for a child of five. (exceptionable, exceptional)
d. The subjects should try to _____ the alloted time. (excel, exceed)
e. Only _____ people should serve on juries. (disinterested, uninterested)
f. A great many _____ enter our country annually. (emigrants, immigrants)
g. _____ professors addressed the conventions. (Eminent, Imminent)
h. Let us not be _____ of our neighbor's success. (envious, enviable)
i. We could not question whether their distribution of property was _____. (equable, equitable)

ANSWERS

1. For a number of years the RDB Corporation has been searching intensively for someone able to manage its daily operations. Recently that search has centered on Hamilton Lyman, Jr., an executive at IT and L. Lyman, it is rumored, desires an executive position with potential rather than the stagnant one he possesses currently. Initial interviews with Lyman indicate that his enthusiasm is matched by his abilities.

3. Group A
   a. apex—tip of an object where all ascending lines converge in a sharp point.
   b. acme—perfection
   c. climax—highest point of interest; the end
   d. zenith—point in the heavens directly overhead
   e. pinnacle—a dizzy height like that of a pointed spire

Group B
   a. concise—stated without any elaboration
   b. terse—said briefly but with elegance or finish
   c. pithy—expressing much in a few words
   d. laconic—stated briefly to the point of brusqueness
   e. summary—main points given without details

Group C
   a. caricature—ludicrous exaggeration or distortion, often pictorial
   b. counterfeit—a copy made with intent to deceive or defraud
   c. parody—treatment of a trivial subject in exact style of a serious one.
   d. burlesque—mimicry that provokes laughter, especially in the theater
   e. forgery—a false signature

Group D
   a. indolent—lazy
   b. inert—lacking power to set itself in motion
   c. idle—not busy at the moment
   d. lethargic—drowsy
   e. languid—weak, sluggish

Group E
   a. proficiency—competence beyond average as a result of training and practice

    b. efficiency—competence in performance; capability
    c. dexterity—adroitness or skill, physical or mental
    d. deftness—lightness and sureness of touch
    e. aptitude—readiness in learning

4. a. The officer was glutted with power.
    b. Gorging is distasteful to see.
    c. The city council was harassed.
    d. Tom habitually obtrudes his opinions upon others.
    e. Some people profane the word "liberty."
    f. Retaliation for injury is natural.
    g. The coach implied that I had been chosen.
    h. Many of us admire Gail's resilient spirit.
    i. This story is a sequel to last month's.
    j. Introspection is wholesome.
    k. On the first page is a chronological list of events.
    l. The article is anonymous.
    m. This statement is ambiguous.
    n. Everyone felt the crisis was imminent.
    o. His speech was interspersed with apt quotations.
    p. The teacher considered the remark sacrilegious.
    q. The man is unscrupulous in his business dealings.
    r. The manager found the apartment dilapidated.
    s. The case I am describing is a hypothetical one.
    t. Politicians must be discreet.

5. a. elude
    b. explicit
    c. exceptional
    d. exceed
    e. disinterested
    f. immigrants
    g. eminent
    h. envious
    i. equitable

NOTE

1. From *Errors and Expectations: A Guide for the Teacher of Basic Writing*, by Mina P. Shaughnessy. Copyright © 1977 by Mina P. Shaughnessy. Reprinted by permission of Oxford University Press, Inc.

CHAPTER NINE

GRAMMAR, USAGE, AND MECHANICS

The final consideration when polishing a paper is to revise it for grammar, usage, and mechanics: You should read over your paper and correct errors you might have made. Those errors will fall into one of three categories: grammar, usage, or mechanics. These categories include such things as placement of modifiers, subject/verb agreement, punctuation, and spelling. In this chapter we will discuss specific errors of grammar, usage, and mechanics that commonly occur in college and university writing. But first we will consider a general technique for locating such errors in your writing.

CORRECTING GRAMMAR, USAGE, AND MECHANICS ERRORS

The technique for grammar, usage, and mechanics revision is to read your paper aloud—slowly—paying attention to what you have written and contrasting that with what you intended to write. You will often find a discrepancy between what you thought you wrote and what you actually put on paper. Consider the essay in Example 9-1.

Example 9-1

English is boring some of the experience I had in some of my English class. Reading novel that are boring to you. But it reads them. I always hated poetry in school because I hate read poetry to self.

This essay was written by a college freshman in a basic writing class.[1] Obviously, the essay has quite a few errors, and upon reading it one might get the impression that its author knew very little about the English language. However, when the author of this essay was asked to read his paper aloud he produced that in Example 9-2.

Example 9-2

English is boring. *I guess because of* some of the experiences I had in some of my English *classes* reading novels that are boring to you. *But you have to read them anyway.* I always hated *reading* poetry in school because I hate *reading* poetry itself.

When the student read his paper aloud, he corrected many of his mistakes. Making errors in writing that you would normally not make when speaking is a common phenomenon. As was explained in Chapter 6, writing is the transforming and translating of thought to print; speaking is the translation of thought to sound. Our minds generate thought, draw conclusions, and see relationships between one thought and another extremely rapidly. Because we can't speak as quickly as we think, speech often lags behind thought. We write even slower than we speak, and as a result, when writing we often write things that we really don't want to and exclude things we want to include. The product is an essay with many grammar, usage, and mechanics errors.

The best way of identifying errors is to read through the paper slowly aloud. Usually doing this will make mistakes obvious. They can then be corrected. It is an even better idea to have someone else read the paper aloud. A second reader can usually identify more miswritings than the author, because the second reader approaches the writing without preconceived notions about what the essay should say.

The general technique for correcting grammar, usage, and

mechanics miswritings is a thoughtful oral reading of your paper. This usually serves to clear up most if not all of the errors. It is also beneficial to be aware of the type of miswritings you are likely to make. This will make you more sensitive to them and consequently more likely to identify and correct them. In the next sections, we will consider various grammar, usage, and mechanics errors you are likely to find in your writing.

GRAMMAR ERRORS

When instructors speak of grammar or syntax errors, they generally are referring to major problems that keep a sentence from making sense. For example, consider the following:

> Everyone was born in July in this room that was not born in April or May.

This sentence does not work. We get the general feel for what the author probably intended, but to do so we must make a lot of assumptions. The problems within the sentence are those of syntax or structure. To understand syntactic errors, you must know some grammar terminology. We have included sections in the Grammar Handbook (see Part 5 of this text) on parts of speech and parts of a sentence. If you are unfamiliar with such concepts as subjects, verbs, and sentence patterns, you should perhaps read those sections before reading the rest of this chapter. In this section we will consider those syntactic miswritings that are most common in student writing. Specifically we will cover:

1. Omissions, insertions, and substitutions
2. Mixed patterns
3. Dangling and misplaced modifiers
4. Overreduction
5. Lack of parallelism

Omissions, Insertions, and Substitutions

Consider the following sentences:

1. I feel that my extending her stay she made the situation worse.

2. Life is really hard today, so you can imagine what it will in the future.

3. I felt that like he was my friend.

All of these sentences contain specific types of miswriting. In sentence 1 there is a substitution: the word *my* is substituted for *by*. Usually a substitution error looks very much like the word it is substituted for. In sentence 2 there is an omission. The word *be* has been omitted from the sentence. Omissions occur frequently, especially in first-draft writing. Sentence 3 contains the error of insertion. The word *like* should not be there. If it were left out, the sentence would be logical and correct. What usually happens when insertions are made is that the writer's mind is considering two or three ways of expressing a thought. When the sentence is recorded, parts of both structures are written.

Errors of omission, insertion, and substitution are almost impossible to avoid. All writers produce them, and the best safeguard against them is a careful reading aloud of your essay. Usually omissions, substitutions, and insertions will jump out at you during this oral proofreading. Other types of grammar errors are not as obvious, however.

Mixed Patterns

Consider the following sentence:

> Statistics show that the average person's future a college education will greatly enhance his earning power.

In this sentence the phrase "the average person's future" doesn't seem to make sense. The writer of this sentence might have had the following two possibilities in mind:

> Statistics show that an average person's future earning power will be greatly enhanced by a college education.

> Statistics show that on the average a college education will greatly enhance a person's earning power.

The author incorporated elements of both structures in the sentence, producing a mixed pattern.

Mixed-pattern errors are similar to insertion errors, except that the former involve larger chunks of the alternative patterns. Mixed-pattern errors can thus be more difficult to correct than insertions. Sometimes you must pull the sentence apart to identify what you actually intended to say. This is best done by trying to phrase the sentence in different ways until you find one that makes sense. Below we've listed a few mixed-pattern errors and rephrased them in acceptable grammatical structures:

a. *Mixed pattern*
   If a person feels that by joining the armed forces could improve his future he should probably look into the Navy.
   Alternative structures
   If a person feels that joining the armed forces could improve his future, he should probably look into the Navy.
   If a person feels that by joining the armed forces he could improve his future, he should probably look into the Navy.
b. *Mixed pattern*
   To take keypunching you must go to a computer school for it.
   Alternative structures
   To take keypunching you must go to a computer school.
   You must go to a computer school for keypunching.

Dangling and Misplaced Modifiers

What's wrong with the following sentence?

Getting into the car, the engine wouldn't start.

It is not clear what the phrase "getting into the car" modifies. There is nothing in the main clause that it could modify: The only noun in the clause is *engine* and certainly the engine wasn't getting into the car. Such a construction is called a dangling modifier, which is a modifying clause, phrase, or word that doesn't clearly modify anything. A general rule regarding modifiers is that they should be placed as close to the word or words they modify as possible. For example, consider the following sentences:

Having been told he was using unacceptable procedures, the judge held the lawyer in contempt of court.

The phrase "having been told he was using unacceptable procedures" is meant to modify *lawyer*, but it is placed in such a way that it looks like it modifies *judge*. Consequently, it is called a misplaced modifier. We can correct the error by moving the modifying phrase as close to the word it modifies as possible—preferably right before or after it. To do this requires some rewording:

The judge told the lawyer, who had been warned that he was using unacceptable procedures, that he was in contempt of court.

Having told him that he was using unacceptable procedures, the judge found the lawyer in contempt of court.

Moving the modifier closer to the word it modifies removes the ambiguity or lack of logic in the sentence. Dangling modifiers occur in situations in which there is nothing stated that can be logically modified. In such cases the sentence must be supplied with something that can be modified. Consider again that first example sentence:

Getting into the car, the engine wouldn't start.

By supplying something for the phrase *getting into the car* to modify, we can correct the problem:

Getting into the car, I realized that the engine wouldn't start.

Misplaced and dangling modifiers can be a negative side effect of reduction and within-sentence expansion. The aim of those two procedures is to generate sentences that have many modifying clauses, phrases, and words, but if this is done without concern for the position of those elements, misplaced and dangling modifier problems can easily result. For example, suppose you had written the following sentences:

The judge told the lawyer he was in contempt of court. He did this after he had already warned the lawyer that he was using unacceptable procedures.

If, when revising the paper to reduce and expand, you had decided to reduce the second sentence to the phrase, "having been warned he was using unacceptable procedures," and attach it to the first sentence, you might attach that phrase to the first part of the sentence and thus produce the sentence with the misplaced modifier. One way to guard against modification errors is to be aware of the placement of modifiers when you are performing reduction and expansion. Another way is to read over and revise a paper specifically for modification errors. This means asking the following question about each modifier: "Does this clearly modify something?" If your answer is *no* you should do some rewording and reshuffling.

Below we've demonstrated and corrected some common modification errors:

Improper modification   Overcooked and tough, I could not eat the meat.

Corrected   Overcooked and tough, the meat was inedible.

Improper modification   Straining under a load of books, his toe
caught on the edge of the step.

Corrected   Straining under a load of books, he caught his toe on
the edge of the step.

Improper modification   After graduating from high school, my
mother bought me a new car.

Corrected   After I graduated from high school, my mother
bought me a new car.

Overreduction

Sometimes students are guilty of overreduction or overconsolidation of ideas, which results in the packing of too many ideas into a sentence. To illustrate consider the following:

> The boy next door, who has been living there for the last ten years which have been very pleasant considering the tone of the times, realized that this peaceful, quiet town is just not exciting enough for an individual like himself, who would like to succeed as much as possible in life and affect as many other lives as possible.

There is nothing technically wrong with this sentence. It violates no stated rules of grammar. There are so many ideas packed into it, however, that it is difficult to understand. As was mentioned in Chapter 7, reduction is not always a preferred editing tactic. Probably the information stated in the sentence above would be better expressed as two or three sentences:

> The boy next door recently came to a realization. He has been living in that house for the last ten years—very pleasant years considering the tone of the times. He realized that this peaceful, quiet town is just not exciting enough for an individual like himself, one who would like to succeed as much as possible in life and affect as many other lives as possible.

These sentences are far less confusing than the original sentence. This is not to say that long sentences are always incomprehensible: Professional writers frequently use very long sentences, but they do in such a way as to express their ideas clearly and unambiguously. The working principle in guarding against overreduction is to read over long sentences and monitor their comprehensibility. Are there so many ideas expressed in them that the reader will get lost? If so, those ideas should be expressed in two or more shorter sentences. Below we've corrected some overconsolidated sentences:

Overconsolidation	I was a poor friendless boy with parents and those who care for me far away, those few acquaintances of theirs, after a little forced notice, growing tired of my holiday visits.
Corrected	I was a poor friendless boy with parents and those who care for me far away. Those few acquaintances of theirs, after a little forced notice, soon grew tired of my holiday visits.
Overconsolidation	An old man with steel-rimmed spectacles and very dusty clothes sat by the road with a pontoon bridge across the river and carts and trucks crossing it staggering up the steep bank that led to the bridge.
Corrected	An old man with steel-rimmed spectacles and very dusty clothes sat by the road. There was a pontoon bridge across the river. Carts and trucks were crossing it, but only after they had staggered up the steep bank that led to the bridge.

Lack of Parallelism

Parallelism means using similar structures to express similar ideas. Consolidating ideas can create the syntactic problem of lack of parallelism. This frequently occurs when verbs from two sentences are consolidated into one statement with a compound predicate. For example, consider the following sentences.

I agree that a father should share his son's experiences. I also think that it is a father's responsibility to help his son when in need.

Logically these two sentences can be consolidated and reduced because they repeat similar concepts—that a father has certain responsibilities and duties to a son. When combining these sentences one might produce the following:

I agree that a father should share his son's experiences and to help his son when in need.

The problem with this sentence is the lack of parallelism of the structures used to express the two verbs (*share* and *to help*). One is expressed as a main verb with a modal (*should share*) and the other as an infinitive. The sentence should read:

> I agree that a father should share his son's experience and help his son when in need.

A general rule of thumb when consolidating or combining ideas is that parallel ideas should be expressed in the same syntactic structures. Below are some further examples of lack of parallelism and corrections for them:

Incorrect	We spent hours doing puzzles and played cards.
Revised	We spent hours doing puzzles and playing cards.
Incorrect	It is easier said than it is to do.
Revised	It is easier said than done.
Incorrect	New York is overpopulated, but there are not enough people in Boise.
Revised	New York is overpopulated, but Boise is under-populated.

USAGE ERRORS

Usage is the second general area to consider when reading an essay aloud to identify and correct miswritings. The most common usage errors are lack of agreement between subjects and verbs and between pronouns and antecedents. Another common problem area is verb tenses. If any of the terms we have mentioned here are unfamiliar to you ("antecedent," "participle," "infinitive"), refer to the sections in the Grammar Handbook on parts of speech before continuing any further.

Subject-Verb Agreement

Usage errors often involve subjects and predicates. When a noun and verb are used together as subject and predicate, they must agree in number: If a plural subject is used, a plural verb must be used; if a singular subject is used, a singular verb must be used.

When you read your paper aloud to yourself you will pick out most of the subject–verb agreement errors that have been made.

There are some situations, however, in which it's difficult to hear these errors. We've categorized and listed those situations below. Each is stated in the form of a rule.

1. A compound subject joined by *and* takes a plural verb, whether the nouns making up the subject are singular, plural, or mixed.

   Gail and her father *cook* delicious family meals.
   The players and their coaches *need* more time for practice.
   Only three girls and one boy *want* to go on the field trip.

2. The number of the verb is not affected by words or phrases between the verb and its subject.

   A *solution* to these problems *is* essential.
   Diplomacy as well as patience *is* crucial.
   The *construction* of more parking lots *is* unavoidable.

3. The following pronouns used as a subject take a singular verb: *anybody, anyone, each, either, everybody, everyone, neither, one, no one, someone, somebody.*

   Everybody wants to learn correct usage for writing.
   Each of the three boys *has* enough money for the tickets.
   Someone has to accept the responsibility for the loss.

4. The following pronouns used as subjects take a plural verb: *both, few, many, several.*

   Both of the girls *are* excellent players.
   Many are supportive of the president's position on foreign affairs.
   Several of the candidates *were* angry with the incumbent.

5. The following pronouns used as subjects use either a singular or plural verb depending on the meaning of the sentence: *all, any, most, none,* and *some.*

   Some of the merchandise *was* stolen from the warehouse.
   Some of the suits *were* stolen from the warehouse.
   None of the construction *is* completed so far.
   None of the buildings *were* completed so far.

6. Whether the subject precedes or follows the verb, the verb must agree with its subject in number.

Has anyone seen Bob?
On the chalkboard were scribbled the test questions.
Here come the players out of the locker room.

7. Singular subjects joined by or or nor use a singular verb; when a singular and a plural subject are joined by or or nor, use the verb that agrees with the subject nearer the verb.

Either the lawyer or the witness has not told the truth.
Either the lawyer or the witnesses have not told the truth.
Either the witnesses or the lawyer has not told the truth.

8. A collective noun used as a subject takes a singular verb when the subject refers to a unit. If the subject refers to the individuals within a group rather than to the group as a unit, use the plural verb.

The audience was thrilled with the performance.
The audience are clapping their hands wildly.
The number of skiing accidents increases each year.
A number of new teachers are leaving the profession each year.

9. When the subject of a subordinate clause is a relative pronoun (which, that, who), that pronoun and the verb in the subordinate clause have the same number as the pronoun's antecedent.

Michael spread a rumor about Jill that was unforgivable.
Michael spread many rumors about Jill that were unforgivable.
Sue is a person who loves to cook for many people.
Sue is one of those people who love to cook for many people.

10. Plural subjects that indicate amount, distance, or other units of measure require singular verbs.

A thousand dollars is a lot of money.
Thirteen inches of snow makes for hazardous driving.
One thousand miles seems like a long distance to travel.

Pronoun–Antecedent Agreement

The function of a pronoun is to take the place of a noun. Without them, we would have to use the same word every time we wanted to repeat a concept. For example:

> Bill likes tennis. He and Mark play it often. They are both fairly good at it. It's a sport that is conducive to friendship.

If we couldn't use pronouns to express the concepts in this paragraph, the sentences would read:

> Bill likes tennis. Bill and Mark play tennis often. Bill and Mark are both fairly good at tennis. Tennis is a sport and the sport is conducive to friendship.

A pronoun must always agree with its antecedent in person, number, and gender. Again, there are situations in which pronoun–antecedent agreement can be confusing. Below we've listed rules for six such situations with examples.

1. When two or more antecedents are connected by *and*, the pronoun that refers to them is plural.

   Michael and Babs are looking for *their* tickets to the opera.
   Millie and I are buying *our* cousins the same Christmas gift.
   Sally and Alex hurt *themselves* at the skating rink last night.

2. When the antecedent of the pronoun is *each*, *either*, or *neither* followed by a plural modifier, a singular pronoun is used.

   Each of the boxers is sure *he* is going to win the match.
   Either of the teachers may lose *his* temper and yell at the class.
   Neither of the students would admit *her* mistake.

3. When the antecedent of a pronoun is *each*, *either*, *neither*, *everybody*, *nobody*, or *everyone*, a singular pronoun is used.

   Nobody in the class turned in *his or her* homework assignment.
   Everyone was keeping *his or her* fingers crossed that the Nuggets would win.
   Each candidate has *his or her* own supporters.

4. Formal usage demands that the pronoun *one* be followed by *one*, *one's*, or *oneself*:

One must be careful when *one* tries to ski for the first time.
One should watch *one's* manners when eating out in public.
One cannot blame *oneself* for the loss of the game.

5. When the antecedent is a collective noun, a singular or plural
   pronoun is used according to the meaning of the sentence.

   The debate team has elected Myra as *its* captain.
   The debate team quickly took *their* positions in the tournament.

6. In a subordinate clause, when the antecedent is human, the
   relative pronoun *who* is used; when the antecedent is
   nonhuman, the relative pronoun *which* is used. The pronoun
   that can refer to human or nonhuman antecedents. *That* is used
   to introduce restrictive clauses. In formal usage, *which* is used
   to introduce nonrestrictive clauses.

   Eleanor is one of those people *who* enjoy watching television.
   My car, *which* is a blue sedan, is my most prized possession.
   This is the crate *that* carried the exotic fruit from South
   America.

Besides the situations mentioned above, one of the most
frequent pronoun problems occurs when the words *that* and *this*
are used to refer back to an antecedent in a previous sentence. For
example, consider the following:

   The world is in a tangle. The oil situation will no doubt
   depress the economy. The Middle East seems to be
   continually on the verge of armed conflict, and the Dodgers
   lost their third straight game. This causes great unrest in my
   soul.

The use of *this* in the last sentence is confusing. Does it refer to the
Dodgers using their third straight game or does it refer to all the
previously mentioned situations?

We commonly use expressions such as *this is* and *that is* to refer
back to a set of statements. However, we also use these expressions
to refer to a single statement immediately preceding their use. This
double use can cause confusion for the reader unless the
antecedent of the pronoun is made clear. A good practice to follow
whenever you use the pronouns *this* or *that* is to state the
antecedent immediately before or after the pronoun. If you are
using *this* or *that* to refer to a set of statements you might, then,

write: *all of this* or *all of that*. In the sample above we might have cleared up some of the ambiguity by writing:

> This nagging habit of my favorite baseball team causes great unrest in my soul.

Verb Tenses

Verb tenses can be a confusing issue. Six basic verb tenses (present/past/future/present perfect/past perfect/future perfect) can be used to express a variety of time relationships. Below are some of the more common uses of the six tenses:

1. Use the past tense to indicate action completed in the past.

   The mayor *lived* in the town for twenty years before retiring to the country.
   Yesterday, the postman *delivered* the magazine I was waiting for.
   Last week, we *watched* the final football game of the season.

2. Use the future tense to indicate action that will happen in the future.

   The newlyweds *will honeymoon* in the Virgin Islands.
   If Mike doesn't get a C on the final exam, he *will have* to take the course again next semester.
   Sam's mother said that he *will have* to get a haircut before applying for the job.

3. Use the present perfect tense to indicate action begun in the past and continuing into the present.

   The candidate *has lived* in the state for the past five years.
   The football team *has* never *won* a home game against the Bears.
   The author *has written* over 200 short stories.

4. Use the past perfect tense to indicate action completed before some other past action.

   Katie *had been divorced* for three years before she *married* Jim.
   The woman *had worked* for more than thirty years before she *retired*.
   If Bill *had been* on time, we *would* not *have been* late for the movie.

5. Use future perfect tense to indicate action that will be completed after another action is completed.

> Our family *will have stayed* at the resort longer than your family.
> By next June, the judge *will have sat* longer on the bench than any other judge.
> After the next game, the shortstop *will have played* more games in a row than any other shortstop.

6. Use the present tense of progressive verbs to refer to an action that is in progress.

> Bill Rodgers *is running* in the marathon today.
> That is my brother who *is playing* the saxophone in the band.
> Kathy *is working* in the reference section of the library.

7. Use the past tense of progressive verbs to refer to an action that was in progress at a specific time.

> Bill Rodgers *was running* in the marathon when he broke his leg.
> My brother *was playing* the saxophone when he was discovered by Harry James.
> Kathy *was working* in the library when I met her.

8. Use the future tense of progressive verbs to refer to an action that will be in progress.

> Bill Rodgers *will be running* in the marathon next week.
> My brother *will be playing* saxophone for Harry James's band.
> Kathy *will be working* in the reference library when she goes to college.

Note that the examples above primarily deal with verbs in the main clause. But many tense problems arise when you wish to use two verbs in a sentence. Below are three common problem situations in which two verbs are used in one sentence.

1. When statements either occur in the present or are "timeless" (true in both the present and the past), use the present tense even though the rest of the sentence or paragraph uses the past.

> Dr. Allan believed that Albert Einstein, who *uncovered* the principles of relativity and *expanded* on other laws of physics, *is* the first and foremost scientific genius of all time.

2. Use the present participle of the verb to indicate an action or state of being that occurs at the same time as the main verb.

Looking carefully from side to side, Mike *led* Harriet across the street.

3. Use the past participle, alone or with a helping verb, to indicate an action or state of being that occurs before the time of the main verb.

Having completed the exam early, Bill went outside for some fresh air.

Concerned by her daughter's sudden unwillingness to communicate, Mrs. Allen sought the help of a professional psychologist.

MECHANICS

Mechanics is the final consideration when revising for miswriting. Mechanics errors occur in the areas of

1. punctuation
2. spelling
3. capitalization

The Grammar and Usage Handbook details the situations in which all types of punctuation marks should be used and explains the rules governing capitalization. In this section we will discuss two specific types of punctuation and capitalization errors that are common in college writing and that commonly occur in conjunction with one another. These are:

1. random capitalization
2. misuse of periods and commas.

Common Punctuation and Capitalization Errors

Consider the following sentences:

First of all the nation really doesn't take Care of its students, school are always overcrowded and students get the feeling that They're not Important. What is, is Basketball. Because it attracts crowds and brings in Money. Which as everyone knows is Important. If education, brought in money you know government would support it Better.

This paragraph contains a number of mistakes with commas, periods, and capital letters. Many of them are logical. For example, consider some of the words that are capitalized incorrectly:

Care
They're
Important
Basketball
Money
Important
Better

These words would probably be emphasized if the author were speaking. When we speak we can emphasize a point or word by raising or lowering our voice. Of course, we can't do this in the written language. Consequently, some people incorrectly and inadvertently use capitalization to emphasize a word. In informal writing, such as a letter or journal entry, this is perfectly acceptable. In formal writing, however, the use of capitals is restricted.

The misuse of commas and periods is also related to the difference between the spoken and written language. We saw in Chapter 6 that when speaking we signal the end of an idea by lowering our voice and pausing. In the written language we cannot do this, so we indicate a pause by using a comma or a period. In the spoken language the pauses we use at the end of sentences are sometimes shorter than the pauses used within sentences. Hence in the spoken language there is no standardization of how long or short a pause must be to signal the end of a sentence as opposed to a hesitation within a sentence. In the written language, though, we do have a standard to follow. Periods are used at the end of sentences; commas are used within sentences. A common error in writing is to use commas and periods interchangeably. If you study the sample essay you will see that this is probably what the student has done. He or she has used commas to mark the end of sentences and periods to mark pauses within sentences. The misuse of periods and commas results in frequent occurrence of fragments and run-ons. Thus, you might find that when revising your essay for sentence sense errors you also correct any comma or period errors you might have made.

Another common mistake involving commas is to omit them entirely. Usually this happens in one of the following situations:

1. When a comma should be used after introductory words or
   phrases:

   Above, the thick clouds began to disperse and let the sun peek
   through.
   As a matter of fact, I am very tired of you too.

2. When a comma should be used to set off words or phrases that
   come after the words they modify:

   Madeline Beaverton, a homemaker and piano teacher,
   pleaded guilty to child abuse.

Spelling

Spelling errors are usually one of the last things to be corrected in
an essay. Again the best way to accomplish this aspect of revision is
to read over your essay carefully, looking specifically for spelling
errors. Some writers have found that it is beneficial to read an essay
backwards when revising for spelling so that they don't skip over
words while reading.

Rely on the dictionary when revising for spelling. If you
encounter a word whose spelling you are not sure of, look it up in
the dictionary. To improve their spelling ability, some people use a
visualization technique. When they want to learn to spell a new
word, they try to see the word in their mind's eye. For example, if
they were learning to spell the word *horizontal* they would try to
see the letters in their mind. The visualization technique for
learning spelling is a powerful method. It utilizes a process that
seems to be connected with all forms of memory storage: forming a
visual image of what you want to store and recall.

Another technique for learning spelling words is that of
mnemonic devices. A mnemonic device is an easy-to-remember
hint that reminds you of how a particular word is spelled. Many
people make these up about words they have a hard time
remembering how to spell. For example, if you had difficulty
remembering how *accompanied* was spelled and continually used
one *c* instead of two, you might make up the following mnemonic
device:

   a is accompanied by two *c*'s in accompanied

A third approach to improving spelling is to learn rules that tell
you how certain sounds in the English language are commonly

spelled. You can then apply these rules to a word you don't know how to spell by concentrating on the sound of the word and using the rules to tell you which letters go with which sounds. We've included in the Grammar Handbook a list of the most useful spelling rules. We've also included a list of the most commonly misspelled words. If you feel you are a poor speller it might be beneficial to consult one or both of those lists.

SUMMARY

Revising of grammar, usage, and mechanics errors is the final step in polishing a paper. Within each of these broad categories there are specific errors you should look for when proofreading. Within the category of grammar errors, you should be conscious of:

1. omissions, insertions, and substitutions
2. mixed patterns
3. dangling and misplaced modifiers
4. overreduction
5. lack of parallelism.

When considering usage, you should be aware of subject–verb agreement, pronoun–antecedent agreement, and verb tense utilization. Mechanics involves the correct use of punctuation, capitalization, and spelling. Other than the errors described in this chapter, the Grammar Handbook in Part 5 of the text contains descriptions of other rules you should be aware of. The procedure for correcting all forms of miswritings is a careful, oral reading of your essay with an eye toward the various types of grammar, usage, and mechanics errors you are most likely to make.

Exercises

1. The following sentences contain errors in grammar or syntax. Some words are omitted. There are dangling and misplaced modifiers as well as faulty parallelisms, mixed patterns, and overreduction. Read through each sentence and correct the errors; then check your answers.

    a. Bob is inclined to act like a clown and always embarrassing his sister.
    b. The search party found the child unharmed at the bottom of a deep canyon after covering the area for two days.
    c. When in high school, classes were not exciting as now.

d. The automobile failed to observe the stop sign and losing control went over the embankment.

e. Carol's main ambitions are to have her own business having enough money to vacation in the Caribbean each year.

f. A recent shipment of flowerpots was found damaged and for which some adjustment should be made.

g. Since returning to my home town, everything appears smaller.

h. In real life there is not always a happy ending such as occurs in most novels but rather one of remorse for those who deserve it later on in life.

i. The baseball game went into extra innings and we had to go home and get dressed for the swim party so we could not stay and watch the rest of the game.

j. Although working twenty hours a week during school, my grades did not drop.

k. The artist continued his work without hope, without pleasure, and having no assurance that the world would understand its significance.

l. For a settlement out of court, I will accept either a cash settlement or having the car repaired as perfectly as possible.

m. After filling out the papers required of me, my university adviser checked the papers to see that I had completed them properly.

n. The robber searched through the closets, but no money.

o. Research shows that male college students like science classes better than female students.

p. The couple advertised their house in the newspaper, but no luck.

q. My mother does not like the crowd which brother associates.

r. My minister believes that, by delaying marriage until after college, the chances of it working are much better.

s. A decision must be made as to whether the intramural fields surrounding the university are important from the standpoint of beauty and practicality or to be converted into parking lost for faculty and students.

t. Because Mike has always been ill and with parents who cater to him, he has never been forced to make a decision on his own.

2. The following sentences contain errors in subject–verb agreement, pronoun–antecedent agreement, and verb tense. Read each sentence and correct it.

a. All hope of finding the flood victims were lost.

b. Bill, along with Karl, brought their fishing gear on the trip.

c. Either Joe or Sandy are going to the mountains this weekend.

d. Gary has received notice of the cancellation before we arrived at the concert.

e. Each of the boxers is sure they are going to win the fight.

f. Both the bull and the calf has won blue ribbons at the state fair.

g. Eighty bushels were all the bin could hold.

h. Kathy is one of the women who works at the department store.

i. There are in many cities a need for law and order.

j. Neither of the students would admit their mistake.

k. Everyone was keeping their fingers crossed that the team would win the game on Sunday.

l. Whenever Mom is away on a business trip she always wrote the family to tell them how she is doing.

m. If Bill had caught some fish, we can cook them this evening.

n. As the crowd increases, we knew that the stadium would be filled.

o. The great musician had played his last performance today.

p. How could anyone bring themselves to hijack a plane full of innocent people?

q. After they are married, the couple moved to New Jersey.

r. The owners have made so much money last year that they bought a second store.

s. Before I was introduced to the person, I heard rumors that she was not to be trusted.

t. The coach, as well as her assistants, were praised for an excellent season.

u. Neither Jacobs nor his doctors was there for the trial.

v. Mary's chief source of enjoyment are books.

w. This is one of those problems that has two alternatives, and I don't know which one to take.   .

x. Everyone should vote for the candidate of their choice.

y. A thousand dollars are being offered for the return of the stolen artwork.

3. The following sentences contain errors of spelling, capitalization, misuse of commas, and misuse of periods. Read through the sentences and correct the errors.

a. Tom said "you are only half right."

b. Bill married Helen and her sister served as the bridesmiad.

c. The casheir at the safeway store is one of my best friends.

d. Mrs. Beasley my favorite teacher has moved to another city I hope she will still teach.

e. Wearing his new robert hall suit Joe looked very nice.

f. Since the man was pennyless we gave him a five-doller bill.

g. The scenery of the american southwest is famous the grand canyon is a beautiful sight.

h. During sundays in the summer I enjoy listening to the symphony.

i. When the new york yankees returned home after the world series they were greated by thousands of people.

j. Neither the halfback nor the quarterback made the last touchdown it was the fullback.

k. Yes I remember when Kaye was what you might call "chubbyness."

l. Displaing no hard feelings the opponents shook hands.

m. The enemy was forced to yield his hold on the town he had to give up.

n. My uncle Harry will recieve the citation for bravery given by the lions club.

o. If you take route 40 and by-pass the city you will reach your destination faster.

p. Until last winter Greg lived in hong kong now he lives in the united states.

q. Wierd noises were heard in the cemetery and we made sure that we left in a hurry.

r. When I went to the doctor's office he refered me to a local pharmacist for mediaction.

s. This is one problem that must be handled with sympathy not harshness otherwise you may cause some serious damage.

t. The repairman told Alex "you need a new amplifyer for your stereo"

ANSWERS

1. a. Bob is inclined to act like a clown, which always embarrasses his sister.

   b. After covering the area for two days, the search party found the child unharmed at the bottom of the deep canyon.

   c. When I was in high school, classes were not as exciting as they are now.

   d. I failed to observe the stop sign and lost control of the automobile. My car went over the embankment.

   e. Carol's main ambitions are to have her own business and enough money to vacation in the Caribbean each year.

   f. Some adjustment should be made for a recent shipment of damaged flowerpots.

   g. Since returning to my home town, I find that everything appears smaller.

   h. In real life there is not always a happy ending such as one finds in novels. Instead, one who deserves remorse may find it later on in life.

   i. Although the baseball game went into extra innings, we had to go home and dress for the swim party. As a result, we could not stay and watch the rest of the game.

   j. Although I was working twenty hours a week during school, my grades did not drop.

   k. The artist continued his work, without hope, without pleasure, and without assurance that the world would understand its significance.

   l. For a settlement out of court, I will accept either a cash settlement or a perfect repair of my car.

   m. After I filled out the papers required of me, my university adviser checked them to see that I had completed them properly.

   n. The robber searched through the closets but found no money.

   o. Research shows that male college students like science classes better than female students do.

   p. The couple advertised their house in the newspaper but had no luck.

   q. My mother does not like the crowd my brother associates with.

   r. My minister believes that by delaying my marriage until after college I will have a better chance of having it work.

   s. A decision must be made as to whether the intramural fields surrounding the university are important from the standpoint of beauty and practicality or should be converted into parking lots for faculty and students.

   t. Because Mike has always been ill and has parents who cater to him, he has never been forced to make a decision on his own.

2. a. All hope of finding the flood victims was lost.

   b. Bill, along with Karl, brought his fishing gear on the trip.

   c. Either Joe or Sandy is going to the mountains this weekend.

   d. Gary had received notice of the cancellation before we arrived at the concert.

   e. Each of the boxers is sure he is going to win the fight.

   f. Both the bull and the calf have won blue ribbons at the state fair.

   g. Eighty bushels was all the bin could hold.

   h. Kathy is one of the women who work at the department store.

    i. There is in many cities a need for law and order.

    j. Neither of the students would admit his or her mistake.

    k. Everyone was keeping his fingers crossed that the team would win the game on Sunday.

    l. Whenever Mom is away on a business trip, she always writes the family to tell them how she is doing.

    m. If Bill has caught some fish, we can cook them this evening.

    n. As the crowd increased, we knew that the stadium would be filled.

    o. The great musician has played his last performance today.

    p. How could anyone bring himself to hijack a plane full of innocent people?

    q. After they are married, the couple will move to New Jersey.

    r. The owners had made so much money last year that they bought a second store.

    s. Before I was introduced to the person, I had heard rumors that she was not to be trusted.

    t. The coach, as well as her assistants, was praised for an excellent season.

    u. Neither Jacobs nor his doctors were there for the trial.

    v. Mary's chief source of enjoyment is books.

    w. This is one of those problems that have two alternatives, and I don't know which one to take.

    x. Everyone should vote for the candidate of his or her choice.

    y. A thousand dollars is being offered for the return of the stolen artwork.

3. a. Tom said, "You are only half right."

    b. Bill married Helen, and her sister served as bridesmaid.

    c. The cashier at the Safeway store is one of my best friends.

    d. Mrs. Beasley, my favorite teacher, has moved to another city. I hope she will still teach.

    e. Wearing his new Robert Hall suit, Joe looked very nice.

    f. Since the man was penniless, we gave him a five-dollar bill.

    g. The scenery of the American Southwest is famous. The Grand Canyon is a beautiful sight.

    h. During Sundays in the summer, I enjoy listening to the symphony.

    i. When the New York Yankees returned home after the World Series, they were greeted by thousands of people.

    j. Neither the halfback nor the quarterback made the last touchdown. It was the fullback.

    k. Yes, I remember when Kaye was what you might call chubby.

    l. Displaying no hard feelings, the opponents shook hands.

   m. The enemy was forced to yield his hold on the town. He had to give up.

   n. My Uncle Harry will receive the citation for bravery given by the Lions' Club.

   o. If you take Route 40 and bypass the city, you will reach your destination faster.

   p. Until last winter, Greg lived in Hong Kong. Now he lives in the United States.

   q. Weird noises were heard in the cemetery, and we made sure that we left in a hurry.

   r. When I went to the doctor's office, he referred me to a local pharmacist for medication.

   s. This is one problem that must be handled with sympathy, not harshness. Otherwise, you may cause some serious damage.

   t. The repairman told Alex, "You need a new amplifier for your stereo."

NOTE

1. Reported by S. Waters, *An Examination of the Writing Process of College Basic Writers*, unpublished masters thesis (Calgary, Alberta: Univ. of Calgary, 1978), p. 148.

part
4

Special Topics

CHAPTER TEN

WRITING THE RESEARCH PAPER: PUTTING IT ALL TOGETHER

Thus far in chapters 1 through 9 we've discussed elements necessary for all kinds of writing. In this chapter we will put all these elements together in the context of a research paper. We will also discuss some writing conventions, such as footnotes and bibliographies, that are specific to research papers.

A *research paper* is a written assignment in which the author is required to study and collect information on a particular topic and then report the findings of that research. To illustrate how to utilize the information presented in chapters 1 through 9, we will walk through the writing of a hypothetical research paper. Suppose that in a sociology course you are required to write a paper on the general topic of family practices. This is an outer-directed assignment in which a general theme has been given. The first step in the process of writing the paper is to deal with motivation.

Motivation

Following the scheme for motivation in chapter 2, you should spend time thinking about your goals for the paper. What grade would you like to obtain for the assignment? How much time and energy do you want to put into it? Assuming that you want to do as well as possible and are willing to put maximum effort into writing, you might decide that each day, while working on the project, you will do some imaging as a form of motivation. That is, you should spend a few minutes each day mentally picturing yourself:

> working with a great deal of energy
> being productive and efficient while you work, yet being able to
>   enjoy social activities
> budgeting time efficiently and thoughtfully
> experiencing success in writing
> experiencing success when the paper is returned.

Doing this systematically for a few minutes each day should help initiate and maintain a positive attitude toward the project.

Topic Narrowing

The next issue is the topic itself. Topic identification is not our concern, because we have been given a general topic: family practices. But we have seen (Chapter 3) that a general theme can be limited in a number of ways. We decide that we want to limit our theme by time, manner, and agent. We accomplish this by asking and answering the questions *when*, *how*, and *by whom*, which for our theme produce the following limitations:

> when—present day
> how (manner)—collective and cooperative settlements
> by whom—Israelis

These answers spring from the writer's personal life. The limitations and answers we choose are a function of our interests and background. The answers selected might be a result of the fact that we have heard of cooperative and collective settlements from friends and relatives. Or we might have seen a documentary on such settlements or read a book about them. The limiting questions are simply an artificial way to jar the mind and bring to the conscious level what is of interest to us.

Applying the limitations to our general theme, family practices, might produce the following topic: "present-day Israeli family practices in cooperative and collective settlements." We now have a researchable topic. It is narrow enough for a short paper but broad enough to facilitate the collection of information.

Audience and Format

The topic narrowed, we now can consider audience and format. As is the case with most college and university writing, the audience is already defined—the instructor. Consequently, we do not have to determine such things as the educational level of the audience, their past experience with or knowledge about the topic, or their interest in the topic (see Chapter 4). However, we do ask the instructor about such things as length of paper, typing specifications, and conventions he or she expects us to follow. From our investigation we find that the paper should be no less than five pages but no more than ten pages in length, be double-spaced, and include footnotes at the end and a bibliography of all sources used.

Having the audience's expectations clearly defined, we can now consider our format and overall purpose. To clarify our purpose as it relates to our topic and audience, we use the test frame introduced and discussed in Chapter 4.

My purpose is to ____(purpose)____   to___(audience)___
(about/that) _____(topic)_____.

Using the test frame in our present context might yield:

My purpose is to *describe* to *my instructor* the *present family practices by Israelis in collective and cooperative settlements.*

Again, this adds focus and clarity to our task. We now know exactly what we want to accomplish and why. This established, we can concern ourselves with specifics, the first of which is the format we want the paper to take.

In choosing a format we must decide which one fits our topic and purpose best. When limiting the topic we decided to describe two types of settlements, collective and cooperative. This seems to lend itself to a comparison-and-contrast format. But recall that comparison-and-contrast formats have a number of variations. They can be organized around subjects (collective vs. cooperative settlements) or they can be organized around charactertistics on which the subjects are to be compared. Using our topic, a

subject-oriented comparison-and-contrast format might have the
following outline:

    Introduction
    Subject 1: collective settlements
        Characteristic 1
        Characteristic 2
        Characteristic 3
    Subject 2: cooperative settlements
        Characteristic 1
        Characteristic 2
        Characteristic 3
    Conclusion

Rather arbitrarily we decide that we want to use such an overall
organizational plan or scheme. This means that we will discuss the
characteristics of each type of Israeli family settlement separately.

This decided, we now try to fill in some parts of the outline. We
know we will need an introductory statement but will wait until
after we have put thought to paper before considering one. We also
know the two subjects we will be discussing—cooperative and
collective settlements. But other than this we have very little
knowledge about the topic. Our lack of specifics point to a need to
begin collecting information.

Collecting Information

As was mentioned in Chapter 5, collecting information for a
research paper usually begins in the library with the *Reader's
Guide to Periodical Literature*. We begin our library search by
consulting the most current *Reader's Guide* (they are published
monthly) under the heading "Families." We find a number of
articles listed under that topic, but most are not relevant to our
topic. Most entries are like the following:

    Child spacing and birth order effect on intellectual ability in
    two-child families. L. Belmont and others, bibl, il. *Science*,
    202:995-996 D'78

The heading "Families" is far too general, and our chances of
finding an articles on family practices in collective or cooperative
settlements are quite small. Consequently, we try consulting the
more specific topic "Collective settlements." Under this heading
we find that the *Reader's Guide* lists a subtopic entitled "Collective

Settlements in Israel." This is precisely what we want. Searching through a few more volumes under this subtopic soon produces an article that looks as though it might yield useful information:

Leisure on the Kibbutz, R. Ronen. *Parks and Rec*, 12, 18-20, Je '77

Continuing the search in this same fashion produces a number of articles that appear related to our topic:

Institution of the family is alive and well on the Kibbutz. L. Y. Ratken, bibl, il. *Psychology Today*, 66-70m F'76

Life on a volcano: Meron Golan Kibbutz. T. Smith, il, *N.Y. Times Mag*, p14-15+, Mr 14 '76

To take the heritage: Israel's biblical right: Gush Eumunim settlement. T. Pristin. *Nation*, 223:233-7 S 18'76

The history of the Mash Hermain Kibbutz. T. Ribull, *Nation*, 245:255-9 F F 6'75

Because we have found each of these articles listed under the subtopic "Collective Settlements in Israel," we are fairly sure they are related to our topic. Performing the same search procedure with the subtopic "Cooperative Settlements" yields the following set of articles:

Life in Israel's Coop settlements. B. Fenlon, *Society* 78:45-60 Sp'78

A model of harmony: the Golan Misha cooperative settlement, R. Goldstein, bibl il, *Middle East Mag*, 90: 23-9 F'76

The success of the alternative way of life. B. Gotlieb and others, *Nation*, 233: 78-82, Je 15'75

We now have a number of articles that will probably provide useful information. We could stop looking at this point or continue our search in the card catalogue. We decide to look further and consult the card file to identify books on the topic. We first enter the subject card file under the topic "Families" and have the same lack of success we had when we used that topic in the *Reader's Guide:* We find a large number of books on the topic, all of which are too general. Again we try the topic "Collective Settlements," but this time we find nothing. We try the topic "Kibbutz" (an alternative name, we have learned, for collective settlements) and have success. We identify a number of books on that topic, two of which look especially pertinent:

> *Kibbutz: Venture in Utopia.* Spiro, Melford E., New York, Schocken Books, (1970), xxii, 266

> *The Kibbutz Experience.* Criden, Yoset, 1916—, New York, Schocken Books, (1976), vii, 208

Searching still further yields some books about cooperative settlements. These identified, we conclude the process of identification of sources.

The next step is to locate those sources in the library and begin reading and recording information. It is at this stage that a great deal of judgment must be used. On any given topic you can usually find a large number of articles and books that relate to that topic. How, then, do we know which information to record when we begin taking notes? Certainly not all the facts contained in three books and eight articles will be used in a five-page research paper. This is where the planning we have done for our paper begins to pay off. We know that we want to write a comparative essay in which we discuss different characteristics of the two types of settlements. Hence, when initially skimming the material in the sources we have identified, we will be looking primarily for characteristics of these types of settlements. Knowing this gives some direction and focus to our reading. We now know what information to skip and what information to take notes on.

Taking Notes

Assume, now, that we begin taking notes by reading the article "To take the heritage: Israel's biblical right." We first find the appropriate volume and issue of the magazine *Nation* in our library. When reading any of the sources we have identified, we will have to record pertinent information and keep track of the source of that information so that we can cite it, if necessary. Hence we must code each note we take as to the source from which it came. One commonly used method of coding notes is to identify each major source by a Roman numeral. Using our sources we might assign the following Roman numerals as indicators of major sources:

I "The institution of the family is alive and well"
II "Life on a volcano"
III "To take the heritage"

When reading and take notes on source I, all we need do, given this coding system, is to put a large *I* on the note, and we can immediately identify which article or book it came from. It is also a good idea to number each note consecutively with an arabic numeral. Thus some of the notes taken from the third source ("To take the heritage") might resemble those found in Example 10-1.

Example 10-1	
III/1 kibbutz definition	a form of collective settlement first founded in the state of Israel in 1941 (p. 233)
III/2 early kibbutz settlements	young unattached settlers primarily immigrants from central Europe (p. 237)
III/3 kibbutz size	usually between 1,000 and 2,000 members (p. 234)
III/4 general characteristics	members agree to subordinate their personal interests to the attainment of communal goals and to seek self-expression only through service to community—at least this was an initial belief of most settlements (p. 236)
III/5 early attitude toward families	from its conception the kibbutz movement realized the risk of conflicting loyalties and set out to curtail family obligations—consequently it took over many traditional family functions (p. 235)
III/6 early devices used to lessen family influence	a) members of family not assigned to same place of work b) all meals were taken in community dining room sometimes called a refectory c) families looked after their

	own rooms but had few other responsibilities (p. 236)
III/7 child rearing in early kibbutz	a) care and rearing of children fell to kibbutz not to family b) children spent time with parents and siblings in off hours (p. 234)
III/8 present kibbutz attitudes	emphasis has shifted from recruitment of volunteers to expansion from within—consequently, there is a need to reinforce the family unit as a provider of new members (p. 234)
III/9 changed attitude toward family	family has now regained some of its lost housekeeping functions a) meals are more of a family function b) maintenance of domicile is more of a family function (p. 237)
III/10 present attitudes toward child rearing	parents now take a more active role than before a) supervise their own children b) spend more time with children (p. 236)
III/11 general present-day characteristics	even with changed attitude toward family, basic orientation must still be considered antifamilistic. (p. 237)

As Example 10-1 illustrates, it is necessary to identify the page from which each note was taken (this helps when you want to cite the source for a particular fact) and to label each note as to the general idea or characteristic it relates to ("kibbutz size," "general characteristics"). Shortly we will see that this is a great aid in the actual writing of a paper.

When you have read through all of your sources, you will have a large number of facts and bits of information, each coded as to its source and each labeled as to the general idea to which it relates. The next step is to put these facts together in some coherent fashion which is in keeping with the overall organizational format selected. For this particular paper we know that we want to begin by discussing characteristics of collective settlements and then discuss those same characteristics for cooperative settlements. It would seem logical, then, to organize our notes by characteristics.

Sorting the Information

One efficient way of doing this, especially if notes are taken on index cards, is to use a sorting approach, which is a variation of the group-and-label technique discussed in chapters 3 and 5. This simply means that we will sort through our notes (index cards) and put them into piles based on characteristics. This is where labeling each note can help. The first sorting might be to separate the notes into two piles: those about collective settlements and those about cooperative settlements. The next might be to take all the notes about collective settlements and try to establish piles representing the characteristics they discuss. We might find that we can sort all the cards on collective settlements into four smaller piles representing four characteristics:

1. present and past attitudes towards families in general
2. present and past attitudes toward children
3. current attitudes toward sex
4. current attitudes toward the state

We would then follow the same sorting procedure for the pile of cards on cooperative settlements. Doing this, we might identify five piles representing five characteristics about cooperative settlements:

1. attitudes toward sex
2. attitudes toward the family
3. attitudes toward the United States
4. attitudes toward children
5. financial considerations within the settlements

Having done this, we could compare the characteristics for the two types of settlements, specifically looking for similar characteristics. The sorting has produced three overlapping areas:

1. attitudes toward the family in general
2. attitudes toward child rearing
3. attitudes toward sex

If we wished to, we could go back to the library and try to fill in the gaps by collecting more information, but let's assume that we feel comfortable with what we already have. We have the necessary information to begin writing, and that information is roughly organized according to our overall organizational format. The outline for our overall comparison-and-contrast format might now be written as:

Introduction: Statement about what our purpose is
Subject 1: collective settlements
  Characteristic 1: attitudes toward the family
  Characteristic 2: attitudes toward children
  Characteristic 3: attitudes toward sex
Subject 2: cooperative settlements
  Characteristic 1: attitudes toward the family
  Characteristic 2: attitudes toward children
  Characteristic 3: attitudes toward sex
Conclusion

We can begin to "put thought to paper."

Putting Thought to Paper

Given the preparation we have done, putting thought to paper should be a relatively easy task. Because we have all our information sorted by characteristics for our two subjects, all we need to do now is reword that information. Following our overall format, we will begin with the characteristic of attitudes toward the family for collective settlements.

Looking over the pile for that particular characteristic we see that we have the following notes that we can use:

Major source I
  Notes 2, 5, 6, 8, 9, 10, 11, 14, 17
Major source II
  Notes 9, 10, 11, 12, 16

Major source III
   Notes 4, 5, 6, 9, 11
Major source IV
   Notes 1, 7, 9, 11, 14, 15, 17
Major source V
   Notes 1, 7, 9, 11, 15, 16, 18, 20

We now have to translate these notes into a coherent whole. We must also decide which notes to use and which to discard. One of the best ways of doing this is to carefully read over a given pile of notes and then put them aside for awhile. This break allows the subconscious to sift and organize the random pile of facts. The next step is to arrange the note cards into a logical sequence and to follow that sequence to write the section of the paper. The reason for putting the notes aside for a short time follows the self 1, self 2 model of the mind discussed in Chapter 2. Reading over the notes allows self 2 (the subconscious) to recall the information. Putting the notes aside allows the subconscious to process and organize the information. Once the information is processed then the writing can take place smoothly.

The result of using this procedure to write the first draft of the section of our paper on attitudes toward the family within collective settlements might have produced the writing in Example 10-2.

Example 10-2

Attitudes toward the family have changed somewhat in collective Israeli settlements since their initiation in 1941. Initially the underlying operating principle of a kibbutz was that each member agree to subordinate his or her personal interest to the common good of the settlement. Self-expression and actualization were supposedly achieved only through service to the community. Consequently there was a move to deemphasize or eliminate some seemingly innocent practices that are actually strong bonding agents within a family. For example, collectives discouraged family meals and instead required all members of the community to eat in a common cafeteria or refectory. They also lessened parental control of children and placed a great deal of authority for discipline and decision making in the hands of the community leaders. In time, however, this initial hard-line stance against the family unit changed and softened. In modern-day kibbutzim, the family unit is considered an important and integral part of the functioning of the community. Family meals are encouraged and even necessary. The disciplining of children is left primarily in the hands of the family unit, with the most authority going to the father or the oldest male within the unit. Despite these changes, however, kibbutzim, even today, can be considered nonfamilistic in their orientation and certainly in their philosophy.

Revising

We will then repeat this procedure (reading over the notes and then putting the information in order) for each section of the paper to produce a first draft of the entire research paper. This, then, would complete the spontaneous phase of writing. This accomplished, we proceed to revise the paper for gaps in logic. There are three parts to this process (see Chapter 6):

1. putting in introductory and concluding statements and making sure that the relationships between sentences are clear
2. paragraphing
3. revising for fragments and run-ons

Looking for fragments and run-ons requires a quick reading through the paper. Usually after this is done it is fairly easy to write the introduction and conclusion to the paper because the paper in its entirety is fresh in your mind. In papers of considerable length it is sometimes helpful within the introduction to explain the format of a paper and the sections it contains. This tells the reader what to expect. For our paper we might use the following introduction:

> In this paper I will compare collective and cooperative settlements in Israel on three characteristics relative to the general issue of family practices. Those characteristics are:
> 1. attitudes toward the family unit
> 2. attitudes toward child rearing
> 3. attitudes toward sex
> In the first section of the paper I will discuss these three characteristics in collective settlements. In the second section I will discuss them as they relate to cooperative settlements.

Such an introduction would establish a frame of reference for the reader and make the paper more comprehensible.

The next step, paragraphing, can be accomplished without actually retyping or rewriting the first draft. Most people simply read over what they have written and put in the symbol ¶ if they feel a new paragraph is needed. They also write in transitional phrases and sentences and mark intersentence relationships while they are paragraphing.

This brings up an important practical point to consider when writing your first draft (the result of the spontaneous phase of writing). It is much easier to revise if you leave room to do so in your first draft: triple space (when typing) or skip two lines (when writing) in the first draft. This usually ensures that there is enough room to signify paragraphs, add transitions, and even expand and revise for vocabulary and for mechanics when these stages of revision are reached. Thus, we have to type or write a paper only twice—once to get ideas down on paper and revise those ideas for the various aspects of writing discussed in chapters 1 through 9, and the second time to produce the finished product.

To illustrate revising for gaps in logic (fragments/run-ons, introduction/conclusion, paragraphing/transitions) let us consider our first draft for characteristic #1 of collective settlements. Revising this for gaps in logic might produce the draft found in Example 10-3.

Example 10-3

Attitudes toward the family have changed somewhat in collective Israeli settlements (called a *kibbutz* or *kibbutzim*, plural) since their initiation in 1941. Initially the operating principle of a kibbutz was that each member agree to subordinate his or her personal interest to the common good of the settlement. Self-expression and actualization were supposedly achieved only through service to the community.

From its initiation, the kibbutz or collective settlement movement realized the danger of a strong family unit to the functioning of a community. Consequently, there was a move to deemphasize or eliminate some seemingly innocent practices that are strong bonding agents within a family. For example, collectives discouraged family meals and instead required all members of the community to eat in a common cafeteria or refectory. They also lessened parental control of children and placed a great deal of authority for discipline and decision making in the hands of the community leaders.

In time, this initial hard-line position against the family unit changed and softened. In modern-day kibbutzim, the family unit is considered an important and integral part of the functioning of the community. Family meals are encouraged and considered necessary. The disciplining of children is left primarily in the hands of the family unit, with most authority going to the father or the oldest male within the unit. Despite these changes, however, Kibbutzim even today can be considered nonfamilistic in their orientation and certainly in their philosophy.

Expansion and Reduction

We can now turn our attention to the process of expanding and reducing. We calculate the Sentence Complexity Index of our paper and find it to be 16.75. We take this as an indication that we have used enough ideas per sentence. However, in reading over the paper we decide that some ideas need to be emphasized. We accomplish this by expanding on the ideas that need emphasis. This has the effect of lengthening the paper considerably. If the original draft was 6½ pages long, the expansion process might lengthen it by a page and one half or two pages.

One particular type of expansion that occurs frequently in research papers is the use of citations and direct quotes. The purpose of a research paper is to state information about a particular topic in a new fashion. If some of the information you mention is not common knowledge, it is necessary to tell the reader what the source for that information was. For example, if we wrote the statement "Some cows are black," there would be no need to explain where we obtained such information—it's common knowledge; the source can be considered life experience. However, suppose we wrote the statement, "It has been estimated that the human brain can store an amount of information equivalent to one hundred trillion words." That is not common knowledge, and because it is not, we are required to tell the reader where we obtained this fact. We would do so by placing a footnote or reference number at the end of the statement and then citing the source in a footnote (at the bottom of the page) or in a note at the end of the paper (endnote). (We will discuss the format of notes at the end of this section.) Consequently, when reading over a research paper to expand and reduce it, ask yourself: "Should I tell the reader where I obtained this information?"

A yes answer to this question indicates that you should put a reference number next to the information in question and then cite the source. But this does not in itself expand the paper. Expansion via citation is accomplished when you back up or validate what you have said by quoting an authoritative source. For example, assume we made the following statement in a paper: "The reading ability of students in America has increased over the last ten years." If we wanted to validate this statement, we could do so by quoting some authority who also believes this fact and has made statements to the same effect. As a hypothetical example, we might find that in a recent speech given by the president of the International Reading Association the following was said:

The fact that reading ability is improving in general across the nation is supported by many studies reported at our recent convention. The highest gains seem to be coming from individuals who live in urban areas with a low socioeconomic status. Possible reasons for this are the increased knowledge of teachers about the reading process and the best methods of capitalizing on that process to teach beginning and remedial reading.

Thus to validate our statement that the reading ability of students has increased over the last ten years we could insert the statement above into our paper and cite the source. Our paper might then read:

The reading ability of students in America has increased over the last ten years. This fact is supported by a recent statement by John Guglioni, current president of the International Reading Association, made at a press conference after the organization's convention in Atlanta. Mr. Guglioni said:

The fact that reading ability is improving in general across the nation is supported by many studies reported at our recent convention. The highest gains seem to be coming from individuals who live in urban areas with a low socioeconomic status. Possible reasons for this are the increased knowledge of teachers about the reading process and the best methods of capitalizing on that process to teach beginning and remedial reading.[8]

Of course we do not have to quote our source directly. We could have paraphrased what he said and inserted that paraphrase directly into the text. In such a case we would have still been obliged to place a reference number at the end of the paraphrased information and then give proper credit in our footnotes.

When a direct quotation is used it should correspond exactly with the original in wording, spelling, capitalization, and punctuation. A short prose quotation is incorporated into the test of the paper and enclosed in double quotation marks. However, if the prose quotation is two or more sentences in length, it should be set off from the text via the use of single spacing and indented in its entirety four spaces from the left-hand margin with no quotation marks at the beginning or end.

Regardless of whether you use direct quotes or paraphrases to validate statements, they are an effective method of expanding. Expanding via quotations using our discussion of the first characteristics for collective settlements might produce the draft found in Example 10-4.

Example 10-4

Attitudes toward the family have changed somewhat in collective Israeli settlements (called a *kibbutz* or *kibbutzim*, plural) since their initiation in 1941. This is evidenced by a recent statement from Jacob Hart, who spent two years on a kibbutz in the 1940s and recently revisited the same community. About his experience, he said: "The importance of the family as a legitimate part of the community has definitely been established. In fact, at that particular kibbutz, the general attitude toward the family has changed one hundred and eighty degrees."[1]

Initially, the operating principle of a kibbutz was that each member agreed to subordinate his or her personal interest to the common good of the settlement. Self-expression and actualization were supposedly achieved only through service to the community.[2]

From its initiation, the kibbutz or collective settlement movement realized the danger of a strong family unit to the functioning of a community. Consequently, there was a move to deemphasize or eliminate some seemingly innocent practices that are strong bonding agents. For example, collectives discouraged family meals and instead required all members of the community to eat in a common cafeteria or refectory. They also lessened parental control of children and placed a great deal of authority for discipline and decision making in the hands of the community leaders. Again, a statement by Hart illustrates this point.

In the early days children obtained their direction primarily from those adults assigned to the care and raising of the young ones. Parents saw their children at night and of course were very loving and close to them. However, they did not, in general, provide a strong hand in the disciplining of their children. Instead they left that function to the previously mentioned adults. This is not to say that children didn't respect and admire their parents. Children simply did not look upon them as dispensers of discipline.[3]

Gradually, however, the view of the family has changed within the kibbutzim . . . .

Mechanics

Expansion and reduction completed, we can now revise for vocabulary. We do so by looking for overused words and for words used improperly. We should also make sure that our terminology is appropriate for our audience, the instructor, and that all unusual terms are defined. This completed, we turn our attention to grammar, usage, and mechanics. We do this by reading our paper aloud, paying specific attention to the structure of sentences and

-1-

INTRODUCTION

_____

_____
_____
_____

COLLECTIVE SETTLEMENTS

Attitudes Toward Family

_____

_____
_____
_____

-2-

_____
_____
_____
_____

Attitudes Toward Child Rearing

_____

_____
_____
_____
_____

_____
_____

the agreement between subjects and verbs and pronouns and antecedents. We also keep an eye out for mechanics errors.

When a research paper is very long, it is sometimes advisable to use headings and subheadings to mark the divisions within the paper. For example, in our paper we have two major divisions, representing our two subjects, collective settlements and cooperative settlements. These two divisions could logically become major headings. Major headings are usually capitalized and centered on the page. For each major heading of the paper there are three minor sections that should probably receive minor headings. Those are signified by typing the heading close to the left-hand margin, capitalizing all important words in the heading, and underlining. Use of headings and subheadings gives an essay an effective visual organization (see page 233).

Adding Footnotes and References

Now the paper is ready for the final touches. These include writing the footnotes, the bibliography, and the title page. Any time you use a direct quote or a paraphrase, you must cite the source from which it came. Citations are handled either through the use of footnotes at the bottom of the page or endnotes at the end of a paper.

The convention for using footnotes is to draw a line twenty spaces long beginning at the left-hand margin under the last line of the text. Then, under this line, type the footnotes, single spaced, in the same order as they appear on the particular page. If endnotes are used, all notes are typed on one page in the same format that would be used if they were footnotes. That page is then inserted at the end of the paper immediately following the last page of the text.

With some exceptions, the information in a footnote or note will contain the elements listed below. Although not every footnote entry will include all items mentioned, it is appropriate to maintain the order given even if elements are omitted.

The sequence of elements when citing a book is:

1. Name of the author or authors, first name first
2. Title of book
3. Name of editor or translator, if any
4. Name of series in which the book appears, if any, and volume number in the series.
5. Facts of publication, including:
   a. total number of volumes, if relevant
   b. number of editions, if other than the first
   c. place of publication

 d. name of publisher
 e. date of publication
6. Page number of quotation

The sequence of information used when citing a periodical article is:

1. Name of author or authors, first name or initial first
2. Title of the article
3. Name of periodical in which article appears
4. Volume and number of the periodical
5. Date of volume or issue
6. Page numbers on which quotation appears

To illustrate how to cite books, articles, and other sources of information, we have listed some examples:

One-author book
 [1]G. Fraenkel, *Writing Systems* (Boston: Ginn and Company, 1965), pp. 202-207.

Two-author book
 [2]M. I. Freedman and M. D. Gowls, *Teaching Reading and Thinking Skills* (New York: Longman, 1980), pp. 101–105.

More than two authors
 [3]D. Burton, et al., *Teaching English Today* (Boston: Houghton Mifflin, 1975), pp. 193–208.

A book with several editions
 [4]W. G. Campbell, *Form and Style in Thesis Writing* (3rd ed.; Boston: Houghton Mifflin, 1969), pp. 202–207.

An edited book
 [5]R. W. Bailey and J. L. Robinson, eds., *Varieties of Present Day English* (New York: Macmillan, 1973), pp. 3–5.

A translation
 [6]P. R. Samuels, *The Logic of Mathematical Principles*, trans. Hector J. Kaet (Munich: Franken and Co., 1962), p. 46.

A work in several volumes
 [7]G. B. Harrison, ed., *Modern British Writers, Vol. 2* (New York: Harcourt, Brace & World, 1959), pp. 14–19.

Article in a professional journal

[8]C. R. Miller, "A Humanistic Rationale for Technical Writing," *College English*, Vol. 40, No. 6 (Feb. 1979), 20–30.

Article from a weekly magazine

[9]P. Ashlock, "Losing Search for a Winner," *Sports Illustrated*, Vol. 50, (May 28, 1979), 36-40, 17-26.

Article from a monthly magazine

[10]C. L. Sanders, "Are Superstars Forgetting Their Roots?" *Ebony*, Vol. 34 (May 1979), 54–56.

Newspaper article

[11]D. Adelman, "Subway Failures Last Year Called Worst in Decade," *New York Times*, January 31, 1980, sec. B., p. 1.

Editorial

[12]"The Peashooter War on Inflation," Editorial, *New York Times*, January 31, 1980, sec. A, p. 22.

Essay in a collection

[13]S. Appleton, "Perceiving Resemblances," in *Writing Exercises from Exercise Exchange*, ed. G. Keps (New York: Fenton Press, 1965), p. 23.

Interview

[14]M. Cope, personal interview with Terry Bradshaw, Pittsburg, Pennsylvania, January 28, 1980.

If you cite an author and title more than once, you need only identify the author's last name and the page number for the second reference:

[15]Appleton, p. 104.

To cite a previously cited author for whom you have already referenced more than one book or article, provide the author and title of the book or article for successive references:

[16]Newman, *Strickly Speaking*, p. 83.
[17]Newman, *A Civil Tongue*, p. 82.

Following these citation procedures with our sample essay would produce the list of notes in Example 10-5.

Example 10-5

NOTES

[1]R. Ronen, "Leisure on the Kibbutz," *Parks and Recreation,* Vol. 12 (June 1977), 18.

[2]T. Pristin, "To Take the Heritage: Israel's Biblical Right: Gush Emunim Settlement," *Nation,* Vol. 223 (Sept. 18, 1976), 224.

[3]Ronen, p. 19.

[4]B. Fenlon, "Life in Israel's Coop Settlements," *Society,* Vol. 78 (Spring 1978), 46.

[5]B. Gotlieb, "The Success of the Alternative Way of Life," *Nation,* Vol. 233

[6]C. Yoset, *The Kibbutz Experience,* (2nd ed.; New York: Schocken Books, 1976), p. 201.

[7]Fenlon, p. 47.

[8]M.E. Spiro, Kibbutz: Venture in Utopia (New York: Schocken Books, 1970), p. 202.

[9]Yoset, p. 230.

[10]Pristin, p. 227.

The bibliography is the last section of a paper; its purpose is to list the sources used in writing. Even if you did not use a quotation from a source, include the source in your bibliography if you obtained information from it. If your bibliography is short, list all sources in alphabetical order without making any distinction among the different types. However, if your bibliography is long, classify the entries. For example, it is a common practice to divide a bibliography into sections, such as books, periodicals, dissertations, book and movie reviews, newspapers, yearbooks, collections of essays. The information included in a bibliographic reference and the order in which the information appears is basically the same for bibliographies as it is for footnotes, but there are differences in typing conventions between the two forms of citations. Footnotes present the author's name in its natural order: first name first. In a bibliography, the author's name is presented with the surname first.

The primary purpose of a footnote or reference is to give the specific location of a source of information; consequently, page numbers are always included in footnotes. The primary purpose of a bibliography is to identify an entire work, as distinct from a specific part. For our sample essay, the bibliography might resemble that in Example 10-6.

Example 10-6

BIBLIOGRAPHY

Periodicals

Fenlon, B. "Life in Israel's Coop Settlements." *Society,* Vol. 78 (Spring 1978), 45–60.

Goldstein, R. "A Model of Harmony: The Golan Misha Cooperative Settlement," *Middle East Magazine,* Vol. 90 (February 1976), 23–29.

Gotlieb, B., et al. "The Success of the Alternative Way of Life." *Nation,* Vol. 233 (June 15, 1975), 78-82.

Pristin, T. "To Take the Heritage: Israel's Biblical Right: Gush Emunim Settlement." *Nation,* Vol. 233 (September 18, 1976), 233–237.

Ratken, L. Y. "The Institution of the Family is Alive and Well on the Kibbutz." *Psychology Today,* Vol. 9 (February 1976), 66–70.

Ribull, T. "The History of the Mash Hermain Kibbutz." *Nation,* Vol. 245 (February 6, 1975), 245–259.

Ronen, R. "Leisure on the Kibbutz." *Parks and Recreation,* Vol. 12, (June 1977), 18–20.

Smith, T. "Life on a Volcano: Meron Golan Kibbutz." *New York Times Magazine,* March 14, 1976, Sec. B, 14–15.

Books

Blackwell, C. *The History of Cooperative Settlements in the Middle East.* 2nd ed. Boston: Houghton Mifflin, 1969.

Spiro, M. E. *Kibbutz: Venture in Utopia.* New York: Schocken Books, 1970.

Yoset, C. *The Kibbutz Experience.* 2nd ed. New York: Schocken Books, 1976.

Our final task is the title page. Title pages for research papers and reports usually consist of the name of the university or college centered at the top of the page, followed by the title of the paper. This is followed by the title of the course, the date, and finally your

name. A sample title page for our paper is presented in Example
10-7.

Example 10-7

SEATTLE UNIVERSITY

A Comparison of Family Practices within
Present-Day Israeli Cooperative
and Collective Settlements

Sociology 113

April 2, 1981

Richard Mosquetta

The paper is now complete and ready to be submitted. Given the
systematic approach we have taken in writing it, we can be fairly
sure that it is of high quality. It will certainly be logical, readable,
and polished—qualities that generally are the prime requisites of a
research paper.

SUMMARY

In this chapter we have attempted to draw together the information
presented in chapters 1 through 9 within the context of a research
paper. If any of the steps in the process seemed confusing it is
perhaps an indication that you should reread the chapter in which
that information is presented. It is important to keep in mind that
the process presented here is not meant to be a model for the way
everyone should write a research paper. It is simply one model.
Most writers have a system that works for them. Of course, this is
the ideal; a system of writing that is specific to you. The
information and process presented in this text should serve as a
springboard which will help you identify your own personal
method of writing.

CHAPTER ELEVEN

WRITING THE ESSAY EXAM

In this chapter we will briefly discuss one final type of writing commonly encountered in college and university settings—the essay examination. Most instructors and professors prefer to utilize essay examinations when testing students' knowledge, because essay examinations allow a flexible response. Usually a question's difficulty increases with the range of possible responses. In an essay answer a student is required to recall bits of information and integrate that information into a coherent whole.

The essay examination constitutes a specific type of writing with its own vocabulary, its own specific constraints, and its own problems. It is a form of writing that can be studied, practiced, and mastered. Unfortunately many students perform poorly on essay examinations, not because they don't know the material but because they are unskilled at taking such examinations. In this chapter we will consider three aspects of writing answers to essay exam questions: (1) preparing for an essay exam; (2) reviewing an essay examination; and (3) writing and revising essay examination answers.

PREPARING FOR AN ESSAY EXAMINATION

In all writing situations there must be some mental input before any mental output can be expected: We must put information into the mind before we can expect to produce anything. In writing essays, research papers, and stories, the input phase usually consists of collecting information from the library, life experience, interviews, and such. The input component of taking an essay examination, however, consists of studying for the test. This usually involves a review of notes taken on class lectures and information presented in the texts for the course.

Even more important than the review of notes, though, is their organization. In an essay exam situation, the examinee is put on the spot. Consider what is required of you in such a situation. You must first interpret the questions. You then must identify the information you have stored in your memory that relates to the questions. You then must determine the manner in which you will present that information and translate it into a short written composition that is brief, logical, and covers all necessary details. And all of this must be done within a given amount of time.

A key component in the process is the recall of pertinent information. This is where organizing one's study notes becomes relevant in preparing for an exam. Most memory theorists believe that the ease with which we can recall information is directly related to the manner in which we have organized that information in our minds. If information is organized and stored in a meaningful way, it will be recalled easily. If information is stored with no apparent logic or order but rather in a random or haphazard way, however, it will be difficult to recall. To illustrate this, consider the twelve numerals below. Look at them closely for a period of five seconds and then cover them with a piece of paper and continue reading:

1   4   9   2   1   9   7   6   2   0   0   1

Now, without looking back at those numbers, try to remember them. Unless you have a very good visual memory, you will probably find that you can't remember all of them. This is because they represent twelve isolated bits of information. Let us now try to organize that information in a meaningful way and see if that helps our recall. The first four numbers (1492) represent the year Columbus sailed to America; the second four (1976) are the year of the Bicentennial, and the last four (2001) are the name of a once-popular science fiction movie. Given this organization, you can now recall those twelve digits easily. The best insurance you can have that you will recall information in a test situation is to organize that information into meaningful units while preparing for the exam. Of course, what is meaningful varies from individual to individual, making the process of organizing notes a highly individual task. Hence there is no such thing as an organization scheme that is *best* for recall purposes. There are some that are commonly used, however.

One of the simplest and most useful organizational schemes is that of major ideas and supporting details. We discussed such an organizational scheme in Chapter 5 when we considered the planning phase of writing. You can use this scheme to organize study notes by first identifying the major concepts your study notes cover. For example, when studying for an exam in a basic accounting course you might decide that the information on which you will be tested covers eight major concepts:

> different types of accountants
> accounting transactions
> construction of account statements
> exchange of assets
> income statements
> accounting ratios
> auditing
> budgeting

The major concepts identified, the next step is to list the supporting details related to those concepts. The supporting information for the first two major concepts above might be:

> Different types of accountants
>> Industrial accountants: employed by big business firms—sometimes called commercial accountants—job is to draw up important financial statements and solve a variety of managerial problems.
>>
>> Government accountants: work for federal, state, and local government agencies—primary task is to handle financial data in organizations that do not seek a profit at a primary goal.
>>
>> Certified public accountants: called CPAs—guardians of accounting principles and procedures—employed primarily in public accounting firms and specialize in verifying the financial records of business and nonprofit organizations.

Tax accountants: familiar with the intricacies of both federal and state tax laws—aid business and individuals in their tax planning programs and in the preparation of tax returns.

Accounting Transactions
An accounting transaction involves any activity that has an immediate and measurable financial impact on a firm.
e.g.: decrease in physical or financial capital
increase in financial obligations

Transactions may be either internal or external
internal transactions are confined to the business itself, e.g., depletion of a firm's inventory or office space
external transactions involve financial relationships between a business and an outside party, e.g., customers, suppliers, nonprofit organizations

For accounting purposes every transaction must be recorded in some fashion
point-of-purchase computer terminal is one way of recording transactions
in small businesses accounting transactions are recorded by hand in journals and ledgers.

When organizing information for a test it is advisable to outline that information in a fashion similar to that above. Minor concepts and supporting details can be indented under the major ideas to which they relate. This provides an excellent visual diagram of your organizational scheme.

The organization process in itself will usually help fix needed information in your memory and make it much easier to recall such information in a test situation. However, some people go one step further and employ some type of memorization technique to help them recall information quickly and efficiently. Most people, without being aware of it, use the worst type of memory technique—rehearsal. When you try to memorize something by rehearsal, you read over the information a number of times in an effort to drill that information into your mind. Given enough repetitions (rehearsals) this technique will work, and you will be able to recall the material in a test situation. However, the process is time consuming, and its effects are not long lasting. A much more efficient and long-lasting memory scheme is *visualization*.

Visualization, as the name implies, involves the mental picturing of what you are trying to memorize. In the case of the first major concept for the accounting exam, we might use the following mental images. We had identified four types of accountants:

industrial, government, CPAs, tax accountants. Using visualization to help us remember these four types and the characteristics of each means drawing a mental picture of each type of accountant that includes all the information we wanted to remember for that particular type. For example, for the industrial accountant we might mentally picture an accountant walking out of a factory (to symbolize industry). He or she might be carrying a briefcase with the titles "industrial accountant" and "commercial accountant" printed on it, to remind us that such accountants are often referred to by two titles. We would picture the accountant working at a desk on a document that had the words "important financial statement" printed at the top. This would symbolize the fact that one function of the industrial accountant is to work on financial statements. We might then picture our accountant sitting with the president of a large company discussing some problem. This would cue us that solving managerial problems is another task undertaken by industrial accountants.

Similar mental pictures could be constructed for the remaining information within the major concept "types of accountants." This could also be done for the information in the other seven concepts identified as relevant to the test.

Another variation on the visualization theme is to try to picture your notes: to make a mental picture of their physical organization. Then when you are in a test situation you attempt to review the notes by mentally picturing each page. With a great deal of practice this technique can be useful, but it is not nearly as powerful or easy as the visualization technique. Unfortunately, many students initially feel that this method is contrived and juvenile. We feel that students should try the visualization scheme at least once before making a decision about its usefulness.

In general the better you organize the information on which you will be tested, the better able you will be to recall that information in a test situation. We also suggest the use of some visualization memory technique to aid in the retrieval of information. Another common sense examination-preparation technique is proper rest. Cramming before a test is successful only up to a certain point. If you cram to the extent that you enter a test situation tired and overly tense, you might hurt your chances of doing well. Systematic preparation a few nights before an exam, coupled with a good night's rest immediately prior to it, usually produces the most favorable results.

PREVIEWING AN ESSAY EXAM

The previewing of an essay examination usually involves three components: (1) reading the directions carefully, (2) interpreting the questions, and (3) planning answers and budgeting time.

Because of the specified time limit on most essay examinations, many students want to begin writing answers as soon as they receive the test. In doing this it is very easy to ignore important directions that might have a strong influence on what and how you write. For example, you might be given a choice of questions to answer; five questions might be given from which you are to select three. Or the point value might be different from question to question. Being aware of the rules can strongly affect how well you perform.

Perhaps the most important aspect of previewing an exam is the interpretation of the questions. In a pressure situation it is easy to misinterpret a question and write an answer that misses the main point of the question. Most instructors have a specific answer in mind for each question and many expect the answer to be couched in a specific format. Usually you can obtain a fairly good idea of what is expected by looking for specific clues in the essay question. These clues come in the form of instruction words that have precise meanings within the context of the question. Some of those words and their meanings in an essay exam are listed below:

Compare   To compare is to identify similar elements or character-istics of the things being compared. Differences can be mentioned, of course, but the main thrust should be to highlight similarities.

Contrast   To contrast is to state the differences between the subjects under consideration. *Contrast* is the opposite of *compare*.

Criticize   To criticize is to judge strengths and weaknesses against given criteria or standards. The standards must be explicitly stated and defined in the answer. It is a common misconception that criticism includes only the negative aspects of the subject under investigation. Criticism can be quite positive.

Define   A definition is a descriptive listing of the critical elements of the subject being discussed. A definition identifies those elements that make your subject what it is. Details are not essential in a definition, but limitations are.

Diagram For a question that asks you to diagram, you should present a drawing, chart, plan, or graphic representation. Generally the student is expected to label the diagram and in some cases add a brief explanation or description.

Discuss *Discuss* is a general direction word that gives you great freedom in your answer. You probably will be expected to give both the pros and cons of an issue and cover as much ground as possible in your answer. Hence you should try to analyze the subject in as much detail as possible within the time limit provided.

Enumerate This means the same as *list*: List the elements of your answer one by one so that each stands out from the rest. In such cases it is also advisable to number the elements.

Evaluate To evaluate is to determine the truth or utility of something by appraising its worth based on given criteria.

Explain To explain is to provide specific reasons why an event occurred. In such an answer it is best to state the why and how, to reconcile any differences in opinion or experimental results, and, where possible, to state causes. Make plain the conditions that give rise to whatever you are explaining.

Illustrate To illustrate in an essay answer is to clarify or explain by presenting a figure, diagram, or concrete example.

Interpret To interpret means to translate. You are commonly asked to interpret such things as a set of numbers that is the result of an experiment, or an event that is the result of some process. *Interpret* in such situations means to explain what is meant by these results.

Justify To justify is to prove or show grounds for the statements you have made. This is best done by validating your opinion using information that was presented in the text or lecture notes.

Outline An outline is an organizational description. To outline is to list the main points of a given concept and some of the supporting details. An outline answer is often expressed in narrative form and not as an outline per se.

Prove A question that requires proof is one that demands confirmation or verification. In the context of an essay question, *prove* means much the same thing as *justify*. It is customary to prove an answer by citing experimental evidence or by the use of logical reasoning.

Summarize   To summarize is to set down in concise terms the major elements or components of some larger event. Usually details, illustrations, and elaborations are omitted in such answers.

Reading over an essay question with a eye for these specific directive words will usually help you determine exactly what is expected of you. Another way of making sure that you understand a question is to rephrase it in your own words. For example if you received the following question on an essay exam:

Contrast the strategies used by Napoleon and Hitler in their respective assaults on Russia.

you might rephrase it in the following way:

Identify the differences in the strategies used by Napoleon and Hitler when they attempted to invade Russia.

Such a rewording makes clear what the answer should contain and gives valuable direction and focus to your writing.

Planning your answers is the last issue to consider when previewing an examination. When you plan, you must first consider the amount of time you will spend on each question. Second, you must consider the format to utilize in your answers. When determining your time schedule, it is usually best to allot a specific period of time for each question. It is also wise to structure your time so that some will remain at the end of the test for revision and for finishing questions you might not have been able to complete. If you have allocated enough time for revision you will be able to complete it later, and even if you don't finish the question you will benefit in the long run. (Six incomplete answers will usually receive more credit than three complete ones.)

Planning your formats is tantamount to outlining what you are going to say within each answer. As time-consuming as this might sound, it is actually a "time saver" in the final analysis because it allows you to write freely and quickly when actually composing your essay answers. It is also a very good idea to include an introduction and conclusion in your answers. Some students even like to insert an outline of their answer within their introduction. This has the benefit of giving the instructor a concise overview of the answer as well as establishing a clear format for the student to follow when writing.

WRITING AND REVISING ESSAY EXAMINATION ANSWERS

Given appropriate preparation for an essay examination and proper reviewing of the questions, the actual writing of the answers is an easy task. When writing answers, relax and trust that the information you are recording is relevant and accurate. It is also important not to concern yourself greatly with such mechanics as spelling and punctuation. Not that these things are unimportant; however, the time to consider them is during your revision time.

When the first draft of the essay answers is completed, the next step is to read over what you have written to consider logic and mechanics. In most essay exam situations you will not have the luxury of recopying your corrected first draft and handing in a polished final draft. Of course this means that your answers will have words crossed out and inserted, corrections, paragraphs marked using the symbol ¶. It is very common to make the following mistakes when writing under pressure:

1. misspell words
2. omit words or parts of words
3. omit parts of answers
4. miswrite dates and figures (e.g., 1353 written 1953, $.50 written as $50)

Consequently, it is very important to reread your essay answer to find and correct such errors.

SUMMARY

In this chapter we have set forth practical guidelines to aid in the composition of essay examination answers. These include:

1. Prepare for a test well in advance by organizing the information you are to be tested on in some meaningful fashion.

2. If possible, utilize some memorization technique other than rehearsal to facilitate the retrieval of that information in a test situation.

3. Before answering questions on a test, preview the test by reading the directions carefully and making sure that you interpret the questions properly.

4. Before you begin writing, set up a time schedule, plan the format for each answer, and outline each answer mentally.

5. When writing answers, try not to interrupt the flow of ideas, and be confident that you are answering the question well.

6. Revise what you have written before handing it in, paying special attention to logic and mechanical errors.

A Grammar and Usage Handbook

A GRAMMAR AND USAGE HANDBOOK

This section deals with topics directly related to the writing process outlined in chapters 1 through 9. All of these topics do not fall under the headings of grammar or usage per se. The information in this handbook should be considered as reference material that can be used to answer some specific questions that may arise when you are editing a paper or encounter a term with which you are unfamiliar. The subsections in this handbook are:

Parts of speech
Parts of a sentence
Spelling
Capitalization
Punctuation
Commonly confused terms
List of trite expressions

PARTS OF SPEECH

In traditional grammar there are eight parts of speech, all of which function differently within sentences. Those eight parts of speech are:

Nouns
Pronouns
Verbs
Adjectives
Adverbs
Prepositions
Conjunctions
Interjections

In this section we will briefly discuss each part of speech and consider some of the roles they play within sentences.

Nouns

Nouns are traditionally defined as names of persons, places, or things. They can be categorized as proper, common, abstract, or collective. A **proper noun** names a particular person, place, or thing (Jimmy Carter, San Francisco, Orange Bowl). A **common noun** also names a person, place, or thing but does not specify one in particular (man, city, game). An **abstract noun** is a common noun that names qualities or characteristics of people, places, or things (anger, courage, bravery). A **collective noun** is a common noun that refers to groups or collections of persons, places, or things (e.g., army, crowd, group, team).

Nouns can be either singular or plural. Another way of saying this is that nouns have the property of number. Most nouns form their plural by adding s to their singular form. There are, however, many exceptions to this rule. Below some of these exceptions are listed:

1. Nouns ending in s, z, x, ch, and sh add es to the singular to form their plurals: bench, benches; box, boxes; lens, lenses; match, matches; and tax, taxes.

2. Many nouns ending in f or fe change the f to v and add s or es: calf, calves; knife, knives; shelf, shelves; wolf, wolves. However, there are some exceptions. For example: grief, griefs; roof, roofs; waif, waifs.

3. Nouns ending in y preceded by a consonant change y to i and add es to form the plural: army, armies; country, countries; lady, ladies, spy, spies.

4. Nouns ending in y preceded by a vowel form their plurals regularly by adding s: alley, alleys; chimney, chimneys; buoy, buoys; monkey, monkeys; quay, quays.

5. Nouns ending in *o* preceded by a vowel form their plurals by adding *s* to the singular: cameo, cameos; radio, radios; studio, studios; trio, trios.

6. Nouns ending in *o* preceded by a consonant form their plurals by adding *es* to the singular: echo, echoes; hero, heroes; potato, potatoes. There are many exceptions to this rule, however: banjo, banjos; piano, pianos; solo, solos; and soprano, sopranos.

7. Some nouns change from singular to plural by altering the stem of the word instead of adding a suffix: man, men; foot, feet; mouse, mice; tooth, teeth; woman, women.

8. A number of nouns have singular and plural forms alike: corps, deer, salmon, sheep, species, trout.

9. Nouns of Greek origin ending in -*sis* form their plurals by changing *i* to *e*: analysis, analyses; diagnosis, diagnoses; hypothesis, hypotheses; parenthesis, parentheses.

10. Compound nouns usually form their plural by pluralizing the fundamental word of the compound:
    a. The final part of the noun is pluralized when what precedes it describes the final element: footstep, footsteps; workman, workmen.
    b. The first part of the compound is pluralized when the first element of the compound is described by what follows: brother-in-law, brothers-in-law; man-of-war, men-of-war; son-in-law, sons-in-law.
    c. The final part of compound words ending in *ful* are pluralized by adding *s* to *ful*: cupful, cupfuls; handful, handfuls; mouthful, mouthfuls.

Within a sentence nouns can serve a variety of functions:

1. As subject:

   The *storm* struck violently.

2. As direct object:

   The storm destroyed many *homes*.

3. As object of a preposition:

   The storm destroyed everything in its *path*.

4. As indirect object:

The instructor gave the *class* a test.

5. As subjective complement:

Mary is my *friend*.

6. As objective complement:

The student body elected Maryanne *president*.

7. As appositive:

Bill, my best *friend*, is the quarterback on the football team.

8. In direct address:

Bill, are you really going to wear that shirt?

Any word or group of words that acts as a noun within a sentence is called a *nominal*, even though that word or group of words may not contain a noun. Below the nominals in the sample sentences have been italicized:

Jogging slowly is my favorite form of exercise.

Whatever you say is acceptable to me.

Pronouns

A pronoun is a word used in place of a noun. Because a noun is a person, place, or thing, a pronoun refers to a person, place, or thing. The word, phrase, or clause a pronoun takes the place of is called the **antecedent** of the pronoun. Pronouns can be classified as being personal, relative, demonstrative, reflexive, and indefinite.

Personal pronouns refer to persons. Pronouns are classified as first person (*I* or *we*), second person (*you*), and third person (*he, she, it,* or *they*). They are also classified as subject, or nominative (*I*), possessive (*mine*), and object (*me*), depending upon their grammatical function. Nominative pronouns function as subjects and subjective complements:

He is the person responsible. (subject)

It was *she* who called. (subjective complement)

Object pronouns serve as direct and indirect objects and as objects of prepositions:

I like *him* very much. (direct object)

Jane gave *me* a present. (indirect object)

Let's give this to *them.* (object of preposition)

Possessive pronouns show possession:

That book is *mine.*

Ours is the red car.

A **relative pronoun** performs a dual function in a sentence: (1) it takes the place of a noun in the clause it introduces, and (2) it joins and relates that clause to the rest of the sentence. The relative pronoun differs from other pronouns in that its antecedent is always in the preceding clause. By definition, then, a relative pronoun cannot be a part of a simple sentence. Relative pronouns include *that, what, which, whom,* and *who.*

This and *that* (and their plurals *these* and *those*) are **demonstrative pronouns.** Demonstratives designate or point out some definite person, place, or thing. *This* and *these* point to objects near at hand; *that* and *those* point to what is more distant or remote.

This is mine. *These* are yours.

That was my old car. *Those* bills were not paid.

The **reflexive pronouns** are sometimes referred to as compound personal pronouns, because they are formed by adding *self* to the singular and *selves* to the plural forms of the simple personal pronouns. The reflexive pronoun first person singular and plural forms are *myself* and *ourselves.* The second person forms are *yourself* and *yourselves.* The third person forms are *himself, herself,* and *itself* (singular) and *themselves* (plural). Reflexive pronouns can function in the following ways in sentences:

Object of the verb: The candidate praises *himself* too much.

Object of the preposition: We found the children playing by *themselves* in the school yard.

Indirect object: Terry bought *herself* a new car with graduation money.

Predicate nominative: The boss is not quite *himself* this morning.

Indefinite pronouns differ from the personal and relative pronouns in that they do not require definite antecedents. These include *none, everything, anything, something,* and *nothing.* They stand for persons, places, or things that are not clearly identified.

Verbs

A verb expresses action, being, or state of being. Verbs can be classified according to their meaning and according to their form. With respect to meaning, verbs can be categorized as transitive or intransitive as well as auxiliary and linking. With respect to form, verbs are classified as either regular or irregular verbs.

A transitive verb is one that always has an object. With a transitive verb, the action is conceived as going across or passing over from a subject or doer to an object or receiver. The verbs in the following sentences are examples of transitive verbs:

The carpenter carried the boards to the house.

The children rode bicycles down the street.

The woman sold the picture at the auction.

When the subject of the sentence is the actor or doer of the action of the transitive verb, the verb is said to be in the active voice. In the sentences above, all the subjects (carpenter, children, and woman) are doers of the action, and therefore all the verbs are in the active voice. When the subject of a transitive verb receives the action of the verb, the verb is said to be in the passive voice. All three sentences above can be changed to the passive voice by changing the positions of the subject and object, adding *was* or *were* to the verbs, and adding the word *by* to the word that was the subject in the active voice.

The boards were carried to the house by the carpenter.

The bicycles were ridden down the street by the children.

The picture was sold by the woman at the auction.

An intransitive verb either shows no action at all or represents action as limited to the subject. The two pairs of sentences below show the distinction between transitive verbs (*a* sentences) and intransitive verbs (*b* sentences).

1a. The artist paints landscapes.
1b. The artist paints very well.

2a. The man smokes nonfilter cigarettes.
2b. The man smokes too much.

One type of intransitive verb is the linking verb. The chief function of a linking verb is to join the subject of the sentence to some adjective or noun that describes, identifies, or defines the subject. The verb *be* in all of its forms *(be, am, is, are, was, were)* is the most common linking verb. Other verbs employed as linking verbs are *appear, come, become, feel, grow, look, remain, stay, smell, taste,* and *sound.*

Auxiliary verbs (also called helping verbs) assist the main verb in the formation of tense, voice, and mood. A main verb with its helping verbs is called a *verb phrase. Shall* and *will* are auxiliary verbs used with verb forms to designate the future tense. *Do* and *did* are auxiliary verbs used to form the emphatic present and past tenses of verbs (e.g., *do go). Have, has,* and *had* are auxiliary verbs used to form the present and past perfect tense, such as *has talked, have talked,* and *had talked.* The various forms of the verb *be* are also used as auxiliary verbs to form the passive voice.

Another type of auxiliary verb is the modal auxiliary, which is used to form verb phrases indicating different attitudes or aspects of mood. The modal auxiliaries are *may, can, might, could, would, should, ought,* and *might.* The aspects of mood include ability, possibility, obligation, and necessity (e.g., *I may go, I must go,* and *I should go).*

The form of a verb can be classified as either regular or irregular. The classification of verbs as regular or irregular is dependent upon the form of the past tense and past participle of the verb. A regular verb forms its past tense and past participle by adding *ed, d,* or *t* to the present tense of the verb. For example, the following verbs are considered regular:

Present	Past	Past participle
walk	walked	walked
talk	talked	talked
move	moved	moved
burn	burned	burnt

An irregular verb is one that does not form its past tense and past participle by adding *d, ed,* or *t* to the present tense of the verb form. There are many more regular verbs than irregular verbs in our language. Nevertheless, irregular verbs cause writers problems, especially when their past or past participial forms are used. Below is a list of common irregular verbs.

Present	Past	Past participle
be (is, are)	was, were	been
begin	began	begun
bite	bit	bitten
bleed	bled	bled
blow	blew	blown
break	broke	broken
bring	brought	brought
burst	burst	burst
buy	bought	bought
catch	caught	caught
choose	chose	chosen
come	came	come
creep	crept	crept
cut	cut	cut
do	did	done
draw	drew	drawn
drink	drank	drunk
drive	drove	driven
eat	ate	eaten
fall	fell	fallen
feed	fed	fed
feel	felt	felt
fight	fought	fought
find	found	found
flee	fled	fled
fly	flew	flown
forget	forgot	forgotten
forgive	forgave	forgiven
freeze	froze	frozen
get	got	gotten
give	gave	given
go	went	gone
grow	grew	grown
have	had	had
hear	heard	heard
hide	hid	hidden
hold	held	held
keep	kept	kept
know	knew	known
lead	led	led
leave	left	left
lie	lay	lain
lose	lost	lost

Present	Past	Past participle
make	made	made
ride	rode	ridden
ring	rang	rung
rise	rose	risen
say	said	said
see	saw	seen
sell	sold	sold
send	sent	sent
set	set	set
shake	shook	shaken
shrink	shrank	shrunk
sing	sang	sung
sit	sat	sat
sleep	slept	slept
speak	spoke	spoken
spring	sprang	sprung
steal	stole	stolen
sweep	swept	swept
swim	swam	swum
take	took	taken
teach	taught	taught
tear	tore	torn
think	thought	thought
wear	wore	worn
win	won	won
write	wrote	written

Adjectives

An adjective is a word used to modify a noun by describing or defining it. Adjectives can be classified according to meaning as descriptive or definitive. A descriptive adjective names a quality, feature, or characteristic of the noun modified. In the sentences below, the italicized words are descriptive adjectives.

Harry is an *honest* man who should be elected.

The *sour* cherries were not put in the pie.

Superman could leap *tall* buildings.

A definitive adjective limits the application or scope of a noun by specifying quantity or number. Definitive adjectives can be classified in the following ways:

1. Demonstrative adjectives limit a noun by pointing out. Examples of demonstrative adjectives are *this, that, these, both,* and *same: That* house needs painting. *Both* girls were suspended from all activities.

2. Numeral adjectives limit the meaning of nouns by showing how many or in what order things are to be considered. Some examples of numeral adjectives are *one, two, three, first, second, third, few, many,* and *all: Two* robins were seen in the yard this morning. The judge said that he heard the story *many* times.

3. Indefinite adjectives may suggest indefiniteness of quantity and number. Examples of indefinite adjectives are *some, every, much,* and *no: Some* people feel that the only way to curb inflation is through wage and price controls. *Much* effort has been exerted in getting the campaign together.

4. Pronominal adjectives are words that are similar to pronouns and used as modifiers of nouns. Some examples are *my, our, your, which,* and *whatever: Our* house is always open to company. *Your* desk needs to be refinished as soon as possible. *Whatever* money I give you is to be used for food.

All descriptive adjectives and a few definitive adjectives have degrees of comparison. That is, when used to compare objects, the forms of adjectives are changed to show degree of quality, quantity, or relation. The three degrees of comparison are positive, comparative, and superlative.

The positive degree is the simplest form of the adjective and denotes a simple quality, quantity, or relation. There is no special ending for the positive degree of adjectives. The italicized adjectives in the following sentences are in the positive degree:

The *old* man in the park is my grandfather.

Our university is a *liberal* institution.

Tim wants to be a *strong* man in the circus.

The comparative degree denotes an increase of the quality, the quantity, or relation expressed in the positive form. The comparative degree is used when two things are compared. Comparatives are formed by adding er to the positive form of the adjective or by preceding the positive form with the word *more.* The italicized adjectives in the following sentences are in the comparative degree:

My grandfather is *older* than your grandfather.

Jackson is a *more liberal* candidate than Myers.

Tim is *stronger* than Harry.

The superlative degree of adjectives is applied to persons, places, and things possessing a quality or quantity in the highest degree. The superlative degree is used when more than two things are compared. Superlatives are formed by adding *est* to the positive form of the adjective or by preceding the positive form of the adjective with the word *most*. The italicized adjectives in the following sentences are in the superlative degree:

My grandfather is the *oldest* person in the retirement home.

Jackson is the *most liberal* candidate ever elected to the Senate from my state.

Tim is the *strongest* person on our team.

Adverbs

Adverbs are closely related to adjectives. Adverbs differ from adjectives in that they modify verbs, adjectives, and other adverbs, rather than nouns. When classified by meaning, most adverbs can be put into the categories of time, place, manner, degree, and cause.

Adverbs of time may express present time, future time, past time, duration, and frequency. Examples of adverbs expressing present time are *now, immediately, today;* future time, *soon, tomorrow;* past time, *before, then, yesterday;* duration of time, *always, continuously, ever, never;* frequency of time, *again, daily, frequently, often, sometimes.*

Adverbs of place may denote position, motion toward, and motion from. Examples of adverbs expressing position are *above, below, here, there,* and *where;* motion toward, *forward, onward;* and motion from, *away, left, right.*

Adverbs of manner usually accompany verbs of action and denote the way or manner in which the action expressed in the verb is performed. Manner adverbs are the most numerous in the English language because they can be made from simple and compound adjectives and from the present and past participles of verbs by adding the suffix -*ly*. Examples of adverbs of manner are *carefully, gladly, nicely, charmingly,* and *pointedly*. In addition to the derived adverbs, there are a number of simple adverbs that denote manner. Examples of these adverbs are *better, fast, how, so,* and *well*.

Adverbs of degree denote measure or extent and usually modify adjectives and adverbs. Examples of adverbs of degree are *just, little, more, very, too, enough, rather,* and *almost.* Some adverbs of degree are formed by adding *ly* to the positive degree of adjectives (*completely, barely, excessively,* and *nearly.*)

Finally, there are a few adverbs that express cause. They usually modify verbs, but sometimes they introduce clauses and entire sentences. Examples of adverbs of cause are *consequently, therefore, then,* and *why.*

Adverbs, like adjectives, have three degrees of comparison—the positive, the comparative, and the superlative. The formation and uses of these degrees are also similar to those of adjectives. The comparative is formed by adding *er* to the adverb or preceding the adverb with the word *more.* The superlative is formed by adding *est* to the positive form of the adverb or by preceding it with *most.*

Prepositions

Prepositions are words used with a noun or a pronoun to form a phrase called a prepositional phrase. A prepositional phrase usually performs the function of an adjective or an adverb in a sentence. In the following sentences the italicized prepositional phrases function as either adjectives or adverbs within the sentence.

Joe enjoys getting letters *from home.* (adjective phrase modifying *letters*)

Most children enjoy riding *on a horse.* (adverb phrase modifying *riding*)

Don't go farther *into the water* or you might drown. (adverb phrase modifying *farther*)

Below is a list of the commonly used prepositions.

about	at	but (except)	into	through
above	before	by	near	to
across	behind	down	of	toward
after	below	during	on	under
against	beneath	for	out	underneath
along	beside	from	outside	until
among	between	in	over	up
around	beyond	inside	past	with

Conjunctions

A conjunction is a word used to join words, phrases, or clauses. In some instances, conjunctions are used to join sentences or paragraphs. Conjunctions are usually classified, according to their function in the sentence, as either coordinating or subordinating.

A coordinating conjunction connects words, phrases, and clauses or sentences of equal rank. The following sentences all contain examples of coordinating conjunctions.

Bill *and* Tom enjoy playing the same sports. (coordinating conjunction connecting words)

We cannot decide if we should go to the mountains *or* to the ocean. (coordinating conjunction connecting two phrases)

Gertrude wore the lavender gown to the dance, *and* Harold wore his pinstripe suit. (coordinating conjunction connecting two clauses)

A subordinating conjunction always joins clauses of unequal rank: it joins a dependent clause to an independent clause. In the sentence, "We cannot decide if we should go to the mountains or to the ocean," the word *if* is a subordinating conjunction that connects the independent clause to the dependent clause. Examples of subordinating conjunctions are *if, unless, because, since, as, in order, though, although, after, when, where, while,* and *as.*

Interjections

Interjections are parts of speech that are very seldom used in formal writing. When utilized, they are placed at or near the beginning of a sentence to express emotion or to emphasize the content of the sentence. Interjections may also be used outside a sentence to form sentence fragments or minor sentences by themselves. The sentences below illustrate the use of interjections.

Hurrah! Louisville scored another touchdown.

Good heavens, inflation has gone up again this month.

Impossible—I never thought he would win the fight.

PARTS OF A SENTENCE

Sentences are groups of words that express complete thoughts. The words within a sentence usually can be divided into different types of clauses and phrases. In this section we will briefly discuss some of those divisions and the various structures found within them.

All sentences must contain an independent or main clause. Most clauses can be classified as one of nine patterns. The first pattern includes a noun used as a subject, the linking verb be, and an adjective.

N	Be	Adj
The soup	is	hot.
The man	was	angry.
The girls	were	smart.

Frequently the adjective in such patterns is called a **predicate adjective.** The function of a predicate adjective is to describe the subject.

The second pattern is similar to the first, but instead of having an adjective after the linking verb, there is an adverb.

N	Be	Adv
The man	was	here.
The pool table	is	downstairs.
The game	was	yesterday.

The third pattern follows closely to the first two. Again, a noun introduces the sentence, followed by the linking verb be and another noun. This second noun is called a **predicate nominative,** and it refers back to the first noun. Predicate adjectives and noninatives may also be referred to as *subjective complements.*

N	Be	Noun
Sandy	was	the culprit.
The dinner	was	a feast.
Marcie	is	the student.

The fourth pattern consists of just two elements, a noun followed by an intransitive verb, which by definition has no object.

Noun	Intr. V.
Houses	deteriorate.
The musician	plays.
The taxi	waits.

In the fifth pattern, the verb is completed by another noun different from the first noun. Within this pattern, the second noun is called the **direct object** and usually answers the question "whom" or "what" after the verb. Verbs in this pattern are transitive.

Noun	Tr. V.	Noun^2
The man	bought	a suit.
The salesperson	sold	the couch.
The mechanic	repaired	the tire.

Notice that in the above pattern the superscript 2 above the second noun denotes a different noun from the first. Also keep in mind that the above sentences can be written in the passive voice. For example, we could change the sentences around to read:

A suit was bought by the man.

The couch was sold by the salesperson.

The tire was repaired by the mechanic.

The sixth pattern uses an indirect object. In this pattern, there is a noun used as a subject, a noun used as an indirect object, and a noun used as a direct object. (For this reason, there are two superscripts denoting the different nouns.) Indirect objects commonly answer the question "to whom" or "for whom" after a transitive verb.

Noun	Tr. V.	Noun^2	Noun^3
The father	bought	the child	a football.
The teacher	asked	Tanya	a question.
The boss	assigned	Jack	the job.

Pattern seven is one that is used infrequently in writing. Sentences within this pattern begin with a noun, followed by a transitive verb, followed by a direct object. The direct object is then followed by either another noun that explains or identifies it or by an adjective that describes it. The noun or adjective following the direct object is sometimes called the **objective complement.**

Noun	Tr. V.	Noun²	Noun³/Adj
The players	elected	Bill	captain.
The committee	considered	the candidate	honest.

Pattern eight and nine are very similar to patterns one and three in that they contain linking verbs. The main difference between these patterns and the preceding two is that the linking verbs (L.V.) used here are not forms of the verb *be* as was the case with patterns one and three.

Pattern Eight

Noun	L.V.	Adj.
The worker	appears	weary.
The child	became	sleepy.
The detective	feels	cautious.

Pattern Nine

Noun	L.V.	Noun
Edgar	remained	a student.
The boys	stayed	roommates.
Ida	became	valedictorian

Again, the adjective in pattern eight is referred to as a predicate adjective and the noun in pattern nine is called a predicate nominative.

All main clauses are made up of one of these patterns. Of course, when we write we use sentences with more than just a main clause: We use subordinate or dependent clauses as well.

All clauses are groups of words with a subject and a predicate. Some examples of clauses are listed below. The subjects have been underlined once, the verbs twice.

1. That <u>man</u> <u>is</u> a friend of mine.

2. <u>I</u> <u>like</u> to walk in the woods.

3. When <u>I</u> <u>come</u> into the house . . .

4. After <u>it</u> <u>rains</u> . . .

As you can see, the clauses in examples 1 and 2 make sense by themselves. They are called independent or main clauses. The clauses in examples 3 and 4 don't make sense alone. They are called dependent or subordinate clauses. They depend on something else to be understandable. When dependent clauses are attached to independent clauses, they become understandable. For example, if we attached clause 4 to the beginning of clause 2, we would have:

After it rains, I like to walk in the woods.

Dependent clauses can be divided into three groups: (1) adjective clauses, (2) adverb clauses, and (3) noun clauses. An adjective clause is introduced by a relative pronoun, and, as the name indicates, functions as an adjective within a sentence. Below are some sentences that contain adjective clauses.

The small girl tightly held the hand of her father, *who was crying.*

The cars *that were filled with teenagers* came cruising up Sante Fe Bouelvard.

My desk is cluttered with debris *that belongs to other people.*

All of the boys *who were going to watch the wrestling match* ran outside.

Pictures *that were selected by students* were displayed in the store windows.

Adverb clauses are introduced by subordinating conjunctions and function as adverbs within a sentence.

Before I went downtown, I finished cleaning my room.

Because Annette was a leader, she took on the major responsibility of the group.

Although we knew the end of the story, we remained quiet.

Since Joe left the farm, the crops have been failing.

When the explorer reached his destination, he was met by the chief and his court.

Noun clauses function as nouns within a sentence and can consequently serve as subjects, direct objects, indirect objects, and objects of prepositions. Most commonly they are introduced by the word *that* but can also be introduced by various subordinating conjunctions, reflexive pronouns, and interrogative pronouns *(how, why, what, which).* Below are some sentences that contain noun clauses.

Whatever you desire will be my wish as well.

Betty said *that she was not going to play tennis.*

Everyone wondered *why the music had stopped.*

Kris wondered *when the plane would arrive in Pittsburgh.*

A sentence that contains a dependent clause is a **complex sentence.** A sentence with no dependent clause and with only an independent clause is a **simple sentence.** A sentence with two independent clauses is a **compound sentence.** And, finally, a sentence with two independent clauses and at least one dependent clauses is a **compound-complex sentence.** Below is an example of each.

He was happy to be alive. (Simple)

He was happy that he was alive. (Complex)

He was happy to be alive, and he was excited about life. (Compound)

He was happy that he was alive, and he was excited about life. (Compound-complex)

In addition to clauses, most sentences also contain phrases. Phrases are groups of related words that do not contain a subject and a predicate. The most common type of phrase is the prepositional phrase, which begins with a preposition and frequently is used as a time or place expansion in a sentence. The other types of phrases all fall into the category of **verbal phrases,** because they begin with a verb form. There are three types of verbals and consequently three types of verbal phrases. They are: (1) participial phrases, (2) gerund phrases, and (3) infinitive phrases.

A **participle** is a verb form ending in *ing, d, ed, n,* or *en* which when used in a sentence functions as an adjective. A participial phrase is a group of related words beginning with a participle and performing the function of an adjective within a sentence:

The students *taking the test* all hoped to make it into college.

A **gerund** is a verb form ending in *ing* that functions as a noun within a sentence. Below is a sentence containing a gerund phrase:

Running in the rain is one of my favorite things to do.

An **infinitive** is a verb form preceded by the word *to: to run, to* *jump*. Infinitives can perform many functions within a sentence, but most commonly they are used as objective complements:

He was happy to see her.

As was mentioned previously, phrases and subordinate clauses are added to main clauses to give them substance. Without them, writing would be very dull indeed. Although it is not necessary to be able to identify such elements as adjective clauses and participial phrases within your sentences, a knowledge of what they are can help improve your flexibility when you perform reduction and expansion (see Chapter 7).

SPELLING

If you think you are a poor speller, welcome to the club. Many people have the same feeling. Actually it's usually not true. You know how to spell thousands of words. There are some words, however, that are commonly misspelled by many people. The following is a list of some of those words. Look them over and identify the ones you know how to spell and those you don't. You'd be surprised at the improvement in your spelling if you could spell all the words on this list.

A

abbreviate	adoption	appearance
absence	advantageous	appreciate
absolutely	advertisement	appropriate
abundant	aerial	approximate
accede	aggravate	arctic
accelerator	allegiance	argument
acceptable	all right	arithmetic
accidentally	allusion	arrangement
acclimated	amateur	artillery
accommodate	among	ascend
accompanied	analogous	ascent
accompaniment	analysis	assent
accomplishment	analyze	association
accumulate	angel	athletic
accuracy	angle	atheistic
achievement	annihilate	attendance
acknowledgment	anonymous	audible
acoustics	answer	audience
acquaintance	anxiety	authorities
acquire	anxious	auxiliary
acquitted	apologetically	awkward
adequately	apparatus	
adolescent	apparent	

B

bachelor	beggar	bore
balance	beginning	boulevard
ballet	behavior	boundaries
bankruptcy	belief	breath
barbarian	believe	breathe
barbarous	beneficial	brilliant
bargain	benefit	buffet
basically	benefited	bulletin
bath	biscuit	buoy
bathe	berth	bureau
battalion	bibliography	business
bear	birth	busy
because	biscuit	
been	blasphemy	
before	boar	

C

cafeteria	changeable	compulsory
calendar	characteristic	concede
campaign	chauffeur	conference
candidate	chief	confidentially
can't	choose	connoisseur
captain	chose	conscience
carburetor	circumstantial	conscientious
careless	colloquial	consciousness
caricature	colossal	consistent
carrying	column	controversial
casualties	committee	corps
catalogue	communist	criticism
catastrophe	comparative	criticize
category	compelled	curiosity
ceiling	competent	curious
cellar	competitor	curriculum
cemetery	completely	cylinder
certain	complexion	

D

dealt	destruction	disciple
decadent	devise	discipline
decision	diary	discrimination
deceitful	diaphragm	discussion
definite	different	disease
descend	dilapidated	dissatisfied
descendant	dilemma	dissent
descent	diligence	dissipate
describe	diphtheria	divide
description	disappear	divine
desirable	disappearance	doesn't
despair	disappoint	dormitory
desperate	disastrous	drunkenness

E

echoes	enthusiastically	exceptionally
ecstasy	environment	exhaustion
efficiency	equivalent	exhibit
eighth	erroneous	exhibition
eligible	especially	exhilaration
eliminate	espionage	existence
embarrass	eventually	experience
emperor	exaggerate	extraordinary
emphasize	exceed	extracurricular
endeavor	excel	extremely
enemies	excellent	exuberant

F

fallacy	fiery	frantically
familiar	finally	freight
families	foreign	friend
fascinate	forfeit	friendliness
fascism	forth	fulfill
February	forty	fundamental
feminine	fourth	

G

gaiety	governor	guerilla/guerrilla
galaxy	grammar	guidance
gauge	grammatically	guild
generally	grandeur	gourmet
genius	grievous	graffiti
genuine	guarantee	
government	guardian	

H

handkerchief	hindrance	humorous
handsome	hoarse	hundred
harassment	holy	hundredths
height	hoping	hygiene
heinous	hospital	hypocrisy
hereditary	horizontal	hysterical

I

ignorance	independent	intelligence
illiterate	indicted	intercede
illusion	indispensable	interesting
imaginary	inevitable	interpretation
immediately	influential	interrupt
inadequate	ingenious	irrelevant
incidentally	initiative	irresistible
incredible	innocent	irresponsible
indefinitely	intellectual	

K

kerosene	kindergarten	knowledge
khaki	knew	

L

laboratory	liable	literature
laid	library	livelihood
larynx	license	loneliness
legitimate	lightning	loose
leisure	liquor	losing
lengthening	listening	luxurious

M

magazine	mattress	mischievous
magnificence	meant	misspell
maintenance	medieval	moral
manageable	mediocre	morale
maneuver	melancholy	mortgage
manual	melodious	mosquito
manufacture	merely	municipal
marriage	millionaire	murmuring
martyr	miniature	muscle
material	minute	mussel
mathematics	miscellaneous	mysterious

N

naturally	neurotic	ninth
naive	nickel	noticeable
necessity	niece	notorious
neither	ninety	nuclear
neighbor		

O

obedience	official	orchestra
obstacle	omission	organization
occasion	opinion	original
occurred	opportunity	ought
o'clock	optimistic	outrageous

P

pageant	phenomenon	prestige
paid	phrase	presumption
pain	physically	prevalent
pamphlet	physician	primitive
particularly	picnicking	privilege
parallel	piece	probably
paralysis	playwright	procedure
pane	pneumonia	proceed
parliament	politician	professor
particularly	possess	prominent
pastime	possible	pronunciation
peasant	potatoes	propaganda
penicillin	practically	propeller
permanent	prairie	prophecy
permissible	precede	prophesy
perseverance	preference	protein
persistent	preferred	psychiatrist
perspiration	prejudice	psychoanalysis
persuade	presence	pursue

Q

quantity	quick	quite
quarantine	quietly	quizzes
questionnaire		

R

rain	referred	reservoir
realize	rehearsal	respectful
really	reign	responsibility
rebellion	rein	restaurant
recede	religious	reverent
receipt	remembrance	rhetoric
receive	reminiscent	rhyme
recognize	repetition	rhythm
recommend	remittance	
reference	representative	

S

sacrifice	significant	succeed
sacrilegious	similar	success
sandwich	sincerely	superintendent
sanctuary	sophomore	supersede
satisfactorily	souvenir	suppress
saxophone	speak	surprise
scene	specifically	surroundings
schedule	specimen	susceptible
secretary	speech	swimming
seize	straight	syllable
separate	strait	symbolic
sergeant	sponsor	symmetrical
sheath	spontaneous	symphonic
sheathe	strenuously	synonymous
siege	strictly	
sieve	stubbornness	

T

tangible	thorough	tremendous
tariff	together	tries
technical	tolerance	truly
technique	tomorrow	Tuesday
temperament	tortoise	twelfth
temperature	tournament	typical
tendency	tragedy	tyranny
than	transcend	

U

unanimous	unnecessarily	usage
undoubtedly	unnoticed	using
universal	unscrupulous	usually
unmistakable	unusually	
unnatural	until	

V

vacancy	various	victorious
vaccine	vegetable	view
vacuum	vehicle	vigilant
valleys	vein	village
valuable	vengence	villain
variation	versatile	vinegar
		volume

W

warrant	welfare	whom
weather	whether	withhold
Wednesday	whisper	woman
weight	whistle	writing
weird	wholly	written

Y

yacht	yield	you're (you are)
yawn	your	

As was mentioned in Chapter 9, some people use a rule approach to improve their spelling. Below we have listed some common and useful spelling rules.

1. *ie* or *ei*
   Use *i* before *e* except after *c* for the long e sound.

believe	priest	*after C*
fiend	relieve	ceiling
grievance	retrieve	conceit
niece	shriek	deceive
piece	thief	receive

   Exceptions: neither, financier, seize, either, species, weird, leisure

   Use *e* before *i* when the sound is not a long e, especially for the long *a* sound.

freight	neighbor
height	weight

2. Adding prefixes: When a prefix is added to a word, the spelling of the word itself does not change.

un + natural = unnatural over + run = overrun
mis + spell = misspell im + mobile = immobile
un + excused = unexcused re + supply = resupply

3. Adding suffixes
   a. When the suffix -ness or -ly is added, the spelling of the word does not change.

   dry + ness = dryness mere + ly = merely
   kind + ness = kindness shy + ly = shyly

   Exceptions: For words that end in y not representing the long i sound, change the y to i before adding -ness or -ly.

   happy + ness = happiness ready + ly = readily

   b. Drop the final e before adding a suffix that begins with a vowel.

   hope + ing = hoping live + able = livable
   use + able = usable

   Retain the final e after c or g if the suffix begins with a or o.

   advantage + ous = advantageous
   notice + able = noticeable
   courage + ous = courageous
   service + able = serviceable

   c. Retain the final e before adding a suffix that begins with a consonant.

   care + ful = careful
   hope + ful = hopeful

   Exceptions: *acknowledgment, argument, awful, dying,* (meaning "changing the color"), *ninth, wholly, wisdom*

   d. For words ending in y preceded by a consonant, change the y to i before adding a suffix. Retain the y if it is preceded by a vowel.

   funny + est = funniest boy + ish = boyish
   happy + ness = happiness enjoy + ing = enjoying
   merry + ment = merriment stay + ing = staying

   Exceptions: Retain the y in words like *babyish, ladylike, studying.*

   e. Double the final consonant before adding a suffix beginning with a vowel if both of the following two conditions exist: (1) the word has only one syllable or the accent is on the second syllable; and (2) the word ends in a consonant preceded by a vowel.

   control + ed = controlled propel + er = propeller
   occur + ence = occurrence quit + ing = quitting

plan + ing = planning   refer + ed = referred
But
cancel + ed = canceled (accent not on last syllable)
prefer + able = preferable (accent shifts to first syllable)
f. Add k before adding *ing, ed,* or *y* to words ending in hard *c.*
picnic + ed = picnicked   mimic + ing = mimicking
panic + ed = panicked   traffic + ing = trafficking

CAPITALIZATION

Below are some capitalization rules to be used when revising a
paper for mechanics.

1. Capitalize the first word in any sentence or in any quoted
   material.
   Everyone agreed that the rooms were nice.
   "Do you think we can do it?" asked Charles.
   But
   "Do you think," asked Charles, "we can do it?"
   (Note: "we" is *not* capitalized, because it is a continuation of the
   direct quotation beginning with "Do you think.")
       Traditionally, the first word of every line of poetry is
   capitalized. In modern poetry this observance is still common,
   but is not a rule.
    I think that I shall never see
    A poem lovely as a tree . . .

2. Capitalize proper nouns.
    a. Capitalize the names of persons: Picasso, Hamlet, Charles
       Dickens, Mr. McDonald
    b. Capitalize geographical names including:
        1. cities, counties, states, countries, continents: San Fran-
           cisco, New York, Weld County, Sweden, South America
        2. bodies of water: Pacific Ocean, Black Sea, Mediterranean,
           Lake Erie, Hudson Bay, Cripple Creek
        3. islands, peninsulas, straits, canals, beaches, mountains:
           Philippines, Florida Peninsula, Bering Strait, Panama
           Canal, Malibu Beach, Grand Canyon, Rocky Mountains
        4. streets, specific buildings: Washington Street, Sunset
           Boulevard, Thirty-second Street, Highway 287, Sears
           Tower, Blair House
        5. parks, forests, dams, canyons, valleys: Sequoia National
           Park, San Juan National Forest, Hoover Dam, Big
           Thompson Canyon, Death Valley

6. Recognized parts of the country or world: the South, the Middle East. The words *north, south, east, west* are not capitalized when they refer to directions.

c. Capitalize the names of ships, boats, planes, trains, awards, and monuments: the Queen Mary, the Delta Queen, the Lucille (name of a boat), the Blue Angels, the Silver Streak, Oscar, Grammy, Liberty Bell, Grant's Tomb.

d. Capitalize the brand names of consumer products; do not capitalize any common nouns that may follow the brand name: Coca-Cola, Kraft, Bell telephone, Chevy Monza, Lay's potato chips, Roman Meal bread, Nabisco cookies.

e. Capitalize the names of specific rooms and other nouns followed by a numeral or letter: Room 222; School District 12; Diagram A.

f. Capitalize the names of school classes; however, the words *freshman, sophomore, junior, senior* are not capitalized when they refer to either a student or a year.

Sue Smith is valedictorian of the *Senior Class.*

They were a fine group of *freshmen.*

David will be a *sophomore* next year.

Al's grade point average rose dramatically in his *sophomore* year.

g. Capitalize the names of specific business firms, and governmental, scholastic, professional, and social organizations or departments: Delta Airlines, Congress, Department of Commerce, United Nations, Kappa Delta Pi, Elks Club, Columbia University, Catholic Central High School.

h. Capitalize the names of nationalities, races, and religions: American, Italian, Oriental, Caucasian, Protestant, Jewish, Catholic

i. Capitalize the names of specific deities or prophets and pronouns referring to those deities: God, Lord, Christ, Buddha, Mohammed, He, His, Him, John the Baptist, Zeus, Neptune.

j. Capitalize proper adjectives, but not the common nouns that follow them: America, American people; Canada, Canadian sunsets; Shakespearean sonnet; Greek alphabet; Romantic literature

k. Capitalize the names of historical events and periods of time: World War II, Spanish-American War, Battle of the Bulge, Iron Age, the Renaissance,

l. Capitalize special events: the Olympics, the World Series, the Rose Bowl.

m. Capitalize political or religious holidays: Fourth of July, Memorial Day, Christmas, Easter, Passover.

n. Capitalize calendar items, including the days of the week and the months of the year: Catholic Education Week, National Secretaries' Week, Monday, June.

Do *not* capitalize the names of seasons unless personified.

I like summer best and winter least.

But

The children were chilled by Winter's breath.

o. Capitalize specific titles of persons when used preceding a name: Press Secretary Powell, Reverend Peters, Dean Thomas, General Patton

p. Capitalize the first word and all important words in titles of books, short stories, poems, plays, periodicals, articles, documents, songs, films, and works of art. Articles (*a, an, the*), conjunctions, and prepositions are not capitalized unless they are the first word in the title.

Have you ever read *The New York Times*?

"The Secret Life of Walter Mitty" is, perhaps, illustrative of Thurber at his best.

Kramer vs. Kramer is a film about a divorced father's right to have custody of his son.

PUNCTUATION

When we speak, we stress ideas and signify the groupings of ideas by raising or lowering our voice. When we write we can't do this; we have to rely on punctuation to show the reader how ideas are grouped and which ideas are stressed. Without punctuation the written language would probably be incomprehensible. Take, for example, the following sentence written without punctuation:

That that is is that that is not is not.

This makes no sense at all, but let's add punctuation and consequently meaning:

That that is, is; that that is not, is not.

Below are some rules and conventions that apply to the most commonly used punctuation marks.

1. *The Comma*
   a. Use commas between items in a series, whether the items are words, phrases, or clauses.

The hall was decorated with paper flowers, streamers, and two giant gazebos.

Paper flowers, streamers of twisted crepe paper, and two giant gazebos decorated the hall.

The wind blew, the clouds appeared, and the rain fell for hours.

b. A comma is placed between the clauses of a compound sentence.

This arrangement would be convenient for me, but you must consider the others in the group.

Let Bill start out on the trip first, and I will follow him later.

You must get in the proper line for registration, or you will not be able to sign up for the courses you want.

c. Introductory words, phrases, and clauses are set off by commas from the main part of the sentence.

Above, the thick clouds began to disperse and let the sun peek through.

As a matter of fact, I am very tired of listening to you.

When you finish playing outside, you must begin your piano practice.

d. All nonrestrictive clauses and phrases are set off by commas.

Harold Matthews, who lives right down the street, is my dancing partner.

Lillie, running furiously through the storm, reached my house in twenty minutes.

e. Appositives, nouns of direct address, and parenthetical expressions used for explaining and interrupting are set off by commas.

Madeline Beaverton, a piano teacher, pleaded guilty to child abuse.

You can be assured, Richard, that your mother will hear about your behavior.

The house next door, as a matter of fact, is for sale.

f. Use commas in certain conventional situations such as items in dates and addresses, and the salutation and closing of a letter.

On Monday, February 6, 1983, the building was razed by fire.

He has lived on 3305 Sunset Boulevard, New York, New York.

Dear Carol,

Sincerely yours,

2. *The semicolon*

Use a semicolon when you use an independent clause without a conjunction, an independent clause with certain conjunctions, and between word groups containing commas.

Walter started walking toward the party; nothing would make him turn back.

The bell usually rings at 3:05; however, today it will ring fifteen minutes earlier.

The composition that Mike turned in was full of humor, life, and happiness; but the manner in which it was written, the many capitalization errors, and the disregard for punctuation rules detracted considerably from its quality.

3. *The colon*

Use a colon at the introduction of a list of items, at the introduction of a formal statement or address, or after an independent clause that is explained by a second clause.

The scout manual recommends the following items: a knife, a compass, a canteen, and matches.

The history books usually include Theodore Roosevelt's famous words: "Speak softly and carry a big stick."

Modern clothing isn't made like it used to be: Seams tear easily, zippers break, and fabric isn't very durable.

4. *The apostrophe*

Use the apostrophe to signal possession, for plurals of numbers and letters, and for omission of letters:

Garry's automobile came to a screeching halt when the light turned red.

The word *occasion* is spelled with two *c*'s.

You *haven't* heard anything yet about the new fee hike.

5. *The dash*
Use a dash when a shift in thought is sudden or when the series ordered by commas is long and possibly confusing.

> The policeman could have—and indeed should have—been a bit more considerate.

> In a research paper you should use sections—table of contents, chapters with headings, tables and graphs, appendixes, and bibliography—to make your paper easy to read.

6. *The hyphen*
Use hyphens in compound words and numbers.

> Bob is acting like a *would-be* movie star.

> Being *thirty-three* years old hardly makes you an old person.

7. *Quotation marks*
a. Use quotation marks before and after a person's exact words. If the person's words ask a question, state a command, or make a statement, use the appropriate end punctuation inside the second quotation mark.

> Bill asked, "Why don't you go along?"

b. When a person's words are interrupted with a quotation stem, place a comma and quotation mark before and after the stem.

> "How would you feel," asked Mother, "if Aunt Ruth didn't even mention your birthday?"
> "Leave me alone," I shouted, "before I lose my temper!"

Place a semicolon outside quotation marks when it is not part of the quotation.

> Alan said, "I don't want to discuss it at all"; however, Dad thought it was an important matter.

c. Place a question mark outside of the quotation marks if the sentence is a question but the quotation is not.

Didn't you tell the teacher, "Forget it"?

d. Use quotation marks before and after words referred to as words.

Don't use "but" or "and" at the beginning of a sentence.

e. Use quotation marks before and after titles of songs, short stories, short poems, essays, articles, and subdivisions of books.

Edgar Allan Poe's "Annabel Lee" is my favorite poem.

I read a fascinating article entitled "Using a Computer for Writing" in the newspaper yesterday.

f. Use single quotation marks to enclose a quotation within a quotation.

"What do you mean by saying, 'Put the symbol in the upper left-hand corner of the first page'?" I asked Mrs. Weber.

COMMONLY CONFUSED TERMS

In Chapter 8 we discussed errors in precision of word usage. Below we've listed some terms that are commonly confused and are the source of error.

Affect, Effect   *Affect* is a verb and means "to influence." *Effect* is commonly used as either a verb or noun. When used as a verb it means "to bring about" (*He effected a change because of his persistence*). When used as a noun it means "result" (*The effect of the storm was felt for quite a few days*).

Ain't   This contraction is still considered nonstandard and is unacceptable in the written language unless used in dialogue. It is, however, becoming more widely accepted in the spoken language in informal situations.

All, all of   In many cases the *of* in *all of* can be dropped. This does not hold true, however, when a pronoun immediately follows: *all the dignitaries, all of them.*

Alot, a lot   Although pronounced as one word, *a lot* is written as two words.

Already, all ready   *Already* is an adverb which means that something has occurred prior to some stated time: *He has already gone. All ready* is a phrase that expresses the state of being prepared. *He was all ready.*

Alter, altar   *Alter* is a verb meaning "to change": *They altered their plans and did not go on the trip. Altar* is a noun meaning a "table used for worship": *The altar was covered with flowers.*

All right, alright   *All right* is correct; *alright* is unacceptable.

Amidst, amongst   These are acceptable substitutes for *amid* and *among*, but are used infrequently.

Amount, number   *Amount* should be used with mass nouns (nouns that cannot be counted), and *number* should be used with count nouns (nouns that can be counted).

The amount of cash he had was amazing.

The number of people I saw was amazing.

Anyplace, anywhere   In the spoken language, these two can be used interchangeably; however, in the written language *anywhere* is more commonly used because it is more formal.

Assent, ascent   *Assent* is a verb meaning "to approve," *ascent* is a noun signifying the act of climbing.

Will your parents assent to your ascent of the mountain?

Awful, awfully   *Awful* is most commonly used colloquially to mean "very bad" (*an awful person*). *Awfully* is an intensifier used before adjectives (*awfully pretty, awfully nice*). Both are informal.

Awhile, a while   These forms can be used interchangeably.

He waited a while.
He waited awhile.

Bath, bathe   Commonly confused spellings. *Bath* is a noun; *bathe* is a verb.

Being as, being that   Both of these phrases are nonstandard forms for *since* or *because*. It's better to avoid them in formal writing situations.

Beside, besides   Both are prepositions but with different meanings. *Beside* means "at the side of"; *besides* means "in addition to."

He stood beside his mother.

Who else besides Joni is going to come?

Between, Among   *Between* is generally used to express a relationship between two things; *among* is used when there are more than two elements. However, *between* can also be used to express interrelationships between several elements when they are considered individually rather than as a group.

He was very popular among the members of the team.

It was between Mary and Bill to decide the winner.

He traveled between Boston, New York, and Chicago quite frequently.

Breath, breadth, breathe *Breathe* is a verb meaning "to take in air," *breath* is a noun meaning "an exhalation of air." *Breadth* is a noun meaning "distance" or "width."

Burned, burnt Both forms are acceptable alternates for the past tense and past participle of the verb *burn*.

Can, may Technically there is a difference in meaning between these two verbs. *Can* means "ability to do something"; *may* means "permission to do something." However, it is becoming commonly accepted to use *can* for both meanings.

Cannot, can not These two forms are interchangeable; both are acceptable in the written language.

Cite, site *Cite* is a verb meaning "to refer to" or "quote"; *site* is a noun meaning "a place or location."

Continual, continuous Although the distinction is gradually being lost, these two adjectives have different meanings. *Continual* refers to events that are a series; *continuous* refers to an event that occurs without interruption.

His back pain has been continual for two or three years; it happens to him about twice a month.

His back pain has been continuous for the last three hours; the pain has not stopped once during that time.

Credible, creditable, credulous These three words are commonly confused; their meanings are distinct. *Credible* means "believable": *His story was credible.* Creditable means "worthy of credit": *His efforts were creditable. Credulous* means "gullible": *You have to be extremely credulous to believe a story like that.*

Desert, dessert A *desert* is a large, dry expanse of land; *dessert* is something, usually sweet, eaten after the main course of a meal.

Discreet, discrete *Discreet* means "prudent"; *discrete* means "separate" or "distinct."

Dissent, descent *Dissent* is a verb meaning "to differ in opinion": *The senator from Texas dissented from the rest of his colleagues. Descent* is a noun meaning "the act of coming down from a high place": *The descent of Everest is treacherous.*

Disinterested, uninterested *Uninterested* means "having no interest." *Disinterested* means "impartial": *We need a disinterested judge to make the debate a fair one.*

Divulge, disclose   Both mean "to make known what was intended to be confidential." *Disclose* usually refers to a general sharing of information; *divulge* refers to a sharing of knowledge with a select group.

Each and every   This phrase is redundant when used to modify a noun: "Each and every person there enjoyed the concert." *Each* or *every* should be used, not both.

Eminent, imminent   *Eminent* means "distinguished"; *imminent* means "about to happen."

He is an *eminent* guest.

The disaster was *imminent*.

Ever so often, every so often   Although very close in pronunciation, these phrases have different meanings. *Ever so often* means "very often"; *every so often* means "now and then."

We go to the movies ever so often, almost twice a week.

We go the movies every so often, usually only two or three times a year.

Farther, further   Once these two words had distinct and different meanings. Now they mean basically the same thing, with *farther* being the most commonly used form.

Fewer, less   *Fewer* is used with count nouns; *less* is used with abstract and mass nouns.

He made fewer errors than I did.

I was less excited than he was.

Former, latter   Both are relatively formal ways of referring to things already mentioned. *Former* refers to the first element previously mentioned; *latter* refers to the second element previously mentioned.

Formerly, formally   *Formerly* is an adverb meaning "previously," *formally* is an adverb meaning "in a formal fashion."

He dressed formally for the dance.

She was formerly a police officer.

Good, well   Interchangeable in constructions in which they are used as adjectives meaning "in a sound state of health." *I feel good; I feel well.* However, when *well* is used as an adverb, *good* cannot be used as its substitute.

Had better, had best, you'd better   All acceptable substitutes for *should* or *ought.*

Had ought, hadn't ought   Both of these phrases are nonstandard and should be avoided in the written language.

Half a, half an, a half, a half a   The first three are acceptable and can be used interchangeably; the fourth is not standard.

Hanged, hung   The principal parts of the verb *hang* are *hang, hung, hung* except when referring to the death penalty. In that case the principal parts are *hang, hanged, hanged.*

He *hung* the picture on the wall.

The murderer was *hanged* for his crimes.

Have got to   This phrase is commonly used as a substitute for *must, should,* and *ought to.* Although acceptable in spoken language, it should be avoided in writing.

Hardly, barely, scarcely   All three mean "not quite" and can generally be used as substitutes for one another. Because all three have a negative connotation implicit in their meaning, it is not logical to use a negative particle with them. For example *hardly didn't know* and *scarcely never listens* are nonstandard.

If, whether   After verbs like *ask, doubt, know, remember, see,* and *wonder,* the two conjunctions are commonly used interchangeably. However, if an alternative is stated, *whether* is acceptable: *He didn't know whether to leave or not.*

Imply, infer   *Imply* means to send out a suggestion; *infer* means to receive a message.

What do you infer from his remarks? (receive)

What are you implying by your remarks? (sending out)

Inability, disability   *Inability* means "lack of ability"; *disability* means a "permanent lack of ability usually due to a handicap."

His *inability* to speak before large crowds hurt his campaign.

His *disability* was caused by an automobile accident.

In regards to, with regards to   Both are nonstandard forms. Correct forms for these expressions are "in regard to" and "with regard to."

Irregardless   Nonstandard form of *regardless* that should be avoided in written composition.

Its, it's   *Its* is the possessive form of *it. It's* is the contraction for *it is.*

The car lost its wheel.

It's cold out tonight.

Kind of, sort of   Colloquial substitutes for *rather* or *somewhat*.

Lead, led   *Lead* when used as a verb means "to conduct" and, although spelled the same, is pronounced differently from the noun "lead," which is a metal. *Led* is the past tense form of the verb *lead*.

Pencils have lead in them.

He led the horse to water.

He will lead the horse to water.

Leave, let   When the meaning is "allow to remain" these two words can be used interchangeably. *Leave me alone; let me alone.*

Lend, Loan   Both are acceptable as verbs in spoken language: "Will you lend/loan me the money." However many writers and speakers prefer the use of *lend* as a verb and *loan* as a noun.

Liable, likely, apt   All three can mean "probable" and in such situations are considered interchangeable.

Lie, lay   *Lie* means "to recline," *lay* means "to place." The past tense form of *lie* is *lay*, which often causes confusion.

I lay down this morning for a nap.

I laid the book down this morning.

Lighted, lit   Both are acceptable past tense forms of the verb "to light."

He lighted the candle.

He lit the candle.

Like, as   In the past *like* was considered a conjunction and *as* a preposition. That distinction is gradually fading. *Like* is now acceptable as a conjunction.

Lose, loose   *Lose* is a verb meaning "to be unable to find something"; *loose* is an adjective meaning "unfastened."

Did you lose your purse?

He has a few screws loose.

May be, maybe   *Maybe* is an adverb meaning "perhaps"; *may be* is a verb phrase meaning "possibly will be."

Maybe he will come.

He may be coming.

Mighty   It is acceptable to use *mighty* in the spoken language to mean "very" (e.g., *mighty nice*). However, it is considered informal and is usually avoided in written language.

Miner, minor *Miner* is a noun meaning "one who works in a mine"; *minor* is an adjective meaning "unimportant."

Moral, morale *Moral* is an adjective meaning "ethical"; *morale* is a noun meaning "mental and emotional attitude."

He is a very moral person.

His morale is always good.

Muchly *Much* can be used either as an adjective or an adverb; consequently the *ly* is unnecessary.

Must At one time this word functioned solely as an auxiliary verb: *He must help us.* However, it is now commonly used as a noun: *Visiting Disneyland is a must.*

No place, nowhere, nowheres *Nowhere* is the most formal of the three. *No place* is used frequently in the spoken language. *Nowheres* is nonstandard and should be avoided.

Of In speech the verb *have* is sometimes replaced with *of: might of, would of.* In the written language this is nonstandard and should be avoided.

OK, okay Both are variations of this now acceptable spoken expression. It should be avoided in formal writing situations.

Pair, pare *Pair* is a noun meaning "two related objects"; *pare* is a verb meaning "to cut down or diminish."

Please pare me an apple.

These socks are a pair.

Per cent, percent, percentage *Percent* is most commonly written as one word. Also *percentage* is now commonly used as a substitute for *percent* to mean "fraction" or "portion."

Personal, personnel *Personal* is an adjective meaning "private"; *personnel* is a noun meaning "employees."

This is a very personal conversation.

I took the assignment because I liked the personnel working on it.

Practical, practicable *Practical* means "useful"; *practicable* means "feasible."

A hammer is a very practical tool.

His plan was practicable.

Pretty This adverb, meaning "moderately," is often overused in the spoken language and consequently should be used sparingly in the written language.

Proved, proven   Both are acceptable past participial forms of *prove*.

Provided, providing   These words are considered interchangeable as subordinating conjunctions.

Quite, Quiet   *Quite* is an intensifier meaning "rather"; *quiet* is an adjective meaning "calm."

Real, really   *Real* is an adjective and *really* an adverb.

Reason is because   This is nonstandard and not appropriate in the written language.

Rise, raise   The principal parts of *rise* are *rise, rose, risen;* the principal parts of raise are *raise, raised, raised. Raise* is used in situations where someone or something is increasing the elevation of someone or something else: it is transitive. *Rise* is used when the person or thing being elevated provides its own motivation.

He rose from the chair to get a drink of water.
They raised me up from the chair because I was unable to walk.

Shall, will   Previously *shall* was the only auxiliary verb that could be used with the pronoun *I* to express future tense: *I shall be there.* However, now the auxiliary *will* has almost totally replaced it.

Sit, set   Very similar to *rise* and *raise* in the differences between them. The principal parts of *sit* are *sit, sat, sat;* the principal parts of *set* are *set, set, set. Sit* is transitive; *set* in intransitive.

He set his cup on the table and then sat down to drink.

Sure, surely   *Sure* is an adjective; *surely* an adverb. In informal situations *sure* is sometimes used as an adverb (*He sure can play the piano*), but this use should be avoided in the written language.

Than, then   *Than* is a conjunction used in comparative statements (*He is taller than I*). *Then* is an adverb designating time (*It happened then*). In speech *then* is often substituted for *than* because of the similarity of sound. This is not acceptable in the written language, however.

That, which, whom   When used as a relative pronoun *that* may refer to persons, animals, or things; *which* may refer to animals and things but not persons. *Who* (whom) may refer to persons only. When choosing between *that* and *which*, *that* should be used to introduce restrictive clauses; *which* is most correctly used to introduce nonrestrictive clauses.

Their, there, they're, there's *Their* is the possessive pronoun form of *they; there* is an adverb indicating *place; they're* is the contracted form of *they are. There's* is the contracted form of *there is.*

It is *their* house.

He lives *there.*

They're friends of mine.

There's gold in those hills.

Though, although Both are acceptable forms when used as subordinating conjunctions and are often used interchangeably.

Thusly *Thus* is an adverb; the *ly* is unnecessary.

Type, type of *Type* is colloquial for *type of* and should not be used in the written language.

Whether, weather *Whether* is a conjunction (see **if, whether**). *Weather* is a noun meaning "climate."

Because the weather looked foreboding, he wasn't sure whether to go sailing or not.

Whose, who's *Whose* is the possessive form of *who. Who's* is the contraction for *who is.*

Whose scarf is lying on the floor?

Who's responsible for this mistake?

Your, You're *Your* is the possessive form of *you. You're* is the contraction for *you are.*

This is your first day on the job.

You're a fine swimmer.

LIST OF TRITE EXPRESSIONS

The following are trite expressions that should be avoided in formal writing:

absence makes the heart grow founder
add insult to injury
age before beauty
all in a days work

all in all
all things being equal
all work and no play
as luck would have it
at a moment's notice
at first glance
at one fell swoop
at the crack of dawn
barking up the wrong tree
bated breath
beat the band
bend over backwards
best foot forward
big as all outdoors
better late than never
bitter end
blood is thicker than water
blow off some steam
blow your own horn
born with a silver spoon in his or her mouth
bright and early
bright-eyed and bushy-tailed
bring home the bacon
busy as a bee
busy as a beaver
butterflies in my stomach
caught in his own trap
checkered career
chip off the old block
clear as mud
cold as ice
cool as a cucumber
cold feet
cry over spilt milk
danger at every corner
dead as a doornail
dead end
dead giveaway
die is cast
dig up the past
dig his own grave
draw the line
drop in the bucket
dry as a bone

dull thud
eat your heart out
eyes as black as coals
eyes like a hawk
face the music
face like an angel
fall on deaf ears
feather in your cap
feeling your oats
festive mood
few and far between
filthy rich
final analysis
fine and dandy
first and foremost
fish out of water
flash in the pan
flat as a pancake
flesh and blood
fly off the handle
for a rainy day
free as a bird
fresh as a daisy
gentle as a lamb
get the ball rolling
God's country
goes without saying
get up on the wrong side of bed
grain of salt
grass is always greener
hand to mouth
happy as a lark
hard row to hoe
head over heels
heart of gold
hungry as a bear
ignorance is bliss
in the face of danger
interesting to note that
in the long run
in the lurch
it stands to reason that
last but not least
lean and hungry

let the cat out of the bag
let your hair down
letter of the law
little did I know
lock, stock, and barrel
mad as a wet hen
make a long story short
make ends meet
make no bones about it
marking time
meets the eyes
method to his madness
miss the boat
more easily said than done
Mother Nature
motley crew
naked city
neat as a pin
necessary evil
needs no introduction
never a dull moment
nip it in the bud
not to be sneezed at
open-and-shut case
over a barrel
pot calling the kettle black
pretty as a picture
proud as a peacock
pull his leg
quick as a rabbit
quiet as a mouse
rat race
rack your brain
raining cats and dogs
raked over the coals
rings true
rubbed me the wrong way
sadder but wiser
second fiddle
seething mass
self-made man
sell like hot cakes
set up shop
seventh heaven

sight for sore eyes
sing like a bird
sleep like a baby
snug as a bug in a rug
soaked to the skin
soar like an eagle
stir up a hornet's nest
stubborn as a mule
take a rain check
tall, dark, and handsome
terra firma
throw the book at
turn over a new leaf
up his alley
upper hand
under the gun
well-chosen words
with bated breath
without further ado
your guess is as good as mine
your number is up

INDEX